How NOT to write a sitcom

100 mistakes to avoid if you ever
want to get produced

How NOT to write a sitcom

to write a sitcom

100 mistakes to avoid if you
ever want to get produced

MARC BLAKE

A & C Black • London

A & C Black Publishers Ltd

1 3 5 7 9 10 8 6 4 2

First published in 2011

A & C Black Publishers Ltd
36 Soho Square
London W1D 3QY
www.acblack.com

A CIP catalogue record for this book is available from the
British Library

ISBN: 978 1 408 13085 8

Available in the USA from
Bloomsbury Academic & Professional
175 Fifth Avenue, 3rd Floor, New York, NY 10010
www.bloomsburyacademicusa.com

Typeset by Margaret Brain, Wisbech, Cambs
Printed and bound in Great Britain by Martins the Printers,
Berwick-upon-Tweed

Contents

Introduction

Welcome to the garage

Situation comedy has existed for over sixty years and is a TV genre that is unlikely to disappear. Established in the 1950s, the format has remained consistent; a domestic arena in which a group of central characters, bonded through blood or necessity, fight like cats and dogs for half an hour a week. Simple ... and yet almost impossible to get right.

The craft of sitcom is possibly the hardest of all screenwriting genres, demanding a complex set of dramatic and comedic skills that must all be in evidence in order to succeed. In the US this is achieved by using a team of writers, their sheer force of numbers pushing the plot escalations further and the gag rates higher until each episode shines with wit and inventiveness. In the UK, a singular mind or pair of comedy geniuses are the norm. The US produced *Frasier*, *M*A*S*H* and *Cosby*, the UK Hancock, Delboy Trotter and David Brent.

In my capacity as script consultant, I read over two hundred scripts a year and am constantly surprised at how many fall at the first hurdle. I will know within ten pages whether or not a script will fly. From page one I come across overcrowded scenes, meandering dialogue, clichéd characters and a lack of wit. Then there's the lack of plotting, drama, comedy; no pace or rhythm and huge errors in basic grammar.

It's a real joy.

You can of course make a script funnier – but if the structure and the story aren't there, the writer is building castles on sand. What the novice has failed to see is that sitcom is primarily a dramatic form – and it is to that end that much of this book is directed.

Rather than being a script doctor, I consider myself a mechanic. My job is to strip a sitcom down to its component parts, to isolate the faults then make suggestions on how to fix them, whilst overcharging wildly.

If you require yet another book that will assure you that you are a beautiful creative flower who only needs just that little bit of watering and nurturing, then please do look elsewhere, as this is not how script editors or producers approach the work of an outsider. They are looking for scripts that *work*. It does not matter if you write beautiful prose or if you are an embryonic genius who will one day reinvent the form and leave us grovelling in the dirt. All we want to see is something roadworthy. Something that doesn't make us all wince and reach for that fifth coffee of the day.

Of the scripts I see, maybe five percent deserve their sitcom MOT, so back your script into the shop and let's take a look under the bonnet.

Marc Blake
Spring 2011

Acknowledgements

I would like to thank all the contributors and interviewees in this book: Simon Nye, Matthew Mulot, Mark Boosey, Esta Charkham, Michael Jacob, and all the production companies with whom I have worked. I would also like to thank Laurence Marks and Maurice Gran, Ron Wolfe and City University, London (where I taught sitcom for 14 years); all current and former students of mine who have endured the red pen, the succinct comment and the lack of mollycoddling; all those who have submitted scripts to me via the comedy.co.uk website: without these, this book could not have been written. Please keep at it and persevere! Finally, to Sara, without whom I would be intellectually impoverished and far less motivated.

Cast list

A guide to contributors quoted and interviewed in this book

S.N. Simon Nye is the creator and writer of UK sitcoms *Men Behaving Badly*, *How Do you Want Me?*, *Is it Legal?*, *Wild West*, *The Savages*, *Carrie and Barry* and *Hardware* (also co-writer of *Reggie Perrin*). He has also written drama for TV including *Frank Stubbs Promotes* and *Dr Who*, as well as literary adaptations of *The Railway Children* and translations of Molière and Dario Fo.

M.M. Matthew Mulot is series producer of *The King is Dead* and a script reader at talkbackTHAMES where he is currently producing and developing scripted comedy for both talkbackTHAMES and Delightful Industries.

M.J. Michael Jacob is currently Head of the BBC College of Comedy and also producer/executive producer of *Inn Mates* (2010), *My Family*, *Two Pints of Lager and a Packet of Crisps*, *Grown Ups* and *The Smoking Room*.

Kev. F. Kevin F. Sutherland is producer of *The Sitcom Trials*. He is a noted illustrator and promoter who has been running the Sitcom Trials for over a decade. His first sitcom script for BBC Radio was *Come Together* starring Ben Miller, Arabella Weir and Kevin Eldon. His second was a sketch show called *Meanwhile*, starring Ronnie Ancona.

D.H./S.W. Declan Hill and Simon Wright are heads of the production company Every 1's A Critic. They took on the Sitcom

Trials for two years but now run their own annual live sitcom competition The Sitcom Mission.

A.B. Andrew Barclay is the producer and co-creator (as well as voice artist) of Channel 4's *Pets*, one of the very few puppet sitcoms produced in the UK.

E.C. Esta Charkham is a former producer of *Birds of a Feather* and *Nightingales* as well as being one of the UK's top casting agents.

Form and format

Half hour comedy will always survive because it's a perfect length for comedy and for TV. I'm not so sure that audience sitcoms will last forever. I hope I'm wrong. The warmth given by the sound of audience laughter, the fusion of theatre and TV, has always been its strength but it's really not cool any more, so most of the creative people are moving elsewhere with exceptions like *The IT Crowd*. The sitcom in general is short of great series at the moment, but as long as there's stuff out there like *The Thick of It* then we're okay.

S.N.

After at least sixty years of always being there in some form or other, I think there's something about thirty minutes of narrative comedy that just 'works'. There have been golden ages and dark ages, though I would contend that most times that some people call golden, some others would call dark. I think the first decade of the twenty-first century was the best for sitcom so far. Some others seem to think sitcoms has been dead since the 1970s.

Kev. F.

1.

What sitcom is – and isn't

Sofa or psychiatrist's couch? Sitcom's identity crisis

Every couple of years, usually in a quiet news period, the press announces the death of sitcom, describing it as tired and moribund, only for some new genius to promptly spring phoenix-like from the ashes to dazzle us all. True, it is an old format; stagey, reliant upon a studio audience, aided by a laughter track and saddled with cumbersome multi-cameras, but these can also be its strengths. The stage is an intimate place, the live audience will boost the performances, the canned laughter encourages the lone viewer to fully enter the world of the sitcom and having several cameras enables every nuance to be captured.

The family sitcom has often been derided for lazy laughs, clichéd characterisation and uninspiring plots, but don't be fooled, the skill and tenacity required to create such a perfect atmosphere is a perilous balancing act. Good sitcom is lightning in a bottle and if this comic charge can be harnessed it will last for years. Furthermore, it has endless repeatability and will continue to be shown for decades after the first run is over. Whether you're in Chicago, Coventry or Cairo, a sitcom will be on a screen near you and you can bet that when the apocalypse comes, it will be accompanied by repeats of *The Simpsons* (Woo-hoo).

Sitcom is a half hour of television or radio that is intended to make us laugh. It has a narrative and a minimal cast of characters in a contained emotional situation. They must never undergo any fundamental change: there is no character arc, no *learning*. The stories are small, usually about life's minutiae, but they are dramatic to its participants. By the end of the show the status quo has been re-established or, if not, the main character will have been left frozen in shame and embarrassment, only for them to begin again the following week with no recollection of the event.

In many American sitcoms there is a clear moral message or learning point that instructs the viewer how to behave; in the UK, sitcom characters offer just the opposite. In this way, sitcom can be seen to act as a social barometer. One of the values of comedy is to poke fun at the powerful, the great and the good; a Dionysian view where the forces of chaos bring down those of order (the Apollonian view). Sitcom, whether intentionally or not, shows us where we are in the social pecking order. It shows us the dysfunctional so that we can compare. We laugh in relief, so that we can be cured of our anxieties. Anything else is not sitcom. It may be a comedy drama or a play, but it ain't sitcom.

The form has always been subject to attack. Many of its notable success were disliked at first. *Fawlty Towers*, *The Office* and *The Seinfeld Chronicles* were all disdained by the press, almost cancelled in their first season due to low ratings, and/ or begrudgingly re-commissioned. It is easy to criticise a new piece while it finds its feet, but what sitcom needs most is time to bed in. As with soap, you need to identify with the main players and with their situation. You need to spend time with them, to befriend them. In today's multiplatform world this is becoming increasingly harder to achieve, but the fast hit or the high concept will never outstrip a considered depth of characterisation. Sitcom is the long game.

What sitcom has over quality drama and soap is repeatability. Once you have seen an episode of a soap, it is forgotten as the narrative paces relentlessly on. The TV drama box set demands a big chunk of time to watch in its entirely. How many times will you return to that? Sitcom is short and self-contained. A single episode can be dropped into the schedules at a moment's notice. It requires little or no prior knowledge from the viewer, which is worth bearing in mind when you create your first episode. Could you turn on and *get it* straightaway? You ought to be able to. Do you need any exposition or back-story to fix your idea? Can you write the show as simply as possible so that anyone can get it before they flip channels?

Does this mean your sitcom has to be bland? Just another family show? No, it just has to be structurally sound. The job

3

of the screen and television writer is akin to that of a carpenter: you design and erect the timber frame of the house. You do the joinery. Your script has all the necessary dovetailing and jointing and all the angles must be correct. It is the job of others to furnish it. The DOP (director of photography), the set builder and designer, the director and the actors are those who put up the wallpaper and the paintings and furnish it. If built well, the audience will not even see the structure. The audience will enjoy the room and the people in it. It's other *writers* who see how well you did your craft.

Still the brickbats come. 'It's too "sit-*commy*"', says the critic. No one talks about film in this way: '*Avatar* was great but it was, like, way too *filmy*.' Sitcom is supposed somehow to be ashamed of itself. It is *light* entertainment; it's frothy, insubstantial fluff aimed at some perceived idea of the lowest common denominator, someone on state benefits, some trailer trash person 'watching her stories'. Deriding sitcom is as easy as punching your Granny, or taking candy from a child, or punching a Granny holding a child or punching a child repeatedly in the face. Remember that next time you sneer at the popular UK sitcom *My Family*. You are metaphorically punching children and that's *wrong*. Anyway, that show gets eight million viewers, easily outpacing the critically adored *Peep Show*.

The Last of the Summer Wine (the myth of Sisyphus played out by aged Yorkshiremen on a hill in a tin bath) may seemingly be for those who cannot reach the red panic cord, but was the longest running sitcom in British TV history. It ran for thirty one series in all, ending in 2010, with every episode written by Roy Clarke OBE (who also wrote *Open All Hours* and *Keeping Up Appearances*). Sitcom, when done well, is the most beloved of all TV genres. These flawed characters, caught in televisual aspic, have become icons. Bilko and Mainwaring, Sir Humphrey and Jim Hacker, Blackadder and Baldrick, Frasier and Niles, Patsy and Edina, Homer and donuts. All of them bring fond smiles like an old lover remembered.

When writing sitcom you tread a difficult line. You want to capture the *zeitgeist* but you also want to create something timeless. You want to avoid bland suburban concerns and yet this is where most of us live. Think not, 'Is my sitcom of now?'

4

But, 'How will my sitcom be seen when I look back on it?' You may be a magnificent storyteller, but you must also think like a producer. A producer who likes simple, funny stories that can and will run forever.

Stretching the form – can the fun last fifty minutes

No. There is a reason why stand-up comedians perform short sets of twenty minutes and that is because it is the length of our natural attention span. After that we require a change of pace. You see this in feature films. Movies are divided into the three-act structure where the action changes direction every twenty to twenty-five minutes. Act One must end within the first half hour, and the longer second act is subdivided into four more-or-less equal periods. The final act (the resolution) is short too. If you find yourself losing interest during a film it is often because these story beats are being messed with.

Back in the 1970s, following their TV success, many UK sitcoms were made into features: *The Likely Lads*, *On The Buses*, *Rising Damp* and *Bless This House* were all made into forgettable movies.*

The problem is that once you go beyond the natural span of sitcom you are in drama territory. This means that narrative structure must take precedence over jokes. The best rom-coms, farces and screwball comedies stay with us because of the quality of the story as well as the characters. *The Life of Brian*, *Some Like it Hot* or *Groundhog Day* are classic films in anyone's book but spoof and parody will struggle to fill eighty minutes. Superior examples of this include *Airplane* or Mel Brooks' and Woody Allen's earlier works but on the whole, once it has exposed the clichéd tropes of its targets, it has nowhere to go. Parody is affectionate and imitative and tends to date quickly. The scattergun spoof – often knocked up by the studios in record time as a cash-in – simply throws a vast number of gags at the screen like a dying stand-up struggling to keep our attention. To

---

*Admittedly, *On The Buses* was the highest grossing film of 1971, beating the box office for *Diamonds Are Forever*, but that does not mean it was any good.

make longer form comedy you must adapt. The dramatic arc is sustainable but the comedic one isn't. This is because in drama the characters grow, learn and change but in sitcom they don't. Sitcom is entropy, stagnation, unresolved emotional issues.

TV drama is different. Being a longer viewing experience (a televisual hour) we expect less of it. All we require to keep us watching for the first thirty minutes is to know that there has been a murder or that a murder is imminent. It is suspense that keeps us going. Comedy does not have this luxury. To write comedy means you have to start with a bang and keep on going for the full thirty minutes (or twenty-one in US shows) so how are you ever going to do that over a full hour?

In the UK, when a sitcom becomes successful, a fifty-minute Christmas special is mooted. The characters are broadened out and a more complex plotline is conceived. On occasion, an outstanding issue such as an ongoing will-they-won't-they get together is resolved. Sometimes this works, as in *The Office* final (Christmas) episode, which brilliantly tied up Tim and Dawn's romance and showed David Brent's maturation in one well-placed expletive. *Only Fools and Horses* was a huge success for writer John Sullivan (who also wrote *Citizen Smith* and *Green Green Grass*), but this show did not gain a fifty-minute time slot until its fifth series. The sixth was its last and many feel that the pathos heaped upon the characters of Del-Boy and Rodney in the extended episodes outweighed the comedy. The default setting when you run out of comedy is to go for sentiment and, in this way, though lucrative, the longer slot is a poisoned chalice. In the US, sitcom producers never waiver from the half hour format. They may deliver a two-part special, but it is strictly two half hours with a cliffhanger in the middle.

Deep down they understand the adage: 'If it ain't broke, don't fix it'.

On comedy drama

Many scripts I receive are trying to be comedy drama rather than sitcom. I have no problem with that but if you want to write for this form you must understand that the comedy will always be secondary to narrative structure, concept and plotting.

6

Comedy drama has at its centre a big question: What do you do when you reach forty? Does thinness equal happiness? If you are of the criminal underclass, is family still the most important thing in life? These UK examples (*Life Begins*, *Fat Friends*, *Shameless*) set out to explore a theme and to offer solutions. US comedy drama too explores concepts: What mysteries lie behind the perfect façade of suburbia? (*Desperate Housewives*) Can an 'ugly' girl survive in a beauty-obsessed culture? (*Ugly Betty*). US comedy drama is more aspirational.

Comedy drama also uses a broad cast of characters and has bigger scope, allowing for multiple storylines, a main 'A' plot, several subplots and four, five or even seven acts throughout each hour-long episode. It is not tied to a single location but rather to the people and their working/domestic lives.

In the UK, it will be location-specific in terms of its milieu, be it Scotland (Scots Whimsy), Manchester (Northern Gritty/Northern Soft), London (Metrosexual, Geezers or Young Professionals) or a rural setting (Generic West Country). There is room for drawn out tragedy too, characters with terrible addictions (sexual or substance based), longings, infidelities and bitter revenge motives. There will be a central protagonist who will exemplify the theme and who has an empathic connection to the audience. It will have an ensemble cast, in which each character represents differing aspects of the issue under discussion.

The style of the piece will differ too. It may be shot on film rather than digital video (DV). The camerawork will often be handheld for intimacy and a feeling of realism. This is in contrast to sitcom, which is studio bound, performed on sets in front of an audience and shot with multiple cameras. Yes, there is a lot of sitcom at the moment that employs *mockumentary* but current commissioners are tiring of this. Sitcom is brightly coloured and sticks to the two-shot and the medium close up, rather than using ECU (extreme close-up). An exception to this is *Peep Show* (created by Sam Bain and Jesse Armstrong) but the concept of this show relies upon facial reactions (and inner monologue).

In comedy drama, scenes run continuously from interior to exterior with no resetting of the camera because Steadicam is used. It will be expensively lit. There may be crane shots, which you do not generally see in sitcom. The scenes will be fast, with a great deal of intercutting, comprising more a jigsaw reality rather than the 'realistic' flow of situation comedy. The action of comedy drama apes film rather than TV. There are sitcoms that look like film (*Scrubs*, *My Name is Earl*) but they are in the minority (so far).

Hybrid examples of sitcom/comedy drama are few. *Green Wing* was a surrealistic masterpiece created by Vicky Pile, writer, producer and creator of female sketch show *Smack the Pony*. Despite its best efforts with multiple plotlines and set comic pieces, towards the end of its second run of nine TV hours, the dramatic questions overrode the comedy.

Examine your pitch with cold precision. If you have an *idea* rather than a core character relationship then you are leaning towards comedy drama. Can it be played out in a living room or on a shop floor, week-in week-out, year-in year-out? If not then think again. If you are asking questions like: 'Why do we stay in abusive relationships', rather than: 'What holds people in a marriage?' then consider the format. If you are thinking in terms of an arcing narrative that covers months or years then be advised that a sitcom episode rarely covers a time period greater than three days. There should be no sense of the passing of the seasons, no September story, no 'a month later'.

Do you want to use flashy techniques such as montage, the slowing down or the reversing of time or split screen? Do you want an exciting (read expensive) opening sequence? Do you want to write a show based on the big idea? If so then you want to write comedy drama.

Finding a home for the orphan script

The main UK markets are the terrestrial channels: the BBC and Channel 4. In the US it's either the networks (Fox, ABC and NBC) or HBO. Launching sitcom is an expensive and risky business and most satellite and cable stations do not produce home grown product. The UK channels make little in-house (ie, using their own studios, production crews and facilities) preferring instead to source their product from the independent production companies of which there are legion. The BBC buys at least two thirds of its product in this way.

Not only are there fewer slots for primetime sitcom nowadays but runs in the UK are also shorter than they used to be – six weeks as opposed to thirteen. Plus of course, there are all those pesky commissioned writers who are still trying to secure their piece of pie – plus the up and coming stand-ups and writing talent all clamouring to be let in.

There was a golden age back in the 1970s and 1980s when if you had gone to the right university with the right people then one of your friends would get a job as a TV producer and you would pop in with an idea on an envelope and walk away with a commission. Either that or you knew a guy who knew someone who was looking for a script editor and you just fell into comedy writing. Perhaps you wrote a play and a TV producer just happened to be in the audience. He would run up to you and gush, 'Hey, this would be *great* for TV'. Maybe you were a pretty writer and the nice producer man took a shine to you?

Yes, this is exactly how it all happened.

Or not.

It has never been easy to get into television. The Old Boy Network, the chance meeting, the decade of hard slog to get the lucky break all occur in any profession. Does going to a good college help? Yes, but only how to learn how to write and drink. Chance meetings occur through precision planning and after much rejection. Applying yourself with diligence to the craft of writing is the entry-level requirement.

Flair is extra. Flair gets you noticed, but only on top of knowing your stuff and getting it in front of the right pair of eyes. So how do you do this when most of the independent production companies will not accept scripts sent in by unrepresented writers? Firstly there is the BBC Writersroom, where everything is read, but the primary intent of which is not to commission scripts. The Writersroom finds and nurtures new writers. Secondly, there are some production companies which will look at unsolicited work, but what you really need to do is to focus on finding a producer.

The producer is, or will be, the person with power. As they move from radio to TV or from a low position to a high one in a network or production company, they will form a coterie of writers whose work they like. It is these writers who will secure the commissions and ensure the production fees, thus enabling the producer to continue. You will want to be one of these writers. But how do you get close to a producer without invoking legal action? Answer: the stalking must be business-like and not creepy.

First you need to find a producer whose work you enjoy and admire, preferably one who is up and coming. Check their credits online (via IMDB) or on the DVD box sets. Call the production company and ask if the producer will accept unsolicited material or if there are any opportunities to write for an existing show which they are producing? Go to places where producers give talks, to writers' groups and industry seminars if you can. Put on a show and send a ticket to the producer or their assistant. Do anything you can to make that first contact. Be polite, get the producer's business card and email them. Do not pester, but do not let them forget you. Be in the background quietly producing good work. In doing this you will get noticed, but please note the proviso – *good* work. If you submit material that is not ready, then you will blow your chances.

In the US it is possible to send a sample script for an existing sitcom series, which may lead to a job as an intern in the writers' room. Staff writers there serve a long apprenticeship before getting the chance to write an episode with their name on it. To create your own sitcom, you really need to be inside the citadel of television, which means your best policy is to write spec scripts for the show you like. In the UK there are currently no team-written sitcoms except *My Family*, and few others 'farm out' episodes, though it does happen. The UK still welcomes submissions from amateur writers, but to be in with a good chance, you need to find your knight in shining armour – your producer.

Guerrilla sitcom

> We don't pay for pilots but we will cast and shoot tasters of shows, if necessary. Increasingly in comedy, just having a script isn't enough and if you can put something on a DVD that will help, then why not?
>
> **M.M.**

The best way of getting a job is to act as though you already have the job. Because the walls of TV and media seem so unassailable, you should consider creating some heat in your own way. If you are serious then you must adopt a guerrilla approach, because being a writer these days is not enough. Just as a stand-up comedian is expected to write all their own material, a writer is expected to network and to push themselves in the marketplace.

Write and cast your sitcom and have it performed live. Make a DVD or a CD of it. DV and HD cameras are now affordable and user-friendly. Shoot your own sitcom and put webisodes on YouTube. Try animated sitcom. Start a Facebook group. Find new ways of getting your product out there. Keep a blog like everyone else in the world. John Weavers, one of my most enterprising students, was tenacious in his attempts to get his work seen. Here is his story.

> On *Blue is the Colour* I found that it was incredibly difficult to get anyone to look at your work. As I understood it, the BBC writersroom gets 2000–3000 sitcom scripts a year and the only one ever commissioned from this process was the *Smoking Room*. What happened with me is I entered the BBC talent competition and came in the top 100 of 5000 scripts. I then started to write more episodes. I joined a group called Scriptank where scripts are read out and criticised by other writers. I put up episode three and was very lucky that there were some great comedy actors there (including Stephen Mangan) who had come to read their friend's script. It went very well so I decided to put on two episodes at the Soho Theatre Studio and then Riverside Studios Hammersmith *and* film them. Steve Mangan generously agreed to do some of the readings and when I made DVDs of them I had his name on the disc, which was an immeasurable benefit as he is a huge, well-regarded star. The cost of hiring the studios was about £250 an evening and £100–£300 for the camera crew who then made the DVDs. It was difficult to get TV people there although Channel 4's Shane Allen did attend and has been supportive ever since. My sitcom is too traditional for Channel 4. Baby Cow heard about it

from a website as their head of development is a big Chelsea fan. Henry Normal took the script to BBC 1 and ITV 1 but they did not bite. A couple of years later I was in the final of a Tap's sitcom writing competition where we had a lecture from Marks and Gran who wrote *Birds of a Feather*. I gave one of them a ten-minute highlight DVD of *Blue is the Colour*. A few weeks later the BBC called me and asked for the scripts. The head of mainstream comedy optioned it for twelve months. We did auditions at the BBC and then a reading for the head of comedy commissioning and the head of BBC comedy, but it went badly and they understandably passed. The latest news is that I have made two YouTube highlights that I have sent out to a TV production company to take to ITV and they have just asked for the scripts.

Blue is the Colour can be viewed on the following link: www.youtube.com/watch?v=Chs9tk0jYgU

There are two companies currently putting on live unproduced sitcom scripts in London, the Sitcom Mission and the Sitcom Trials. You will not be paid for putting your work on – nobody is. What is so important about getting your work shown is that you will see it objectively and should you reach the final of a competition it will be seen by the right people. TV executives, producers and agents *will* attend these showings because it is easier than reading scripts in their office and there is no onus on them to provide detailed feedback. They are always looking for new writers and an afternoon of their time spent at a showing is easier than ploughing through the slush pile.

You do not need to be in London to do this. With the ubiquity of email, your comedy career can be masterminded from Orkney if you so wish. Theatre and live performance are thriving in the UK. Why not put on two or three sitcom episodes in your local arts theatre studio space? Why not set up and run your own regional competition? But remember, this does not mean you get to win every year! Be enterprising. Don't wait for producers to come to you.

Interviews with the Sitcom Trials and the Sitcom Mission

Sitcom Trials

Kevin F. Sutherland has been running the Sitcom Trials for over a decade.

What are the Sitcom Trials and what is its function?

The aim of Sitcom Trials is to test sitcom scripts live in front of an audience in a format that keeps the audience engaged and involved. So we have scripts no longer than ten or fifteen minutes, with the audience voting for the best, and featuring a cliffhanger ending so the audience only sees the ending of the winner.

Have you had any notable successes?

It began in 1999, growing from a show called Situations Vacant which showcased complete half hour scripts that I began in 1995. The Sitcom Trials went to the Edinburgh Fringe in 2001 with one of our stars being Miranda Hart. The sitcom she presented in that show is the template for her current BBC series. Our 2002 Edinburgh show featured Laura Solon who went on to win the Perrier, and James Holmes who now co-stars in Miranda. Many of the writers and performers in our London, Bristol and Edinburgh shows have gone on to TV and stage success, with such names as Justin Lee Collins and Russell Howard passing through the ranks. In 2003 we had an eight week TV show on ITV1 made by Carlton in Bristol. It went out live on Friday nights at 11.30.

What does a writer need to know in order to make a submission?

Sitcom Trials stipulates a tight format regarding the length, number of actors, the cliffhanger ending etc, though these change depending on the venue and production. The bottom line is that we're always looking for funny sitcom that will work in front of a live audience.

What is the process thereafter?

The selection of scripts has happened in many ways, from a script reading team to peer-review online. In 2009 we had over 400 scripts, from which only twenty were performed, so whatever method we use, we can be sure to disappoint the greatest number of entrants.

Who will see the work of the successful applicants?

In the recent Trials seasons we have run a series of heats, semi-finals and a final. If those shows all sell out, each script can be seen by a few hundred punters. Clips of all the sitcoms are then showcased on the website, some proving very popular in their own right. The audience includes representatives from the TV and comedy business, not the least of those being our panel of judges, who help choose the winner.

Do you offer feedback to those who are not successful?

The experience of the Sitcom Trials is the best feedback you can get. Seeing how an audience reacts to your writing, and how actors and a director can interpret your work is an invaluable learning process which most writers struggle to achieve.

Who judges the competition?

The audience's vote has always been a key part of the process, and we never let the audience lose their part in the process. For the recent seasons, since 2007, we've introduced a panel of judges from the TV and comedy industry. They have the casting vote and the final say, with their votes and the audience votes being tallied together. In the recent season two sitcoms would go through from each heat, with a wild card highest scoring runner up also going through. This allows for audience favourites not being judge's favourites getting a chance, and ensures there's no chance of ballot stuffing derailing the vote if, heaven forefend, one writer fills the audience with their friends!

What sort of scripts will get rejected from Sitcom Trials?

Scripts need to adhere to the guidelines set out for each season. These usually stipulate cast size, length of script etc. If a script is funny but needs some changes to become performable, it would be sensible for us to suggest changes rather than reject it out of hand.

For more on the Sitcom Trials go to sitcomtrails.co.uk/

The Sitcom Mission

Declan Hill and Simon Wright of production company Every 1's A Critic have created a competition that is both audience and industry friendly. Avalon, Baby Cow, Hat Trick, Big Bird Films, Rough Cut, So TV, talkbackTHAMES, Tiger Aspect and BBC Radio Comedy have all been to see Sitcom Mission live performances.

What are the aims of the Sitcom Mission?

The Sitcom Mission aims to get live sitcom in front of producers and executives where they would not normally have an opportunity to see them. Someone once said that sitcom is a really difficult art form, because for every good one there are nine bad ones. So it would make sense to try them out in front of a live studio audience first before committing hundreds of thousands of pounds on them for TV. Channel 4 currently showcases seven new comedy pilots a year, four of which were sitcoms in 2010. We showcase sixteen sitcoms, with five in the Grand Final.

How many scripts do you receive, and how many are accepted?

Last year we received over 500. Initially we accept thirty-two, of which we have rehearsed readings, and then we whittle that down to sixteen for performance.

What makes you want to reject a script straightaway?

One-dimensional characters are a massive turn off. If they're in a flat-share sitcom they never go to work and if they're in a workplace sitcom they never go home. Think of Frasier Crane or Alan Partridge and how much is revealed about them by showing them both at work and at home. Frasier goes home to a luxury apartment in the Elliott Bay Towers. Partridge to a travel tavern near Norwich. Most people reading this will have a job as well as somewhere to go home to. Why shouldn't your characters? We have a three-strikes and you're out rule, so if you break three, you're in trouble. However, if what you've written is laugh-out-loud funny, we'll keep reading. Our maxim is 'funny, interesting and marketable'. If it's not funny or interesting, why would I want to turn the page?

15

How often do you hold the competition?

We hold it once a year, but it's an on-going process. We put the call out for scripts in July, and then have a closing date in December, and we hold writing workshops – if you attend one of these and follow the advice we give, you've got a good chance of getting in the top 10–15%.

Who have the judges been?

We've had a number of TV and radio comedy producers including Dawn Ellis, Karen Rosie, Carlton Dixon, Chris Carey and Esta Charkham. This year we've tried to get more TV press involved, so we've had someone from *Time Out*, and we had TV critics from *The Sunday Independent* and the *Daily Telegraph*. For the grand final in 2010, we had Cheryl Taylor, Comedy Commissioner BBC TV; Shane Allen, Head of Comedy, Channel 4; Michaela Hennessy-Vass, Commissioning Editor, Scripted Comedy, ITV; Lucy Lumsden, Head of Comedy, Sky TV; Pete Thornton, Comedy Commissioner, Comedy Central; Jane Berthoud, Head of Comedy Production, BBC Radio and Tim Arthur, Comedy Editor, *Time Out*.

What success have the writers had?

A couple of the finalists look like they're going into development with production companies. The winner of a sitcom competition that we used to run had a half-hour non-broadcast pilot commissioned by BBC Radio. When we produced that competition, we set ourselves the target of getting a radio script commissioned, which happened. This year, we've set ourselves the target of getting a TV pilot commissioned.

The most successful writers use us as a stepping stone, not as an end in itself, so one writer who got through to the heats but not to the semi-finals wasn't so worried about that, because she'd managed to get a top TV producer to see her work.

More information can be found on the following website: www. comedy.co.uk/sitcom_mission/

Radio: limited budgets but better pictures

A brief history. The earliest known British radio sitcom is *That Child*, which consisted of six ten-minute episodes broadcast in 1926 starring Florence Kilpatrick (who wrote the script) in which a couple – Netta and Henry – struggled to cope with their daughter. Radio comedy was later popularised by the long-running *ITMA* (*It's That Man Again* – a title referring to the relentless advance of Hitler), which ran from 1939 to 1949. The creation of comedian Tommy Handley, scriptwriter Ted Kavanagh and producer Francis Worsley it had, by 1942, gained an audience of sixteen million. Three hundred editions were broadcast and the show ceased only on Tommy Handley's death. It spawned the first BBC television sitcom, *Pinwright's Progress*, which aired in 1946. Ted Kavanagh was the script editor and this movement from radio to TV still exists to this day.

Radio has always been a proving ground for comedy writers and the sublime *Hancock's Half Hour* introduced the world to two of the finest exponents of comedy writing the UK has ever produced. Ray Galton and Alan Simpson created Anthony Aloysius Hancock of 23 Railway Cuttings, East Cheam and 102 radio editions made him the most popular comedian in Britain. Since then, BBC Radio has continued to make transferrable comedy shows. Comedians such as Harry Hill, Sanjeev Baskar (and the *Goodness Gracious Me* team), Baddiel and Newman, the League of Gentlemen, the Mighty Boosh and Mitchell and Webb all began their careers in this medium (I even had *my* first break with a self-penned BBC Radio 2 series *Whining for England*). Many of these comedians performed sketch comedy, but sitcom has also fared well with shows such as *After Henry*, *On the Hour* (which became *Knowing me, Knowing you*, then *Alan Partridge*), *The Hitchhikers' Guide to the Galaxy*, *Red Dwarf* and *The League of Gentlemen* (a hybrid sitcom/sketch show) which all transferred. This proving ground is unique to the UK and continues to thrive, as long as BBC TV and radio co-exist in their London production bases at White City and Portland Place.

Sadly, radio offers little in the way of remuneration, hence sixty years of jokes about the BBC and small cheques, but it is a great test-bed for sitcom. Without the visual distractions of sets or attractive actors, the listener only has voice and sound to fall back on. A whole world must be created with contrasting voices, stresses, pauses, beats and nuances. Silence is used to great comic effect as well, as the listener will fill in the gaps. There are no nods or winks to camera, but it does not preclude slapstick humour either: listen to the recordings of the Goons or the Monty Python CDs to see how sound effects can be even funnier than dialogue. There is more on writing for radio in chapter eight.

Likely Lads Peeping Badly. Is your lad-com hard enough?

If I'd started *Men Behaving Badly* now, I would probably have asked to do it single-camera without an audience. Although they are both rubbish with women, the *Peep Show* guys are more sophisticatedly rubbish and less innocent, just as Gary and Tony were probably a bit more clued up than Bob and Terry. I liked *The Likely Lads* but always felt it was very specifically northern, however stupid that sounds. I was influenced by the banter in *M*A*S*H* or the film *Animal House*.

S.N.

One of the most common things for new writers to write about is just 'a bunch of guys', either at university or living together in an apartment. Oh, the hilarious scrapes, the accusations over washing up rotas, the thinly veiled attacks on 'wimmin'. This is perhaps because if you are game-obsessed, testosterone-fuelled screenager, this *is* your world and how funny it seems. To you.

The alchemy required to make this work is to turn this raw material into a successful long-running comedy about siblings, for that is how these relationships must play out on screen. Sitcom is always about familial relationships, whether through blood or subtextually. When pitting man against man, you have the choices of father against son (Steptoe/Sanford and Son, Frasier and Martin Crane) or brother against brother (Frasier and Niles, Earl and Randall Hickey, Charlie and Alan Harper (*Two and a Half Men*). US sitcom is unafraid to explore the rivalries of the fraternal situation, and we often see it played out between characters who are faux-brothers, such as Ross, Chandler and Joey (*Friends*) or Leonard and Sheldon (*Big Bang Theory*).

In the UK, because men only show emotion through sports, their music collections or in their taste for trivia, the heat of the brotherly battle is played out in the 'best mate' scenario.

Bob and Terry (*The Likely Lads*) 1960s/70s
Rimmer and Lister (*Red Dwarf*) 1980s
Gary and Tony (*Men Behaving Badly*) 1980s/90s
Mark and Jeremy (*Peep Show*) 2000s

These men are brothers in all but name and their character dynamics share many similarities. One is nominally intelligent and controlling and tries to occupy the high moral ground; the other is slovenly, cunning and catnip to the ladies. The former is aspirational yet desires the chaotic love life of the other; the latter revels in his apathy and ridicules the stability of his 'brother' because he craves it. This is the literal expression of the Dionysian versus the Apollonian view. It is control versus chaos, stability versus change. It is classic comedy in the true sense of the word.

The role models of 'lad' comedy are Laurel and Hardy – the silent masters whose attempts to earn a crust of bread during the American Depression were both hilarious and heartbreaking. In many of their shorts, the story is the same: Olly sees an opportunity for employment, perhaps babysitting, carting a pane of glass about or delivering a piano (*The Music Box* won the first Live Action Oscar for Comedy Short in 1932). To this end, he inveigles his companion Stanley into the plan. Stanley, once coerced or tricked into it, becomes engaged in the task and is then inspired to improve and industrialise the method. He is a child, a pure creative force, pretty much an *idiot savant*. Due to his meddling, circumstance gets the better of them. Lacking foresight and incapable of talking their way out of their dilemma, they proceed toward chaos. This results in the trope of reciprocal revenge. All dignity is lost as they are dumped on the street, no wiser and no better off. Stan and Ollie were pure sitcom and a close study of their work will pay dividends.

The fraternal dynamic continues into each new decade. In

the US, *Two and a Half Men* and *My Name is Earl* are ratings winners and in the UK, *Peep Show* has become a huge hit.

Can you write the next brotherly battle? Remember that for your lad-com to be convincing it has to have strong women to temper and offset the puerile nature of the lads' existence. *Men Behaving Badly* had Debs and Dorothy; Bob (*The Likely Lads* and *Whatever Happened to the Likely Lads*) had Thelma; Lister (*Red Dwarf*) had Kochanski (the honey-voiced Clare Grogan); *Peep Show*'s Mark has Sophie, his unfortunate, sensible partner. You need the womenfolk to be credible. Sure, they are in essence long-suffering spouses but like Marge Simpson they must have believable inner lives and flaws. It can be argued that females civilise us, as so often they act as a rudder, steering the boys away from extreme behaviour. If there are no women you get *Bottom*, which descends into pure anarchy. *Two Pints of Lager and a Packet of Crisps* works because of its strong women. Writer/creator Susan Nickson (who also wrote BBC's *Grown-ups*) created flawed but likeable women: women other women would relate to, which is why it has become such a big success for the BBC. They are needed for balance. Men on their own soon degenerate into infantile farty bum-bum behaviour, which is only amusing to other men.

If your sitcom is all about men – and you have a thinly veiled version of yourself in there as the voice of reason – then think again. There are some things that ought to remain the preserve of the stag night rather than in the in-box of the producer waiting to be deleted. Women cannot be ciphers or mere attitudes rather than characters. Women are great consumers of sitcom and to risk alienating fifty per cent of your potential audience might not be a good thing.

I have bolted some sketches together

INT. FLAT LIVING ROOM. NIGHT
MATT is asleep in front of his Wii. A BURGLAR enters, sees him and backs off. Pause. He re-enters, bends down and tosses a peanut at him. No reaction. The BURGLAR tries to prize the Wii from his hands. MATT stirs ...

MATT

Who the hell are you?

BURGLAR

Jehovah's witness ... paramilitary wing?

MATT

You're a bloody burglar.

BURGLAR

Very good. The balaclava was it?

MATT

You're trying to take my stuff.

BURGLAR

Observant. Look, you're insured, nice place like
this. Chill. Go back to sleep. Don't get involved.

MATT

I know that voice.

BURGLAR: (*lowering his voice*)

No you don't.

MATT

Chris. Chris Henshall?
Mobury Secondary School?

This is a sketch. The premise that Matt and Chris the burglar
were classmates at school has some potential. There might
be some good dialogue, an argument – possibly a neat comic
resolve – but after that, what happens? On what basis do they
form a long-lasting relationship? Was Chris the school bully or
even Matt? How does a fossilised relationship – which ended for
a good reason – play into adulthood? Other than the comedy
inherent in the unlikely juxtaposition of this meeting, where can
this go? Perhaps Matt will offer to help Chris sort out his life, but
under what circumstances would he do that? Only if he felt he

owed him a debt. And how would this impact on his family? It feels contrived.

Sitcom is more about character, less so the situation. When it comes to the latter it ought to be something simple and long term; something in which you find yourself, not something thrust upon you. Sitcom asks: if we make our choices in life, then what trap do we willingly choose? Where are the sitcoms about an unwanted flatmate or best friend or clinging parents?

Sometimes, a script introduces 'sketch' characters. These are not fully rounded people but cardboard devices created to shoehorn in a comic idea. They are often written by fans of *Seinfeld* or *Curb Your Enthusiasm*, both of which employ a great comic template of taking a simple life problem (double dipping, dating someone with a loud voice, arguing over who pays for dinner) and running them out like an extended sketch. The difference is they are filtered through *character*. It's not the 'contest' problem itself; it is how Jerry, George or Elaine dealt with the problem. They are inside the situation, rather than in a sketch. The writer is asking: 'How does George Costanza *feel* about a bubble boy …?' Rather than 'If there was a boy in a bubble …?' Temper your comedic ideas by putting them through the forge of character. If they prove themselves there then you can take them anywhere.

My sitcom is so good, here are ninety pages …

Some writers, eager to prove their worth, write like mustangs, galloping over the forty and fifty page mark, hurtling through bluster and banter, trampling the foliage of action description then cantering across plains of arid plot-free scenes. Seventy pages pass without sign of resolution or characterisation and the analogies become even more tortured than this one. These scripts are often about students or men hanging out in bars.

The writer is convinced that their magnum opus is genius and sends the whole thing out unedited. A heavy parcel arrives in my letterbox or, more likely, the postal service leaves me a card telling me they are sorry I was out and that I will have to go and pick up the parcel from the sorting office at a time more convenient for them. Not knowing the offending item is a script I go along, sign for it and lug it home. I tear open the envelope and slap my hands together in giddy glee. How amazing that this writer has eschewed the restrictions of form and so trampled the conventions of sixty years. I set about making a shrine to them that I call 'recycling'.

It is not brave or original to over-write. It's dumb. All it does is tell a script editor that you do not understand the form and that you do not respect them or the profession enough to give them what is asked for.

A sitcom script should be around 6000–7000 words, or around thirty-to-forty pages when double-spaced. Once you have written yours, read it out loud, doing the funny voices, at normal speed, and include all the stage directions. If you are still reading once the light has gone and the wolves are howling then it is too long.

I ask for hard copies of scripts for two reasons:

1 The sender has to think about paying more for a heavy package
2 I am too mean to print them all off

Never print on both sides of the paper. We may be trying to save the planet but TV people are not. They want a nice easy read.

- ❖ Be clear on form: are you are writing narrative situation comedy or comedy-drama? Understand the genre.
- ❖ Do not write long or short.
- ❖ Sitcom is not sketches but rounded characters in relationships that trap them together. Ideally forever.
- ❖ The comedic situation ought to be recognisable to us on a resonant emotional level.
- ❖ Consider radio to hone your skills, and as another route in.
- ❖ Opportunities with main terrestrial channels are limited, so go DIY. Get it on the Net or in a theatre.
- ❖ Write about family even when it isn't a family.
- ❖ Take responsibility for your own success: don't ever expect the producers to come to you.

2.

Grammar: the grammar of sitcom

> So often people rush to finish a script, to get it out there and it seems like they haven't even bothered to read it back themselves. Be patient. Make sure you think the script is perfect, or at least as good as it can be before you send it out.
>
> **M.M.**

Without a basic understanding of the grammar it is impossible to speak a language. Screen, television and radio have their own syntax and a writer with access to scripts and format notes at the click of a mouse has no excuse for not learning its rules. Spelling errors and the odd typo are not enough to scupper a seaworthy script, but will give pause to the reader. More serious concerns such as purple prose, massive over-writing and unreadable work, will have a reader hurling your masterpiece at the bin.

Spolling errors, typos and bad grandma

INT: KICHEN: DAE
Martin is wearing a fevvar boa. He is sat on a pouf and looking all around him at the firy kitchen. At any moment it could catch fair and if it becomes a crisis he will picnic.

Put yourself in the position of a professional reader, someone who went to college and is most likely still paying back the fees. They spent three years learning how to drink and how to get their heart broken but somehow pulled it together at the last moment and obtained a second-class degree. They are someone who was going to do something useful and productive with their life but right now is treading water as a reader for an independent

24

production company. Being creative and capable, they are also writing their own sitcom/blockbusting novel or angling for a directing job. Most of their time is taken up with assessing the rubbish they receive from you.

What the reader loves is to find a script that is so badly written from page one that they are able to toss it into the nearest receptacle with no feeling of guilt or any sense that they have missed out on the next *Office* or *Friends*. Their job is to find good material or at least a writer with potential: a writer with whom they can work. What follows are some practical ways in which you can stop them from reading your work. These mistakes are real. I cannot say if the writers are genuine morons or if there is something very wrong with the UK schooling system, or both.

BRIAN
I gotta bare witness is all.

He stop's, see's what is happening, trip's up and then shoot's hisself in the face. He then falls off of the wall.

Spelling
If you are not sure of how to spell a word or if you have written a word that you *think* may be erroneous, then check it. Do not rely on your spellchecker because your computer will make assumptions, just as predictive text does. No one is totally accurate on spelling (except perhaps Stephen Fry) and there are many words, such as occasion, practise or entrance, with which we all have problems. The most common of these are those words with double consonants or with vowel choices, -ance/ence endings and the basic there/their choice.

'Their' is a possessive determiner, used to define to whom something belongs. 'There' is an adverb, a noun and an inter- jection. It tells you where a thing is located.

Even more irritating is the confusion of 'its' and 'it's'. 'Its' is used to define ownership and 'it's' is the contraction of 'it is'. Learn them or you don't have a career as a writer. There are roughly a million words in the English language. Words are lovely and ought to be your friends, your lovers even. In technical terms they are scalpels which when wielded with skill will define

25

any object, feeling, time or action to a point of precision; if used badly they are a blunt knife that results in butchery. Sitcom writers are not expected to be Shakespeare but there is an entry level and that entry level is 'good written English'.

In sitcom, you will not be using long words unless you employ the rococo flourishes associated with Blackadder or some of Frasier's more eloquent barbs, so make sure that the short ones you do use are the right ones. Also, please check the meaning. If it looks wrong it probably is wrong. I was once writing a script for a big two-part TV drama and misused the word *erstwhile*, confusing it with 'esteemed', only for the director to point this out. It was my first big commission and the shame of it stays with me to this day as I weep over my erstwhile career.

Write what you know and use the words that you know.

'I meant beloved *aunt*, not beloved c***.'
Larry David, *Curb Your Enthusiasm* (2000)

Typos
A typo is a misspelling by the author or a printer's mistake.

No one minds the odd typo but an easy to correct spelling mistake is a speed bump in the reader's journey through your script. I notice all of them and if I find myself juddering through a staccato series of bumps – a rumble strip of bad spelling if you will – I will stop reading.

My attitude is this: if you cannot be bothered to send in a properly written piece of work, then you obviously do not care enough about it to want it to be any good, so why should I? A script reader can always put the badly spoiled peace of writting aside and get on with the next won.

If you are unsure of spelling or presentation or have dyslexia then get a professional to read it first. It takes under an hour to proofread a thirty-five-page script and it will ensure that your work is looked at beyond the first few pages. Why sabotage yourself?

Bad grammar
Bad grammar comes in many forms. Clumsy phrasing, mixed tenses, poor punctuation and the use of incorrect words. Again,

all I can do is suggest you get someone to cast a professional eye over your work. If you are a non-native English speaker, then you must have someone to hand with a good working knowledge of British or even US English, including some dialect, slang and idiomatic phrases. Misheard or amusingly incorrect English is fun if you are creating a 'funny foreigner' but the humour can only work if *you* know that what they are saying is wrong even if *they* don't.

Use the present tense because we are watching now

All writing for the screen is written in the present (or present continuous) tense, with the exception of dialogue if a character is referring to the past. You write as if you *are* the viewer. You write exactly what you would see on the screen and only this. This means that when it comes to the slug-line (the scene descriptor which tells us whether we are inside or out, the location and the time of day, also if the scene is running continuously on from the previous one) or scene location, you only need put in enough to give us a general flavour.

EXT. WOODS. LATE AFTERNOON
Tall trees close together. In fast-fading sun, it is growing SCARY.

Or

INT. LIVING ROOM. MORNING
A room just like the one you lived in as a student with all the accumulated trash, plates and unwashed clothes. NICK enters, hung-over and tousle-haired. He stumbles to the fridge, grabs a stale beer and takes a long pull on it. He sprays its contents all over the calendar girl on the wall.

NICK
Lucky I had you laminated.

There is no room for prose. Prose is a poetic description of the physical or emotional scene or setting, often involving the inner thoughts of the protagonists. You reveal character through action. Nick is a slob, that's all we know right now. We do not know why he was drunk the night before. He may have had a legitimate reason, say his sitcom about students was rejected once more. Since he is drinking in the morning we may assume he's unemployed or a writer or most likely, both.

Strong verbs

JAMES strolls uneasily along the grass verge of the verdant area. He seems confused, asking himself if she has any feelings for him or not?

Or

JAMES walks across the park.

The second one is what you see. You cannot write in a sense of unease or confusion because these are inner feelings. If you want to show these feelings then you have to make him do something that demonstrates them. Also, it isn't clear what he is uneasy about. The grass verge? Does he have an extreme form of vertigo? All we can show is the walk in the park. We might overlay some sad music and have him put his hands in his pockets, but that is about it. There are no substitutes for clear, strong verbs and each adjective or adverb you use must be treated with suspicion. They must earn their place. If you can lose them then do so. We will understand. We're clever too.

The best writing is readable writing.

Avoid adverbs carefully

He just carefully reaches out and takes her wine glass as she walks prettily and carefully across the lovely shiny dance floor. She kisses him lovingly, and starts to dance frantically, before slipping on her cute ass.

Adverbs slow things down. These descriptive words, instead of giving us a clearer picture, add unnecessary verbiage. What we want to read are strong verbs and nouns.

The tough script with jokes and a plot makes me want to read on.

> *He reaches out and takes her wine glass as she teeters onto the dance floor. She plants a kiss on his cheek before starting to dance. Then falls on her cute ass.*

Redundant feisty bubbly adjectives

> *SUZIE, the bubbly blonde secretary giggles as she enters the boss's office. As usual, he is sitting at his mahogany desk smoking a cigar almost as fat as himself. Unusually, standing beside him is his feisty new PA.*

> *JULIE is standing with a hand on her hip. SUZIE wilts. Her old school seduction technique is going to be no match for this post-modern feminist ball breaker.*

There are certain adjectives that are so overused they have become drained of meaning. True, TV and film still on occasion trade in stereotypical portrayals (the iron-willed but privately flawed career woman, the sensitive gay best friend, the black salt-and-pepper haired judge) but we still strive for authenticity and freshness. Take for example, the idea of a boss. Some of the adjectives you might attribute to an employer may be:

Middle-aged, overbearing, pompous, self-satisfied, stuffed shirt.

Physically, he is overweight and balding, dressed in a smart pin-stripe suit with a waistcoat. He strides around issuing orders and retires to his corner office to slaver over a catalogue of top of the range sports cars.

Boring and trite.

Let's look at the descriptions of the bosses in *The Office*, both in the UK and the USA, according to the British Sitcom Guide website.

David Brent is an irritating man who tells bad jokes and fails to earn the respect of his staff. He is inept, egotistical, hypocritical, two-faced, and gauche, constantly finding disaster and making faux pas. He is a lonely deluded man who lies to himself about how popular and talented he is.

Michael Scott is a single, middle-aged man who believes he is the office funnyman, a fountain of business wisdom and his employees' cool friend. He has no clue that his employees tolerate his inappropriate behaviour only because he signs their paychecks.

These are nothing like the sitcom bosses of old. Their folly is that they are all too human; they want to be liked as we all do. They want to be our friend, which is a difficult trick to pull off in the complex status exchange of boss and employee. They want to be the office joker whilst still retaining control of the workplace. They want it all. This makes them flawed and a delight to watch – but how do you get this across in the script? When you introduce a character for the first time you need to describe them so the reader has some idea of the character. Later on, action and dialogue will do the rest of the work but for now, you need to give us some telling characteristics. First, include their rough age in brackets – 20s, 30s, whatever – then select no more than two adjectives to describe them, either that or a short phrase. For example:

Enter SALLY: (40s). Newly dumped and cynical, she's a breath of bad air in any situation.

TOM: (mid 20s). Your best friend when he needs to borrow something.

KEVIN: Bar hanging guy who can't even commit to non-commitment.

The intention here is to interest the reader. You don't want to be too cute with every description but make each word punch its own weight. Remember, too, that most sitcoms are going to fit a generic situation, for example, a gang of guys in their 20s or a middle class family. What makes yours stand out must be *character*, and this needs a defining hook. What makes *you* remember the guy with the funny laugh, the big ears or the meat cleaver?

Friends and *Seinfeld* were great at using outward characteristics as signifiers, each character being a cameo of a behavioural type. Ross was lovelorn, Chandler pathologically sarcastic, Joey a combination of vain and dumb. Rachel was a JAP (Jewish American Princess) incarnate, Phoebe the complete flake and Monica an obsessive-compulsive. George Costanza was a 'meatball of rage' whereas Jerry was the cool guy you wanted as your friend.

When describing women (if you are a male writer), do not be tempted to be politically correct or to effect positive discrimination. Women are flawed too, and to write them as either super heroines or ball breakers is inaccurate at best. The observation that in times of stress they like to collapse into a petal-strewn hot tub with a glass of chilled white wine and a fireman is a tad patronising. Perhaps they like to run half marathons or kick box or sculpt. When women are feeling down its not all about chocolate ... though most of it is.

I have also read scripts where women writers assume the worst of men. Sure, you can't go far wrong in calling us sport and fart obsessed Neanderthals but we do have some range. We like music and games too, and we like to put women on pedestals so we can see up their skirts. ☺

Your script has to show you at your best and you get only one chance to make a good impression. Make it count. Make the characters intrigue and impress us from the start.

Brand name comedy

I could murder a Ginsters, said the lorry driver.
She sucks like a Dyson.
Fat? He never passed a Gregg's in his life.

The judicious introduction of brand names introduces a sense of familiarly and folksiness to a script. It is not something to be overdone, but instead of necking a beer, if our character's favourite tipple is a pint of wife beater, then he might 'throw down a Stella' before storming off. As we are becoming increasingly defined by the brands we choose (*Sex and the City* is *all* about this), the writer must sift through our homogenised global culture for material. The big brands hold little; Apple, MacDonald's and Starbucks are too ubiquitous to offer much comedy but the little places, the regional ones, earn our affection. It is in the details, for example in the way every local hairdressing salon has to have a punning title, or quirky spelling and odd syntax; this is the gold.

In the UK, northern writers Victoria Wood (*dinnerladies*: *Acorn Antiques*), Alan Bennett (*Talking Heads*), Craig Cash (*Early Doors*) and Caroline Aherne (*The Royle Family*) have all made careers out of referencing the local and mundane. In their mouths, a cherry Bakewell is delicious (actually, it *is* delicious). The current king of this is Peter (*Phoenix Nights*) Kay, who has captured the spirit of a generation with his stand up routines on 'yer mam's pop' and 'Garlic … Bread'.

There is a danger that some might feel alienated by the use of local expressions, dialect or colloquialisms, but the benefits of audience loyalty cannot be over-stressed. *My Name is Earl* and *King of the Hill* both make great capital by getting all 'down home' and the *Big Bang Theory* makes as much out of its nerdiness (quantum physics gags for those who never got to Princeton) as Frasier and Niles (*Frasier*) did out of wine, psychobabble and snobbery. It all adds to the verisimilitude.

Brand name comedy is a regional not a cosmopolitan trait. The metropolis is too diverse and populated for us to find the necessary communality. I could refer to the kim chi in my local Korean deli, the antipasti in Waitrose or the balti in my high street, but you still won't know where I live (thank God).

Of course you can use mall produce, high street chains or supermarket products with impunity. There are always easy laughs to be garnered at the expense of Aldi's or the Piggly-Wiggly; any downmarket shopping experience too – Poundland, Iceland, World of Leather – anywhere as ubiquitous as a DFS half price sale on a Bank Holiday Monday will garner laughs. However, it is always good to mint new observations. Look at how your parents refer to shopping experiences, the dated phrases they use, and derive comedy and truth from them. Look at the language you and your friends use for shopping, eating and going out.

Find the communal experience. It will endear the characters to the reader.

BOLD, underlining and what italics can do

How do we express emphasis in a written form???!!! Correct. The use of triple question/exclamation marks look great on the page if you are six years old. In an ideal world, the meaning of each line of dialogue and its subtext should be clear from the context of what you have written or from your expert characterisation. However, you may find yourself in a situation where you wish to employ irony, sarcasm or some complex emotion and need to find a way of showing this without resorting to:

INT. APARTMENT. DAY
BIFF sticks his finger in the socket, receiving 140 volts.

BIFF
(*Ironically*)
Whoa. Guantanamo dude.

BOLD, underlining and *italics* have their uses. Bold is shouting, plain and simple. You can shout in CAPITAL LETTERS, too, but the number of times you might recourse to doing this ought be roughly ... zero. It jumps out at you, doesn't it, the one **bold** word? Considering that caps have already been used for the slug lines (INT/EXT) and for the action/description then it is rather gilding the lily. Underlining a particular word will certainly emphasise it but again it is a trifle clumsy. *Italics* are often used in novel writing to separate the inner thoughts of the protagonist from their outward behaviour.

You mean, a bit like writing in the subtext?
Yes, that's right.

However, this is prose. In the novel, italics offer the author an opportunity to change perspective. If the author is telling their story from the first person subjective, italics can be used to introduce another character.

You mean like a ghost?

Or someone with another viewpoint. They can then intertwine the dual narratives and add depth and resonance to their story.

But how does this work in sitcom?

You cannot use it in the same way because sitcom is not a prose form. A sitcom script is as much of a blueprint as a screenplay in that it is not designed to be appreciated as it is, but to be changed to another media, that of film. In our simplified script, we can recourse to using italics in subtle ways to imitate the pattern of stressed *words*.

BOB

Oh, you are *so* smart. *Really* bright.

Hopefully the sarcasm is evident. But would it be true of this line?

JANE

Oh, that's so *funny*.

I think it works against us here. In placing Jane's emphasis on the word *funny* rather than *so*, she comes across as more genuine. Had she said ...

JANE

Oh, that's so funny.

With no emphasis at all, we would know that she hasn't a funny bone in her body. But again, if you overdo it ...

CHANDLER

I'm *so* not going. *Not*! See? I fooled ya. *Smart boy*.

We are asking the script editor to play hacky sack with his eyeballs. There are no rules for the usage of italics, bold and underlining, but the key is to be judicious. Emphasise only when it's right to do so. *Cabron*.

34

Beats and pauses – what they mean

A 'beat' has different meanings depending on the form and format. In screen writing, the script reader may refer to story beats, which are the moments of emotional resonance that the characters are expected to hit at certain points throughout the story. Beats and pauses, when used in a TV script, can be confusing. The beat is very comedy and very sitcom. In a comedy sketch it is clear where to hit the lines. It is the pause between the set-up and the punch. Comedians take an intake of breath at this point as they prepare the audience for the actual joke. It's an invisible nudge.

> BRIAN
>
> I've always hated her. Those teeth and that horrible stupid piggy laugh. Your mother is ...

BEAT

> BRIAN
> Standing right behind me, isn't she?

In plays, pauses are often written into the folio. They are a clear signal for the actor to take a few seconds before speaking again. Look at the work of Harold Pinter. The dramatic pause is laden with meaning and presages an emotional or physical catastrophe. It has no real place in the area of situation comedy unless it is a moment of great pathos or drama. Use beats by all means but be judicious: if you litter your piece with them it will begin to look like a stand up routine.

Leaving a white space in your typescript does not always convey the necessary hesitation.

> BRIAN
> I think your mother is going to hit me now ...

> Ow.

Is clear. But:

BRYONY

So I said to him, 'That's the biggest cock I've ever seen'.

Of course he's not always farmed roosters.

Looks as though you might have censored a line. How your script looks on the page will not necessarily sell it, but a clear, sparsely laid out page will predispose your script editor to enjoy it. They want to be able to read it as if they were 'seeing' the entire episode in their head.

Less really is more.

INTERIOR/EXTERIOR and continuous shooting

You have three choices of location in screen writing: interior, exterior and continuous shooting, which is moving between the inside and the outside, using a Steadicam or digital video camera. The latter would only be used in a single camera setup, not in the studio.

Traditionally, sitcom has always been shot on a sound stage; *I Love Lucy* is credited with the first use of the multiple camera set up, which means that several cameras (three or four, sometimes more) simultaneously record and broadcast the scene. Two outer cameras shoot 'crosses' of the two most active actors at any one time, and a central camera gives us a wide master shot to capture the action and establish the geography of the set/room. This reduces editing time and scenes are shot 'as live' without the need to reset the lights or to obtain alternative camera angles. This is also why sets are colourful and drenched with light – so there are no tricky dark places. The director is up in the gallery pasting the shots together in real time. This method has proven to be most effective and continues to this day.

Friends was shot on 35mm film, rather than on standard videotape. This was done to 'future proof' against HD – as film is more easily transferable to this medium. Nowadays, videotape has fallen out of use with the advance of digital video (DV) and most sitcom is shot with single camera. In the US, *Two and a Half Men* and *How I Met Your Mother* are still shot with multi-camera, and in the UK, so are *Miranda* and *The IT Crowd*.

Sitcom evolved in part from the comedy play and is still a stagey medium. This gives rise to the problem of cast members hanging about with nothing to do. Too many people in shot can be confusing so when you are writing, try to think of the blocking. This means where the characters are on the set and how they are going to move around it. What will they be doing when they aren't speaking? Don't make them static and note that in US sitcom, the main speaking characters are always brought to the fore as the others melt away, out of shot.

Some actors sometimes don't know what to do with their hands if they are not performing and nerves will lead them to grab a prop: a glass of bourbon, a cup of tea, a stuffed rodent. Anything will do to occupy them. Look at old black and white films and marvel at what the actors could do with a simple smoker's pipe. The humble briar, the rural clay or the flamboyant Meerschaum were all fiddled with in myriad ways. The pipe (surely Sherlock Holmes was the progenitor) implies wisdom and honesty and is at once paternal and reassuring. It can be lit, tapped out, drawn on thoughtfully, re-filled and re-lit and jabbed to make a point, 'My God, Caruthers. If you bods at the Ministry go ahead with this there'll be hell to pay'. Cigarettes too were once, unbelievably, not a filthy habit and cancerous health risk but a godsend to the insecure actor, 'Got a light Doc?' 'Of course, young fellow. Do have a smoke whilst I whisk out that bothersome lung'. If an actor is not contributing, tuck them at the back or get them off the stage.

Write as many exits into the main set as you can. Count the exits in the *Frasier* apartment.

Front door
Bathroom (by the front door as you come in)
Frasier's bedroom
The balcony
Corridor to Dad's and Daphne's rooms
The kitchen

It's a lot more than the lousy motel room that you live in.

Exterior shooting is expensive and is traditionally shot on film before the rest of the series and then played in on monitors during the studio recordings. In this way the whole episode can be shown to the audience in chronological order and the laughs are consistent. Note that most US sitcoms do not actually shoot anything outside, instead using stills for the outside of the *Friends* apartment, Monk's Cafe (*Seinfeld*) or for *Big Bang Theory*'s somewhat Italianate scenic backdrop. The outside, in sitcoms, is usually a stage set. Do the best you can to make it all as cheap as you can. The set builders can knock up an alleyway, but the frozen tundra may cause problems (in commissioning for a start).

Each time you need to move the camera to a new location, this will be a new scene. You need to mark this by writing a new slug line.

EXT. TIM AND DAISY'S FLAT. DAY 1

Is fine. Leave the fancy continuous shooting for the movies. If you take a scene out of the living room to go into the hallway or the lift then that is a new scene. If you place a character in the kitchen or bathroom then that is a new scene. To look into a room from the outside means that a camera must be present outside that room and if that room is a set, then another set will have to be built.

Continuous shooting is sometimes used. *Curb Your Enthusiasm* in the US employs this and in the UK, *The Thick of It* and *The Office* both do so (single DV camera as already mentioned) but note that in general, the camera is kept inside the office location because the light changes when you move from room to room. See this for it yourself. Get a DV or video camera and walk out of your lonely apartment, go past the winos and the dumpsters (or Biffa bins), past the burning cars to the nearest heavily graffittied public space. Before you are mugged and relieved of the camera, play it back and see how the light keeps changing. This is because the camera adjusts its aperture automatically unless you add extra lighting and extra lighting costs.

Avoid flashbacks. Avoid, avoid avoid ...

JIM BOB
Why, I remember when I was just a young boy.
Back at the old swimmin' hole ... hole ... hole ....

CUT TO:

EXT. THE OLD SWIMMIN' HOLE. DAY.

JIM BOB swims in dappled sunlight. A big croc moves lazily towards him ...

The apparent advantage of the flashback is that it gets rid of clunky exposition. It *shows* rather than tells us, it uses voice over which is so extremely handy for giving out information when you don't notice it and it can be a cool way to do a bunch of visual gags. What's not to like? After all, *Scrubs* uses them all the time.

We do not have flashbacks in real life. We tell a story. Sometimes a long boring patronising story but a story nonetheless. The flashback is shorthand for this, but what it does in visual terms is to throw us out of the reality you have painstakingly created. A feature film has room for this, but a half hour sitcom struggles. There isn't time. If you need to fill us in on some relevant back-story, then – before employing flashback – see if you can't come up with some other way of getting the information across. Ideally you might leave it out altogether. Sitcom is better when it moves forwards and tells a story in the now. Also, technically speaking, a flashback means that another set will have to be built and populated. If it is childhood or college years (which they often are), then it will have to be shot and dressed differently. This makes a lot of work for the art and costume departments, and impacts on the budget: all this for something that takes up less than a few seconds of screen time.

Breaking the fourth wall (making light of the artifice or showing your working) is seductive to the writer, inviting cute tricks like showing us a different reality to the one the character *says* they experienced. However, being postmodern for the sake of it tends to pale after a while. It tends to fall into the realm of cerebral *clever* comedy and thus avoids the gut laugh we crave as an audience. The flashback trope is rather tired and predictable; to get much more out of it, the writer must think hard to justify its inclusion. Of course, all this will change once you are a produced writer and the budget has increased; then you can use it all you like. Right now though, with the aim of selling your pilot, I ask you to avoid ... avoid ... avoid ...

The curse of the cell phone

SCENE 1. INT. LOUNGE AREA, PUBLIC HOUSE. DAY

REG sits with a pint and mobile phone to his ear.

REG

All right, Nigel. Did you get the text I sent earlier? The one about me getting this new job? Yeah. I'm starting tomorrow. What? No, I don't know nothing about the law. No, no qualifications at all ... they said I can learn on the job. Why would I want to wear a wig? I'm not in court. I don't play tennis. I'm not a lawyer either – what you going on about? ... Barrister? No, I said Starbucks. I said in the text that I was going to become a *barista*.
Yeah, yeah ... yeah alright then. Bye.

Funny   [ ]
Dull   [ ]
D'Oh   [ ]

When I receive scripts where people are constantly on their mobile phones I want to harpoon them and the mobile phone user with a swordfish. The cell phone has caused big problems for writers of slasher films wherein beautiful semi-naked teenagers wander round deserted forests waving bits of metal saying, 'OhmiGod, there's no reception ... I can't get a signal'. For the rest of us, the ubiquity of the cell has left social mores floundering.

What do we actually *see* during this interminable speech by

Reg? Not being party to the other side of this conversation we are at best only half interested in what is being said. We do not know Nigel. We don't care about the texts so this turgid speech must either be jazzed up or kept to a minimum. A great actor will convince us that there actually *is* someone on the other end of the line. A great writer will write in the other side of the dialogue and then erase it, and keep cutting until all that is left is the necessary information and the emotional punch for the scene.

Also note that no one says goodbye on TV, either when they exit or at the end of a phone call. There isn't time. We don't need that silly high voice that you do in real life (*Byeeee*) unless we're using it as a character tic. There are better ways of imparting vital information via the phone than the above. First, if we are only seeing the recipient and not the caller, keep the dialogue short and the responses natural.

REG

Nigel. Get my text? No, it's really important …
You're always leaving your phone off … no … No.
I'm not telling you … yeah AND your mother.

CLICK

Secondly, you can use split screen, so that we see both sides of the conversation. A good example of this is in the film *When Harry Met Sally* (directed by Rob Reiner and written by Nora Ephron) and before it, *Annie Hall* (written and directed by Woody Allen) where the disparity in what the couple are doing adds to the comedy and helps to flesh out character. The third and most common way is to cut between the two parties. These latter two ways of portraying phone calls are visual. You should never just let a call happen. It must function either as a way of delivering exposition or as an opportunity for drama or comedy. Let's not forget also that though it is being dramatised as a 'real' conversation, it is not. It is an ersatz call with all the attendant possibilities for comic misunderstandings, for example:

- One party thinks the other is alone but there is an eavesdropper.
- One party is in a compromising position.
- One of them is trying to get off the line.

41

- The call must be kept secret from an authority figure or partner.
- The timing of the call is inappropriate.
- One party cannot remember who the other one is.
- The battery is running out.
- The phone is needed for another call.

Remember that the cell phone is only a device.

- It may be used to drink and dial.
- It may be used as a missile by supermodels.
- It can be left in embarrassing places.
- It can be left on during a show or during lovemaking.
- It can be switched off and therefore vital information is withheld.

A call is a great opportunity. Don't waste it.

Descriptive methods

TEENA, a 17-year-old girl gets into the car. She is dressed in black. Her long hair has been dyed jet black, her fingernails are black, her face is white but she is wearing black lipstick. She has a crucifix around her neck, although it is upside down. She has tattoos and piercings. She wears a black T-shirt, skinny jeans and enormous black platform boots. She looks miserable.

Or

Teena, A GOTH, enters the car.

Description should be as simple and clear as possible. Give the relative age of the person (20s), allowing for the fact that the casting will vary. In series three of *The Inbetweeners*, the actors playing 18-year-olds were around 26. It has already been mentioned that a couple of adjectives will suffice or a pithy statement about how the character comes across, but other than that do not resort to prose. Don't write oddly about the surroundings as in this example.

42

INT. BEDROOM. DAY

The bed has a Dr Who duvet (Tennant era) plus there are posters of Amy Pond, Tron and Battlestar Galactica: also a cardboard standee of Homer from the Simpsons Movie and littered around are figurines of Leatherface, Sam (Trick r Treat) and various Nightmare/Freddie Krueger ephemera.

It may be clear what type of person lives in this bedroom but it is a little too specific. There is nothing wrong with giving a flavour of the person, but this amount of detail is unnecessary. It is the set designer's job.

When describing action, keep it simple.

EXT. STREET. NIGHT

JOHN is walking home, drunk. He realises that there is a young woman in front of him by the clacking of her high heels. He keeps a discreet distance. She senses him and crosses over.

After a moment he too crosses over.

JOHN (V/O)
Oh God, she must live near me. But she doesn't know that and she probably thinks I'm a weirdo.

She starts to walk more quickly.

JOHN (V/O)
Maybe I should catch her up and tell her I'm not following her. I can't just hang back in the shadows ...

He walks faster. She turns a corner into

EXT. ANOTHER STREET. NIGHT

She is half running now. JOHN goes after her but he is

43

out of condition and he starts to wheeze. He runs faster
until he's almost caught up with her. She drops her bag. He
reaches for it.

JOHN

Sorry. I'm not a rapist. I just live over there. You
shouldn't have started running. It's your fault
really.

She sprays him in the face with pepper spray.

You need nothing more complicated than this. Simple clear
description of what the camera sees.

Verbal and very writerly tics and habits

'OK. Well, honestly. Actually, I don't think I have any tics – you
know? Yeah, right. OK. Umm, maybe I do say I hate things like
so much? And I guess I do like raise my voice at the end of a
sentence? Duh.'

In writing this book I have removed several hundred 'wells' and
'howevers', not to mention tortured analogies and nice lovely
adverbials. Were it not for my slimmed down prose style and
wonderful editor this would be a piece of prolix to vie with a
Stephen King novel.

We all do it. Sitcom should be an easy read but repeated actions
or comments begin to jar after a while. Some sitcom characters do
speak repetitively, but unless this is a catchphrase (You plonker!;
Stupid boy; We were on a break) or intended trait, then it's best
not to overdo it.

One successful example of using a verbal tic was in the UK
sitcom *The Vicar of Dibley*, in which the character of parish
council member Jim Trott replied to every question by saying no,
no, no, no – yes. His wife Doris was later revealed to do the exact
opposite. A nice running gag.

In general, give us a flavour. If a character has an amusing
regional dialect then we will get that from the phrasing. Don't

write it all out phonetically as it will be impossible to understand. An exception to this is the BBC Scotland sitcom *Rab C. Nesbitt* (currently on series nine, written by Ian Pattison), which is written in heavy dialect rather like an Irvine Walsh novel. This is specific to Glaswegian and no doubt the actors and writer are in collusion over its pronunciation.

'That lad wants smacking' is a clear direction that the speaker is from the north of England, just as 'Ma momma told me 'bout boys like you' is clearly of the Southern States rather than the North. Vernacular and the occasional use of slang are fine, an important social signifier even, just don't overdo it. This is particularly true of writing in Estuarine English, which is now near-ubiquitous in Southern England, but when written phonetically comes across as 'geezer' speak. Give a hint by all means but don't go full on with clichéd utterances: e.g. 'Ee dun me up like a kippa'.

Note that Del-Boy and Rodney (*Only Fools and Horses*) were both proper South Londoners (as is writer John Sullivan) but that in their speech they did not overdo dialect. Del-Boy was known for his tortuous ways of rising above his linguistic station, as he applied malapropisms in what he considered to be high class (what would have once been courtly) French. In general, specific regionalism tends to be ironed out in sitcom as it alienates large sections of the viewing public. (See 'Northern soft'.)

Another spoken form of English in South Eastern England – especially by the young – is a mix of Jamaican patois and rap-speak, some of it indigenous, some learned from MTV and other US TV stations. It is in essence an attempt to talk 'black' whether you are black or not.

In the US, there is a significant subgenre of African American sitcom, which began with radio shows *Amos 'n' Andy* and *Beulah*, continuing on TV with *The Cosby Show* and *The Jeffersons*, through *Benson* and *Diff'rent Strokes* to the *Fresh Prince of Bel Air* and *Everybody Hates Chris*. The US networks had been heavily criticised by the NAACP for failing to portray African Americans (as regards *Amos 'n' Andy*, certainly) in a positive light. In response *Steptoe and Son*, a very British sitcom about rag and bone men, was bought up and recast as *Sanford and Son* with a black cast. It was a huge hit. US black sitcom is still, to an extent, ghettoised and there is precious little Latin American or Asian sitcom, despite growing examples of tokenism. True black–white crossover audiences came to pass with Cosby and more recently Chris Rock, who mocked the situation by saying, 'Everybody loves Raymond but everybody hates Chris'. It became the hook for his show.

In the UK, we have had *Desmond's*, which was set in a Peckham barbershop, but little else. Today's white and Asian kids have learnt to flatten their vowels and hammer every consonant. This was comprehensively satirised by comedian Sasha Baron Cohen (*Ali G*) but seemingly to little effect. A new sitcom, Phil Bowker's *Phone Shop* features a young white salesman Ashley (Andrew Brooke) who talks in this affected way around both black and white and no one seems to notice or care. This may be a growing linguistic development or a nod to simple faddism. In the 1970s many youths adopted 'hippy speak', just as the 1980s Australian soap *Neighbours* resulted in a generation using the phrase 'no worries' and adopting a rising inflection.

Today, like, everyone, like, is like, trying to speak like a Valley-girl, like.

By all means give a nod to how we speak and write the truth, but don't let it overwhelm. The character must shine through. And don't use the N word; leave that to *Nathan Barley* or Larry David (*Curb Your Enthusiasm*). More about profanity later ...

Metaphor and simile and stuff like that

As big as a house. A few sandwiches short of a picnic. The lights are on but there's no one home. As dry as a camel after five weeks crossing the Sahara followed by a day in the sauna with only a doughnut to eat.

The trouble with metaphors and similes is we rarely use them in real life. There are of course the common phrases and idioms that have bled into everyday speech such as 'raining cats and dogs' or 'spitting feathers', 'dry as a bone' or 'pissed as a fart' and these are fine to use. In fact, many British idioms are about states of inebriation. If Eskimos truly have fifty-five words for snow then we have an equal number for being bladdered, mullered or mashed.

46

Unless you are a student, a wastrel or a student wastrel with too much time on your hands it is too much effort to try to conjure up some new way of conveying meaning. When we do try to conceive of a good simile we are often left scrabbling for words and rely on the tried and tested. As tight as a gnat's chuff, as thin as a WAG, as thick as shit, as thick as a WAG. If you can come up with something inventive and natural sounding then by all means use it. Regionalisms are great, especially northern ones akin to those in the *Viz Profanisaurus* – an indispensible guide to bad language.

Few sitcoms use the rococo turn of phrase, though *Frasier* and *Blackadder* are two examples that spring to mind. In the second series, Rowan Atkinson's Edmund Lord Blackadder's tortuous analogies were an integral part of the show (as written by Ben Elton and Richard Curtis) and were heaped upon luckless stooge Baldrick. This and the overwrought prose of Lord Melchett (Stephen Fry) seemed to suit the Elizabethan times. Surely no one ever really spoke like that – but with period sitcom we *might* just believe it, and credibility is all.

Likewise, *Frasier* makes great play of the competing intellects of the brothers, Frasier and Niles. Each tries to out-do the other in matters of elocution, cultural taste and sartorial elegance, despite their living in Seattle. This was in contrast to the embarrassment of their ex-cop father, Martin Crane – a true blue-collar hero. As to whether it is likely that Crane Senior could have sired such effete siblings is open to question, but the cymbal crash of cultures worked. Marty liked to shoot pool; the boys would have preferred polo. Both sitcoms are delightful exceptions to the norm, and it is wonderful to hear language put to its fullest use. If you use simile and metaphor, ensure that it is congruent and germane to the piece and character. Mnaaah!

Timescale. Three days was enough for Jesus OK?

CUT TO: Five years later …

An entire sitcom episode should not be stretched over more than one or two days. The plots are about the minutiae of life – issues

47

that can be solved over the time it takes to start and conclude a row. Don't go flashing forwards two months or back six years unless you want your audience to get whiplash thinking they are in a remake of *Back to the Future*. The half hour slot cannot accommodate a lot of time shifting unless it is a vital element to the show, and even then its internal logic must be so fixed that the audience gets it immediately (I'm thinking of *Scrubs* or *Red Dwarf* here.) If, during the ad break, you were to fast-forward to three months later, the audience would be lost. A lot happens in three months. Certainly, whatever the problem is now, in a few months' time it will either have been dealt with or you will be sitting amongst the rubble of your life. Imagine you are having a catch up with a girlfriend – that's a girl who is a friend rather than a sexual partner – and she asks:

' Hey, remember that cute guy I was dating about three months ago ...?'

Your response ought to be.

'No, not really.'

Both of you are safer that way. Otherwise you get ...

'That Bob guy? He was awful. He had hygiene problems and he treated you real bad. You were in *tears* most of the time. So, anyway, what hap ... oh, God – is that a *ring*?'

Tempus fugit. Sitcom is of the here and the now. It rarely references its past and the characters never learn from their mistakes. They never even recall their life events. Sitcom characters suffer from mild autism at best: at worst, Alzheimer's.

Camera directions

INT. APARTMENT. DAY

Ross is playing with a banana. He becomes aware of a strange smell. He sniffs the banana. It isn't that. He does not realise that behind him is ...

We pull back to reveal the grizzly bear, a small hat perched on his head at a jaunty angle.

You do not need to write in camera directions unless they are so specific to the scene that it will not work on the page unless you do so. Write as if you are the viewer and not the camera and avoid terms like mid shot or close up unless the scene will not work without it. For example, if an actor speaks, but is off screen, then say so: write OS after the character's name. Include what is necessary but no more. Remember, you are writing a writer's draft not a director's draft and you should not be telling them how to do their job (they won't like that). Clarity is all-important. The script you submit must allow the reader to understand without clutter what is happening and no more. You do not need to specify how to stage (block) the scenes except in general terms. It is best not to go into detail about where the actors are in a scene, just give us the words and let the director figure it out.

> *PAUL enters to the left and stands near KEVIN. KEVIN walks across to the bar and takes a drink. JUDY enters and stands by KEVIN. PAUL crosses over to them. A DOG enters stage right and wanders across to JUDY and KEVIN who pet him. PAUL tries to shoo him away. Failing that he places a small hat on the dog's head with an elastic band at a jaunty angle.*

These are traffic directions. Just give clear instructions where necessary.

> *PAUL pats the bedspread, indicating to JUDY that she sit by him.*

Or

> *GARY throws a ball just as TONY enters.*

> *He deftly catches it without breaking stride. Then falls over the sleeping dog.*

> *They laugh, and then attach a small hat to the dog's head with an elastic band.*

Setting the scene

In sitcom, two or three small sets are the norm. Look at *Friends* or *The IT Crowd*. There is one main setting, which is either the living area or the office of the cast. A common secondary set might be a café (*Seinfeld*, *Frasier*, *Friends*) or the apartment of the second lead. That's about it. It is a contained emotional arena. Most of your life is lived at home and at work, and sitcom reflects this.

Sitcom is not considered to be a director's medium. They are an undervalued breed and names like Martin Dennis (director of *Men Behaving Badly*, *Coupling* and *Is it Legal?*) or Tony Dow (*Only Fools and Horses* and *Birds of a Feather*) are almost unknown to the public. The sitcom director does not need to throw the camera around like an action or a horror director, but needs merely to express the comedy in the clearest way, whether catching reaction shots or setting up visual gags.

As much as the cast needs a talent for comedy, so does the director. However, this is not your job. Edgar Wright, director of Channel 4's *Spaced* worked in tandem with star Simon Pegg, as both were movie buffs and wanted to include as many visual nods and references to their favourites as possible. They are exceptions and anyway, postmodern and ironic pop culture references were at the heart of this brilliant (and much missed) slacker comedy.

It would be expedient for the novice to think of their piece in terms of the traditional studio-bound multi-camera sitcom. This means the action will take place in either the INTERIOR or EXTERIOR. It will be DAY or NIGHT and CONTINUOUS or LATER.

You don't need anything more than that.

Mockumentary

It is a mistake to assume that just because digital video camera can shoot endless takes of broadcast quality footage (*The Office*, *The Thick of It* and *Curb your Enthusiasm* have all used the medium) that you can do it too. It's over.

The documentary format was re-popularised by the emergence of TV reality shows in the late 1990s. This was due to the technological advancement of DV but it soon became so over-used that the grammar of these shows – the confessional piece to camera, the hidden POV and the 'emotional moment' – fast become clichéd. To have one person speaking without guile to the camera and then to show they are either lying or too stupid to realise the lie has become a common trope, an easy visual gag. It is no longer a surprise, just as the false jeopardy in any documentary/chef/competitive show is now so obvious and hackneyed. We are beyond parody on this. Mockumentary is not new. The brilliant *Spinal Tap* 'rockumentary' introduced it in 1984. It has been used so often that the format is tired. The ironic take is always slightly sneering and distanced and sitcom needs to bring you in and make you part of its family, not leave you peering and sniggering through the windows. In the UK, a script editor will not look kindly on yet another spoof doc or mockumentary.

Off screen

The directions OS (off screen) or OOS (out of sight) mean that, although the character may still be in the scene, they are not in the frame, which is to say that the camera does not see them. You may use them interchangeably.

Voice over

> HERMAN (V/O)
> I wonder if they'll ever realise I have no idea what
> I'm thinking about.

Voice over (V/O) means we are hearing the inner voice and thoughts of the character. While it is a convention in TV and film terminology, I advise the judicious use of this technique. In the US it's common to use voice over as a framing device for the introduction to a show. *How I Met Your Mother*, *Scrubs* and *My Name is Earl* all do this and it cannot be denied that it is effective. This is in part because the American way of storytelling attempts to be universal, to paint on a big canvas, whereas UK sitcom is more parochial (more on this in the next chapter). The American voice over is both the universal narrator and also a folksy device to bring you into the story, the buddy at the bar. UK sitcom does not operate in the same way. Britons are not accustomed to trumpeting their tales or putting their heads above the parapet. This humility may be only one beer deep but even such great sitcom horrors as David Brent or Reggie Perrin are more confessional in their approach. Also bear in mind that the monster character would not be the one doing the voice over, as that is the role of the slightly flawed hero/protagonist. A British example of this is in *The Inbetweeners* in which Will McKenzie narrates (as if it were his teenage diary) the necessary exposition about his new life as a fish out of water.

One show that is totally reliant on V/O is *Peep Show*, wherein we are constantly hearing what Mark and Jeremy are thinking, and laugh at the contradiction between this and how they then act. Without this device the show would have been considerably weakened (and probably not commissioned). Putting these exceptions aside, UK sitcom tends to throw you into the action without spelling out the situation. It does not spoon-feed. It says, Like them or hate them, here they are, unfettered.

Another reason to be careful about voice over is that it may be seen as intrusive, placing a block between the viewer and the action on screen. Some believe it helps, others that it hinders. It's your call. With cartoons the rules are different because what is inside Homer Simpson's head can simply be drawn – and turns out to be no more than doughnuts or a monkey playing a drum. We don't need to get inside Frasier's head and nor should we want to: we can read him like a book. A pompous book.

Montage

Montage is a device used to illustrate the passage of time and may be used in sitcom in the following ways:

- To show us a dating disaster as described to others.
- To show us how a project was completed.
- For the opening credits to explain how we got here.

Montage is such a common trope of film that when sitcom tries to do it (remember the compacted time scale) it is only left with parody. Montage becomes a series of visual gags that show time passing or some necessary exposition, but little more. Montage makes us aware of the form and anything that does this should be treated with care. We tend to look at the screen and not the box it came in; the classic sitcoms did not play with the format itself until it had tired of character, great storylines and all the comedy inherent in the situation. If you find that you are building jokes based on deconstructing the form rather than on character then beware. It is character that will sell your script, not camera tricks.

Subtext

Dialogue reveals character, but we reveal more about ourselves not in what we say but by our subtext.

> JAMES
> I see you are talking about my receding hairline.

This has no subtext. Try:

> JAMES
> What about my hair?

This has some emotion to it. We know he is hurt. He is saying, Are you being cruel about my vanity? I am wounded. I might have to hit back. In fact, if I don't hit back then you will think less of me. Help! That is a lot of meaning for four words. The first line of dialogue only has one interpretation: I am concerned. It is an opening gambit but there is nothing more. It is almost Germanic in construction.

Good sitcom dialogue is full of suspicion, hidden truths, secrets, double meaning and dramatic provocation. As an exercise, why not try writing some trite dialogue – just everyday stuff – between two people. Jot down what others are saying in front of you on the bus, for example. Then when you get home, rewrite it but replace every line with the actual meaning of what was being said. Quite often, we are saying to someone: Like me, please. I want to be accepted. I want to feel safe with you. However we cover up the raw, emotive, honest words with evasion and subtlety. Think of how children talk to one another. Until they learn to lie effectively (in effect, using subtext), it's charming, guileless, and innocent. As we grow up we realise that it is expedient to cover our feelings, to allude and imply and, if a politician, to lie through our teeth and believe it. What you need to be doing in each line of dialogue is to get across what is said and what is meant: in the gap between them we will find both comedy and drama.

Don't text: subtext. You know what I mean.

Multiple perspectives

Most comedy is subjective and often told from the single perspective or first person point of view. It is the story of a man or a woman in a situation that they may or may not resolve. In drama and crime, there is often the dual perspective of the criminal and the detective, Holmes and Watson, Morse and Lewis, Jekyll and Hyde, Columbo and his guest star, the Id and the Ego, the two sides of a coin. We are asked to sympathise with the detective but our concern is with how to solve the puzzle itself, rather than with the characters.

In sitcom we follow the life and misfortunes of one main character. This is enough. There are subplots and minor players, but they are always subservient to the main story. Because sitcom is often centred on a monster character, they are sometimes not at all empathic (Brent/Scott or Fawlty), so we range around looking for another to engage with (Rodney, Baldrick, Martin Crane) but it is not their story; otherwise the sitcom would have been called *Baldrick*, *Martin Crane* or *Tim's Office*. We can and must see things from their point of view but the story and plot does not begin and end with them. It revolves around the main character. The others are satellites.

Can you have a multiple perspective story? As mentioned earlier *Green Wing* was successful but was not true sitcom, more a hybrid comedy drama. Despite having a collective cast, we were being asked to follow the central love story between Dr Todd (Tamsin Greig) and Dr Macartney (Julian Rhind-Tutt). Does *Friends* have a true multiple perspective? It began with the story of Ross and Rachel: a couple whose emotional thermometer had broken and who could no longer be together. Once that dynamic was resolved, we moved on to Monica and Chandler and then later Joey and Phoebe. The latter were not particularly well-developed characters: if anything they remained as the echo couple once Monica and Chandler moved centre stage. This show is intriguing in sitcom terms as there was no real monster. They were all rich beyond their means despite having mundane jobs. They lived in an impossible apartment and had no real issues in their lives and yet were collectively dysfunctional. It marked a sea change in the desire to be aspirational, which has seemingly spread across the globe (*Sex and the City*, *Ugly Betty*).

Where *Friends* succeeded is that it described a time in one's life when you sever the apron strings and no longer rely on your parents. Your friends really are 'so good for you'. They are your complete world and woe betide anyone who tries to storm the citadel of your charmed circle. Any predator was summarily despatched – look at Janice or poor jilted Emily. What happens next in life is that we pair bond and form a family with our new partner and our alliance to our friends weakens. This is what happened in *Friends* and thus inevitably signalled its demise.

As an audience we crave to be told who to like and why. We cannot empathise with more than one person at a time, which is why in a divorce there is always one bad guy.

The new writer sometimes tries to make all of their characters either entirely monstrous or unanimously likeable and in this way they are all clamouring for our attention. As a result we lose interest in all of them. It's like a roomful of comedians (there is nothing worse). Trust that one fine character is enough. Not by accident did sitcoms get to be known by one name alone, from *Hancock* to *Cosby*, *I Love Lucy* to *Roseanne*, *Shelley* to *Seinfeld* and *Frasier* to *Miranda*.

The ensemble/workplace comedy are also dominated by a single perspective. Often it is the lowly pen pusher (Mr Lucas in *Are You Being Served?*, Tim in *The Office*); sometimes it is the wiseacre know-it-all guy (the Alex Rieger character played by Judd Hirsch in *Taxi*) but the writer's intent is clear. One pair of eyes.

❖ Learn the grammar of writing for TV.
❖ Download scripts and study them.
❖ Strip your work down to its most simple and readable.
❖ Write as though you are the viewer or the camera.
❖ Respect your work by ensuring that it is as perfect as you can make it before you send it out.

3.

Sitcom in the US and the UK

Social realism versus escapism

British sitcom has ties to social realism (film and television which portrayed social and economic hardship, racial injustice and ennobling or heroic depictions of the working classes) and with it shares a point of view of pessimism and failure. A line can be drawn from *Hancock*, Alf Garnett (*Till Death Us Do Part*), and *Steptoe and Son* in the 1950s and 1960s, to *Butterflies*, *Rising Damp* and *The Good Life* in the 1970s. It continues with *Only Fools and Horses* and *Birds of a Feather* in the 1980s and on to *One Foot in the Grave* and *The Royle Family* in the 1990s. Its latest flowering was perhaps *The Office* where little men lead disastrous lives in dead end jobs in a dead end town.

In these sitcoms (and many others) there is an element of nostalgia, wallowing in a past perceived as 'better,' a simpler time when the ordinary working class bloke would be out to overthrow the unfairness of the landed gentry or the officer classes. Until the 1990s and the advent of docu-soaps and reality TV, there was little irony or self-regard in sitcom (save perhaps the punk attitude of *The Young Ones*). Michael Bracewell, in his excellent essay in *Frieze* magazine, notes, 'In the mid-to-late 1990s the cultural insistence on authenticity had become the single peg upon which many of television's hopes were hung and the world of the sitcom – beyond a zappy, ironic version of itself – was allowed to decline.'

Before this, a lot of British sitcom was about Us and Them, harking back to the Kitchen Sink Dramas and the 'Angry Young Men' of the 1960s. Contemporary dramatists of that time, Ken Loach and Mike Leigh, could have easily gone on to make sitcom, though it might have been just too miserable. UK sitcom is resolutely suburban, centring on people lost or crushed by domesticity and the nine-to-five, the trap for them being not only in the relationships they inhabit, but in being themselves. Mainwaring mourned his marriage to the unseen Elizabeth but toiled daily at the bank despite the bombs. Rigsby lived in the B&B equivalent of Dracula's castle, trying to suck life from his young tenants. Rossiter's next incarnation, Reggie Perrin, was a suicidal businessman, who was a template for the suburban man of that time. Jim Royle just gave up, raging in the light of the TV screen, filled with self-hatred, doom and Northern gloom. Ironically, he was one of Ken Loach's regular acting troupe.

Whilst this went on, in America there was *The Dick Van Dyke Show*, *The Mary Tyler Moore Show*, *Taxi* and *Cheers*. Not a lot of introspection there. That teenage nation is all brash and brawn, and quite convinced of its place in the world. Homer Simpson, Frasier or Larry David may have their dilemmas, but they never doubt their right to exist. Hancock, Shelley, Perrin and Meldrew are melancholic, disheartened and full of an almost existential angst.

The locations too are different. British sitcom is about the boarding house, the corner shop, the holiday camp and the department store. These do not exist in the same way in America. Think just how many UK sketches are set in a shop. It is one of the reasons why Monty Python flopped on US TV. Parrots, arguments or Hungarian phrase books? They lack the cultural recognition.

There is also something in UK sitcom about the aftermath of the Second World War. The war, to a degree, levelled out the classes, but the 'know your place mentality' prevailed for decades after. This is plain to see in *Dad's Army* and *On the Buses*, and the office hierarchies presented in *Are You Being Served?* remained clear cut, despite a torrent of innuendo and high camp.

British sitcom avoids the feel-good factor of US sitcom. Our 'Golden' era, the 1970s, brought us *Butterflies*, a sitcom about an unappreciated unhappy woman (Wendy Craig), with a depressive husband (Geoffrey Palmer), who considers an affair but never consummates it. It also gave us *The Fall and Rise of Reginald Perrin*, which dealt with middle class mid-life crises, as did *The Good Life*. When the soaps appropriated the catchphrases and the camp aspects, sitcom shied away, flowering into fantasy with *Red Dwarf* and *Blackadder* or farce with *The Brittas Empire* and later *Only Fools and Horses* episodes.

When reality TV and documentary grew in the 1990s (due to lower costs of production values brought about by digital technology) sitcom bit back with more fatalism and social misanthropy in *One Foot in the Grave, Keeping Up Appearances* and *The Royle Family*. The latter masterpiece brought us full circle. Sitting around watching the telly, frustrated by the lack of social mobility, yet resolutely knowing your place and too lazy to protest: it was 1974 all over again.

Comedy in UK sitcom is often black humour, an extreme example being the brilliant *League of Gentlemen*, a sitcom/ sketch hybrid that takes the tropes of stereotypical British life – the shopkeepers, the bed and breakfast owners, the butchers and landlords – and makes grotesques of them all. UK sitcom is *always* about underachievers and incompetents, people trapped in unpleasant situations or in dysfunctional relationships. It is also more adult orientated (*Yes, Minister, The Thick of It*) as opposed to US sitcom, which is more folksy and good-natured.

This is perhaps because of a fundamental difference in the way the two countries see themselves, which makes for uneasy bedfellows when trying to translate UK sitcom into the American style. British writers tend to poke fun not only at authority and institutions (the army, the law, politics and the media) but also at the foibles and the downbeat nature of the British soul. A British person is a born pessimist, knowing that if they are in a lower class, they are unlikely to rise through hard graft or legal means. If they are middle class, they are full of self-loathing and smug self-congratulation in equal measure. As for the upper classes they do not fare well in any kind of fiction, being reduced to either simple-minded buffoons or the kind of evil tyrant that would make Mr Burns sneer with envy.

The British do, on the other hand, enjoy a rags-to-riches story and for a time will tolerate modest success, but it sticks in their craw. As the Australians have their tall poppy syndrome, the British love to see the high and mighty brought down, which is why their literature is full of this – from Shakespeare to Dickens to P.G. Wodehouse. Whilst business or banking successes get away with it (by virtue of not sticking their heads above the parapet), the visible celebrity even at the point of his greatest triumph is heading for a fall. The British Olympic gold medalist, in a moment of arrogance, stepping onto the podium has experienced the beginning of the end of his career. Success, to the British, is preparation for decline and inevitable failure.

Basil Fawlty (*Fawlty Towers*) will never see his dream of running the perfect boutique hotel because his guests can never live up to his expectations. Del Boy Trotter (*Only Fools and Horses*) may have gained his millions in the end, but did he know what to do with it? Did he invest wisely? Would David Brent ever get to be a chilled-out entertainer? The comedy is in the struggle. It is in every fibre of failure, every thread of self-loathing and distrust. If these people ever obtain whatever it is that they do not deserve, then it's all over.

This is why it's no good trying to relocate it. *Red Dwarf, Men Behaving Badly, Coupling, Absolutely Fabulous* and most notably *Fawlty Towers* all failed in the US. With the latter they tried three times, first with a show called *Chateau Snavely* (1978) but the pilot remained unproduced, then *Amanda's* (1983) where they had the brilliant notion of removing the main character of Basil Fawlty. Bea Arthur played the titular role thus eliminating the central conflict between man and wife. It was finally tried as *Payne* (1999) and was again dropped by the network.

It does, however, work the other way round, bringing US sitcoms to the UK, the most notable successes being *The Simpsons, Friends, Frasier, Roseanne, Cheers* and *Taxi*. You may howl to include *Seinfeld* but it had a rough ride with the BBC, shunted around the schedules and never garnering a large audience. It is remembered and loved chiefly by aficionados. American sitcom is different, firstly in that each episode runs for only twenty-one minutes, leaving eight minutes for commercials, so a UK sitcom cannot jump the pond in its original format as the show runs too long. US sitcom also has a longer run at twenty-two episodes a year to the UK's six or seven (with an additional hour-long Christmas special). The UK used to produce series runs of thirteen to coincide with autumn, winter or spring TV seasons but this is now rare.

US sitcom is relentlessly positive and upbeat. Nowhere would you see a drunken man confessing to his granddaughter that he has 'fucked up his life' (*The Royle Family*) or the kind of splendidly appalling behaviour that you will see in *Rab C. Nesbitt*, *Ideal* or *Pete vs. Life*. Instead, urban socialites (*Sex and the City*, *Friends*, *How I Met Your Mother*) live in impossible apartments with invisible means of income, and friends and relatives who support and cherish them no matter how selfish or vain they are. Every word that escapes their perfectly orthodontic mouths is a crafted *bon mot* or witty barb that is beyond the linguistic abilities of the rest of us. Physically, too, American sitcoms tend to feature perfect specimens even when they dress it down. The star and creator of *30Rock*, Tina Fey (as Liz Lemon), is neither ugly nor fat as she so often claims and nor is America Ferrara in *Ugly Betty*. She is a glamorous woman in glasses and a retainer. Women in sitcoms are beautiful and the men need never worry about paunches, baldness, hearing or memory loss, disease, loss of erectile function, dizziness, vertigo, hypertension, seepage or memory loss. Sure, there will be the odd fat friend (always the buddy role or the wacky echo couple) but they're rarely the lead. He is Norm in *Cheers*, George Costanza in *Seinfeld* or Jeff in *Curb Your Enthusiasm*.

Perhaps this is narrow-minded. Once we get away from the city sitcoms there's more of a downbeat acceptance of life. There's *My Name is Earl*, *Arrested Development* and *South Park*, first aired on Comedy Central on 13 August 1997 with the pilot episode, 'Cartman gets an anal probe'. There's *Seinfeld* and *Curb Your Enthusiasm* to explore the underbelly of the narcissistic American, and thank God for the blue-collar sitcom of Roseanne and Dan Connor and their bunch of ingrate kids. Fundamentally though, the US and Britain differ in their views of class. The US has at its summit politics and Hollywood/celebrity culture, Ivy League (Princeton, Harvard, Yale) and old money. The wealthy professions are dominated by industry, banking and law, then below that a billion small businessman and then the poor. Below this there is what you might loosely lump together as the immigrant class – service jobs and store clerks. These jobs have no shame attached, whereas in Britain being a waiter or any kind of service operative is to be the subject of disdain. In Britain there are still too many signifiers of class. Many white Britons avoid anything that has connotations of 'service'; in London, the minimum wage jobs are nearly all filled by immigrants or foreign students. The UK has for so long been tied to the old three-tier system of aristocracy, the merchant/tradesmen (middle class) and the working man or woman that despite all attempts to modernise or create a unified society, there is still a sense of one's place being defined by class. Society has of course changed tremendously since the 1960s. For the first time, the working class had the opportunity of escaping poverty by becoming actors, photographers, boxers or footballers. Now there is huge mobility but class still gnaws away at us. Samuel Johnson once said:

> So far is it from being true that men are naturally equal, that no two people can be half an hour together, but one shall acquire an evident superiority over the other.
>
> Boswell, *The Life of Samuel Johnson*

UK sitcom has become more middle class, less adventurous, safer and may well be a reflection of our times and growing affluence. On the other side of the Atlantic, US sitcom remains aspirational. It accepts the promise of the American Dream in that anyone can be a success. In Britain it is believed that anyone can be a failure.

Different markets, differing requirements

In the US there are large teams of resident scriptwriters who do the lion's share of the work in big round table sessions. Some episodes are written by a 'guest' writer but this is not the norm. Most of these writers are highly educated: *The Simpsons'* staff contains both Harvard and Yale graduates. They must be team players and are continually competing to raise their game and not to get fired. Whatever your strengths as a writer, be it characterisation, plotting, story lining or writing great one liners, you will need to produce a cracking sample script in order to be considered.

In the UK, this is not the case. Most UK sitcoms are written by a pair (from Galton and Simpson (*Steptoe and Son, Hancock*) to Bain and Armstrong (*Peep Show*)) and they don't need an outrider. There are those lone writers who write every script episode (David Nobbs (*The Fall and Rise of Reginald Perrin*), Roy Clarke (*The Last of the Summer Wine*) and Simon Nye (*Men Behaving Badly*)) but there are others who, faced with other commitments (wheeling their money to the bank) may agree to farm out the work once the series is established. At present only *My Family* and *Two Pints of Lager and a Packet of Crisps* are written by guest writers. Perhaps you might try writing a spec script and sending it in?

British and American writing styles are very different. In the US many eyes have been on each script even before the actors get their hands on it; each scene and every line has been fought over by committee. This has its strengths and weaknesses, the former being you get a consistency across the board, plus a higher gag strike rate and slicker plotting, the latter being that there is a degree of homogeneity and a lack of originality to individual characterisation. In the UK, the lone writer brings a unique sensibility to their work and often it is the writer who becomes the brand, for example Carla Lane (*Butterflies*, *Bread*) or John Sullivan (*Citizen Smith*, *Only Fools and Horses*, *Green Green Grass*) who have been rewarded with a great deal of power. The double act too creates a hybrid sensibility, but this relies on the pair always working in tandem. It allows for idiosyncrasy, quirks of character, plot and mannerism, which in a team situation might be ironed out. British writers are peculiar and eccentric and somehow this survives translation to another country or language. *Keeping Up Appearances*, a very British sitcom by Roy Clarke, is a big hit in South Africa, where the petty snobberies and jealousies of aspirational middle class people has struck a chord. Who knew?

In the UK, it's the one-man band or the double act. In the US, it's a spec script and for that you really need to be in LA and to be prepared to spend several years writing before you get your first solo credit.

The spec script

The speculative script is the only way in – a correctly formatted script for an existing show, which you send to that show's production team. As with many jobs, the way to get a job is to act like you already have the job. This means that your work must be indistinguishable from the real thing or as near as you can manage. If you can achieve this then it's a no-brainer for them to consider your work. They aren't after 'your take' on the show. They don't want to know how this character ought to bring out her innate lesbianism or how this other person might be funnier if sent into space, nor do they require a plotline that involves the cast departing from their usual surroundings (Hey – what if they go to France?). They want something that can be slotted into current programming. It won't sell, but it may get you in the door.

Joke rhythm and wisecrack

In US sitcom, everything is subservient to the laugh and sometimes to the laughter track. Jokes and wisecracks are its bread and butter. Remember artist Al Jaffe's snappy put-downs in *MAD* magazine? This example of set up and punch is the purest form of how sitcom comedy is expressed. All jokes are based on the set up (information, question) and the punch line (the twist). As regards the set up, the information conveyed should be only what you need for the joke, no more, no less. The set up contains the word that will be twisted, or the hope that will be dashed. The dialogue may imply that the speaker is a moron, or is hubristic or plain dumb so that the punch just has to 'knock him down'. In US sitcom this is the norm. Almost every line will either be or be leading to a joke. You can, if the twist is an emotive one, use pathos and litotes for this, building a picture, setting a scene for the punch to tear it all down.

Each character will have his or her signature way of delivering the gag, be it sarcasm (think Chandler or Ross in *Friends*), backhanded compliment and/or snobbish put down (*Frasier*) insult (*Scrubs*, *South Park*) or plain old weirdness (Phoebe, Kramer from *Seinfeld*, etc). Many of the stars of US sitcom are or have been stand-ups and are most comfortable with this rhythm. Jerry Seinfeld used vignettes from his act as the basis for each episode in the early series, using real life situations to effectively illustrate the punch line. There is an echo of this in *Curb Your Enthusiasm* (Larry David had a dry run for his uber-irritating character in *Seinfeld*, where he heaped defeat and opprobrium on George Constanza, the Costello to Jerry Seinfeld's Abbot), which if you remove the sitcom element is an exploration of the social mores and foibles of latter day California.

To this end, the punch is engineered as a knee-jerk reaction. The audience knows where the punch should be and fills it with laughter. There are many shows, such as *Big Bang Theory*, that are delivered in this way. The cast pause at the punch and leave a silence. The laugh track is later laid on. Contrived? Morally OK? Television is no more a contrivance than a magic show. We know we are not being shown reality and it is the job of the producer and director to present a simulacrum of it, not the real thing. All TV cheats. The audience is expected to laugh in all the right places, particularly as so much time and money has been invested in each show. Not to laugh as an audience member is seen as churlish at best and not showing the team spirit expected of you.

All is subservient to the joke or the perceived joke and it is to this end that the writer will be expected to deliver: this and sentiment.

Character serves plot

From the above it might be theorised that character is subservient to plot and jokes, and there is an element of truth in this. Many of the great lead sitcom actors (Lucille Ball, Phil 'Bilko' Silvers, Bill Cosby, Jerry Seinfeld, Roseanne Barr, Chris Rock) came from a stand-up background and are reluctant to let go of the laugh. For an eponymous sitcom to show the character in an unflattering light is unacceptable as it would also reflect badly on the show. They can have foolish moments or be shown up, or be surrounded by lovable mop-top kids who baffle and amuse them, but overall they triumph. They succeed through quick wit and warm humanity but they aren't fully rounded individuals. They are extensions of their act, a *persona*. Ironically, the most fully rounded three-dimensional sitcom character is Homer Simpson. What other sitcom dad would pay his kids to go away or refuse to go to church ('Homer the Heretic') or question seriously whether he still loved his wife when she had just lost him a million dollars ('Bart Gets Hit by a Car')?

If sitcom characters are subservient to the joke, then we have to ask if they are not also in thrall to the plot? Gordon Allport, a founding father of the study of personality, rejected the deep psychoanalytical approach of the person, instead focusing on a behavioural one. Through this he created Trait Theory. Using a lexical hypothesis, he went through the dictionary and made a list of four and a half thousand words to describe human behaviours, which he organised into three levels.

- Cardinal traits. These shape and dominate a person's life as a single theme and are rare. These include justice, devotion to God or revenge.
- Central traits. These are general characteristic found to some degree in everyone. They are the basic building blocks that shape most of our behaviour, for example empathy or honesty or optimism.
- Secondary traits. These are particular likes and dislikes which only close friends will know, that give us a complete picture of the person.

When you are creating your sitcom characters from the ground up, it may be useful to use traits to help define them. Allport spoke of functional autonomy, which I believe is germane to the sitcom character. He drew a distinction between motive and drive, suggesting that a drive, formed as a reaction to a motive, might outgrow said motive. This means that the drive becomes distinct and autonomous from it. Allport gives the example of a man who is dedicated to perfection. A sense of inferiority is ingrained from childhood (via the parents), which drives him on. His motive is to please them but he fails in this. Even when the parents are no longer a direct influence on him he is still driven to succeed and therefore the drive keeps going regardless of motive. Struggling writers may recognise this.

Perhaps we have several drives that employ our time which have in truth outlasted the motives behind them. This being the case we could, if we so wished, address these issues and through cognitive behaviour therapy, modify how we deal with our thoughts, emotions and behaviour.

Sitcom characters have no arc and should not and must not change. They remain subservient to their desires, however you write them. This means that they are of necessity limited and not fully rounded 'people'. If you understand that their behaviour is being driven by outmoded desires then this ought to help with their characterisation. It also means that what you can do with them in terms of plot has its limitations and it is via this reasoning that I suggest that character is ultimately subservient to plot.

British sitcom tends to be less plot-heavy and more character-based. The audience enjoys watching them wallow in their failure and shame. American sitcom continually bombards us with dynamic plots for the characters to become engaged in. I suggest you watch four or five episodes of any US sitcom and see if the plots aren't, well, fairly *interchangeable*?

Cute story to end on. Gordon Allport once met with Sigmund Freud in Vienna. Nervous of meeting the great man, he broke the ice by telling him an anecdote of how he had met a boy on the train who was afraid of getting dirty. The boy refused to sit down despite his mother's reassurances. Allport suggested he had learned the dirt phobia from her, a neat domineering type. Freud studied him for a minute and asked. 'And was that little boy you?'

Morality lessons: aspiration syndrome

The US has enshrined in its constitution that any US-born citizen (sorry, Arnie) can become President. Also implicit in the 'American Dream' is that everyone has the right to succeed and to be happy. Yeah, right. It is a country that has never been invaded or had its borders breached, save by recent terrorist attack. It is vast yet homogenous. West coast and East coast are clearly defined, as are north and south, but within these divisions there are millions of people who are very much the same in their manner of speaking, dress and customs (read Bill Bryson's *Mother Tongue* for more on this). In contrast, a Brit can be identified by class, dialect or occupation. Britain is full of grey areas, a secular society which takes in migrants and refugees as a matter of course and which prides itself on its sense of fair play and good humour.

The US is a 95% Christian country; 60% of its inhabitants have never left the country or even the state in which they were born. There is a fundamental belief in salvation, in the Protestant work ethic, in Catholic and Jewish guilt, in original sin. This has created a society that follows Christian or Judaic morals even if it does not hold to them. These principles are strongly in evidence in the TV networks, and they are not about to rock the Christian boat.

TV drama does not tell Americans how to live their lives and nor do its soap operas – their soaps offer charmed and opulent lives but also lives in crisis. They imply that you can have it all but it will cost you your soul. Films are about a heroic journey, redemption, revenge, and the defeat of external or internal nemeses. Sitcom does not have that journey. Sitcom is where Americans learn their fireside morality tales.

- This is what happens if you lie to your partner.
- This is what happens if you are greedy or wasteful.
- This is what happens when you look for love in the big city.
- This is how a single woman manages.
- This is how a family copes.

This is the lesson and in case you don't get it, the homily is explained to us – without subtext – a couple of minutes before the last gag. It is a sentimental manipulation of the heartstrings but it tells the audience what the point is. You might, as a sitcom writer, take one of these homilies and expand upon it to develop the plot you are trying to write.

This is not true of all sitcom: *Seinfeld* was the first to promise no hugging and no learning and in its wake comes *Curb Your Enthusiasm*, *The Larry Sanders Show* and *Modern Family*. *South Park* and *30Rock* too are keeping the cynical flame alight. You need to decide which side of the white picket fence you are on or if you are trying to burn down the fence and trample it into the mud, you crazy kid, you.

In Britain, a healthy cynicism is taken for granted. In America you may find you have to earn it.

Other transatlantic problems

One script problem arising with more frequency in British writers is their attempts to Americanise their work. US vernacular is adopted and placed patchwork throughout the piece. Colloquialisms or

American grammar are used – the yard, out back, different than – perhaps in the hope that a big American executive from CBS or NBC will pass the London-based production company and exclaim, 'Dis is genius. This Briddish guy rilly knows us merkins. We gotta have it'.

There are too many differences in the underlying structure of the two forms for this to fully succeed. Only when *adapting* a script should you to try to change its cultural form and only then in partnership with a native American speaker. It is hard enough writing in your own language, let alone attempting some kind of cultural anthropomorphism. Stick to what you know for now.

Animation

The US has an excellent pedigree with animated sitcom, beginning with *The Flintstones* (1960–66), created by William Hanna and Joseph Barbera. It was the first primetime animated sitcom to last longer than two seasons. It was said to be an animated version of the then popular sitcom *The Honeymooners*, placing the dumb paterfamilias and his wily wife in Stone Age times. Hanna-Barbera also created *The Jetsons*, which ran for twenty-four episodes in 1967 (and was brought back in the mid 1980s) and started the science fiction sitcom sub genre, which goes from *My Favourite Martian* to *Mork and Mindy* to *ALF* to *Third Rock from the Sun* to *Futurama*.

Animated sitcom more or less died out until its rebirth in the 1990s with *The Simpsons*. Matt Groening conceived the idea for America's first dysfunctional family in the lobby of multi-award winning producer and screenwriter James L. Brooks' office (the creator of *The Mary Tyler Moore Show*, *Rhoda* and *Taxi*). He named the characters after his own family and submitted only basic sketches, assuming that they would be cleaned up in production. They weren't. *The Simpsons* made their debut in 1987 as shorts on *The Tracey Ullman Show* (a UK comedienne). Two years later they were adapted into half hour shows for the Fox Broadcasting Company. *The Simpsons* is, to date, the longest running sitcom in the US and the world's most successful TV show. Following in its wake – with computer animation replacing costly labour-intensive single cell animation – came *South Park*,

Beavis and Butthead, *Family Guy* and *King of the Hill*. These animated sitcoms sell worldwide and in the case of *The Simpsons* has passed five hundred episodes with no end in sight.

The UK has produced one animated sitcom, *Popetown*. However, after protests from the Roman Catholic Church it was never shown. Ten editions were originally made for BBC3 in the early 2000s and was pitched as a kind of *Father Ted* meets *South Park*. It has more recently obtained a DVD release but has only been broadcast by MTV in New Zealand, Germany and Lithuania, where it incited opposition from religious authorities. It is not, in fact, a searing indictment of the Catholic Church, but rather puerile – maybe its time will come. Stop motion clay animation has fared slightly better with *Crapston Villas*, which was produced by Spitting Image Productions and lasted twenty episodes but these were only ten minutes each and do not really count as true sitcom. Puppets, too, have been tried in Channel 4's *Pets* (Fit2Fill Productions), which ran for twenty-six episodes in 2001, but they too were only eleven minutes each. A late showing time made it hard for it to find an audience. A similar idea, named *Mongrels*, has recently been shown on BBC3 and has been commissioned for a second series despite accusations of plagiarism.

Put simply, the UK has not so far been able to obtain the funding to produce animated sitcom in the quantity or quality that is possible in the United States. *The Flintstones* had Winston cigarettes as sponsor and Fox Broadcasting has deep pockets. The BBC cannot justify spending huge sums of money in-house and the independent productions companies, in times of recession, are risk-averse.

However, software programmes are now much more sophisticated and cheaper to operate and it is becoming possible to create your own animated shorts – and sitcom – and to broadcast them on the net. The day cannot be far off when it will be possible to do this with a good script, a solid idea, a small cast of voice artists and a team of people dedicated to produce it all on a Mac. There is undoubtedly an audience for it, the question being how broad? The advantage is that the potential audience is worldwide, the disadvantage being finding a concept with the appeal of *The Simpsons* or *South Park*.

Only a couple of years ago, servers and home computers simply did not have the capacity to stream more than a few minutes of video, but now it's all on-line, and it's tempting to believe that this is where the future of broadcasting lies. US animated sitcom succeeds in being family-orientated and universal. It is playful, colourful and witty. If you are of an artistic, ambitious sensibility – then go for it!

Interview with Andrew Barclay

Andrew Barclay is the co-writer and producer of *Pets*, the UK's first puppet sit-com for adults, which aired in 2001 on Channel 4. The series was sold around the world and also had its own spin-off, *Pet Show*, on MTV Italy. Here he talks about how it was commissioned.

Channel 4 had a nighttime strand, *4 Later*, which was tasked with bringing new and original talent to the screen. We sent in a pilot episode of *Pets*, which we'd made for about £1,000 and a lot of favours, and the commissioning editor invited us in for a meeting. By the end of that meeting, we were asked to deliver twenty-six episodes of the show. It was as simple as that. The commissioning editor had the power to say yes or no, without having to spend three years pondering the decision or taking our idea to endless committees. With screening times very late at night, there was no risk to the channel's ratings and at the same time we learned a great deal about how to produce a TV series! I believe the same thing happened to the writers of *Father Ted*. Channel 4 gave them a very late slot to try out their material and to learn on the job.

How did you capitalise on your success with *Pets*?

Despite being lucky enough to sell the show abroad, and to license a couple of the characters to MTV Italy for their own use, we really wanted to make more *Pets* programmes or a completely new show with different puppets. We approached the BBC to make a new UK series of *Pets* as we knew our idea was still fresh and original, but were told by a member of their comedy department that the BBC would 'never, ever make a puppet sitcom for adults'.

Why is it so hard to get puppets/animated sitcom produced in the UK?

It comes down to cost. It is assumed that animation will cost millions of pounds to produce, that it won't make its money back, so that scares people off. The exception is kids' TV – you can sell a *Scooby-Doo*-type show to every station on the planet, so the costs are more than recouped. Thus, nobody has the confidence to invest in animation for adults. Despite the fact that Oscar-winning British animator Nick Park has an astounding four Oscars to his credit! Despite the massive, international success of *Family Guy*, *The Simpsons*, *South Park* and *American Dad*! So, it's all down to cost. As for puppets – well, I suspect that they're not taken very seriously outside children's programming. More depressingly, there seem to be few broadcasters prepared to take the sort of risk that our commissioning editor did, plus many channels are all now chasing different audiences.

What advice would you give to people creating their own animated webisodes on the Net?

Spend all your time and effort in creating great characters with funny dialogue! Nothing else matters as much. Nobody cares if it's 2-D, 3-D, stop-frame, puppets or stick men but they will start to care if they are watching identifiable, believable characters being funny. In *Pets*, although our main characters were a couple of dogs, they were written as real people facing real dilemmas that our audiences understood. It wasn't just a load of jokes about fetching sticks.

* ❖ British sitcom has a background in social realism. American sitcom is far more optimistic.
* ❖ The two are almost incompatible stylistically, because of the joke rhythm, playing time, season length and the fact that US sitcom has the morality tale at its heart.
* ❖ US sitcom is team written, British is not.
* ❖ To write for the US you must produce a spec script episode for an existing show.
* ❖ British humour loses something in translation.
* ❖ Animated sitcom is cost-effective in the US, but not in the UK.
* ❖ Make your own animated sitcom and put it on the Net.

Character
and plot

4.

Character

> Character is the most important thing and often you feel the writer doesn't really have any affection for their characters and if they don't, why would anyone else? More often than not with unsolicited scripts there will only be one tone of voice for all the characters, like watching an episode of *Friends* starring six Joeys. Not good. We need character-based dialogue.
>
> **M.M.**

> Most scripts we get sent are written in the author's voice so the characters all sound the same. We get a lot of scripts that are essentially stand-up written by people who are too scared to do stand-up. It's just observational humour with no storyline whatsoever. And about a quarter, 125 or so, are about two 25-year-old blokes sitting in a room discussing their inability to get laid. If you're going to send us that, make it brilliant, because we're going to reject it very quickly otherwise.
>
> **D.C./S.W.**

> Character and story are of prime importance. You must establish the world quickly and sparsely but never forget that the audience will empathise with the character every time, even if the story is an unusual one. It is also not a good idea to go along the route of 'that's never been done' and so come up with odd situations and locations (youth hostel, local village hall) as it will run out of steam. Better to work with something that has been done (couples, families, workplaces) but do it with a new spin.
>
> **M.J.**

Let me introduce myself ...

SAM (V/O)

Hi. I'm Sam. Not Son of Sam the serial killer, because
that would mean my dad would have to be called Sam
and he's not. He's called Colin and he's genetically
responsible for making me short, nerdy and pear-shaped.
Because of that I don't have any friends, but I don't mind.
I don't need anyone. I just like sitting in my tree house all
day, watching people, making observations in my little
notebook. Maybe one day I'll do something. I just don't
know what.

Solid characterisation is at the heart of all good sitcom. Without
it there is a vacuum that cannot be filled by any number of
fast-paced plots or zinging one-liners. Sitcom is *all* about the
characters: people at odds with themselves and with the world.
The most reductive answer on how to write a character is this:
learn what it is that they want and ensure that they don't get it.

The character above tells us nothing and does not introduce
any drama into his world. He tells but does not show. The only
hook we have is his father, Colin. If he hates his father then we
have a situation. If we are going to permit him a monologue then
he must introduce some drama: let dad come along and spoil his
arboreal reverie. Have dad pull him out of the branches and set
him to work. Create a relationship in which young Sam must act.

You must place obstacles. If a character wants a partner
(Frasier), success (Del-Boy: *Only Fools and Horses*) or respect
(David Brent/Richard Scott: *The Office*) then make sure it eludes
him at every turn. The sitcom character is unfinished, protean,
striving for something unattainable. Once the journey is complete,
there is nothing more to say. There is nowhere for them to go.

The sitcom story is collusion between the writer, the characters
and the audience. It is a lie we all share and the lie is this – that
there is a journey, because we know that sitcom characters must
not learn. They are emotionally stunted. They are caught in
aspic. In real life we like to believe we are maturing, learning,
moving on to the next stage. We see our lives as a series of
projects: the education project, the job project, the pair-bonding

project, the raising a family project, the creative projects and the drinking-yourself-senseless project. Sitcom bucks all this. The main character has all the same desires as us but he never satisfies them. He fails to complete the projects or if he does they are so riven with bad planning and so unsuited to him that they soon collapse. Sure they need to be *seen* to be striving and this is the fun of it. Basil Fawlty (*Fawlty Towers*) attempts to run a hotel. Rigsby (*Rising Damp*), Sam Malone (*Cheers*) or Simon (*The Inbetweeners*) all attempt to win the unattainable girl. All are doomed to failure.

My Name is Earl is a good example of governing how to get what you want. Earl, a habitual criminal, sees the light and decides to seek redemption for his bad deeds. In order to do this he draws up a list to right all the wrongs he has done to his victims and to all the people close to him. He inveigles his brother Randall, his ex-wife Joy and her partner Darnell into the scheme and works his way doggedly through the list, the completion of which will be his salvation. Only then, he believes, will he stop being a recidivist screw-up and only then can his life propel itself forwards. 'Believe' is the key. Earl is trapped by his own dogma. He thinks it is fate. He thinks that he can control his destiny. He is an OCD criminal. The wonderful thing about dogma or a belief system is that because you created it (there is no external force), you can change the rules anytime you like. This is exactly what Earl does. Anytime he is close to completion, he adds another set of tasks. It is a self-fulfilling prophecy, governed only by how long the audience wants to keep watching.

Then there are those sitcom characters who crave security, inertia or to simply be left alone (Victor Meldrew in *One Foot in the Grave*, Shelley in *Shelley*, Tim in *Spaced*, Mos in *Ideal*, Jim Royle in *The Royle Family*). Apathy is their comfort zone and so having identified this all the writer needs to do is throw events at them, which require them to act. Life is against them. No one can be left to do nothing. Sometimes the novice writer thinks we must get to know their lead character before the action begins. Scrap that. Start with the action and we will get to know the character along the way. Trust the audience to get it or at least to *want* to get it. Enthuse us.

You need to demonstrate who the lead character is. I admit

that this is a big ask of a first script, which is often concerned with exposition and scene setting. I recommend that the novice writer does not write a pilot script or if they do, then they should put it aside and write a second selling script. As a viewer, I am not looking for all that information: where are we? How did these people meet? How did they all get into this terrible mess? I don't care and I don't want to know. I don't want to be told to do all the work. I am relaxing in my sweatpants with a beer. Two beers. All I want to know is – are these people funny and interesting? Do I like them? What is the problem I am being invited to share each week? Where are the nachos?

When you start a new job there is a degree of triage which must be employed with all your new dysfunctional colleagues. You dismiss those who do not make that good first impression by job title (regional sales rep, bought ledger clerk, consultant), sometimes by dress (comedy socks or tie), sometimes because they skulk away from you like rats, have a limp wet handshake or a sniffle problem. It is of course wrong to do this, and you may one day find that the snot-nosed human resources officer naked up on the roof at lunchtime with a rifle, but we do make these early decisions through expediency. The same is true of reading a fresh script. I want to meet someone new and interesting otherwise why would I be here? How do we show the world an interesting character? We show it in how they *interact* with others, through dialogue, via their context with the world and in the very real drama with which they are struggling.

That's me in the spotlight

Sometimes the writer is a frustrated performer and all those things they never said at school or to their family or in their hilarious stand-up routines which would have oh-so-cleverly skewered the pretentions of their school teachers/army drill sergeant/the bullies are going to turn up on the page – whooh boy, then we'll sit up and listen or it's the lunchtime guy with the rifle and his comedy socks all over again.

There is nothing wrong with using a bit of yourself in the script but there is a line between honed characterisation and a rant. True, David Renwick used Victor Meldrew (*One Foot in the Grave*) as a mouthpiece for venting his bile and spleen on all that was wrong with the world, but he was a damn fine stooge. Sitcom is not soapbox; neither is it stand-up. You can't just shoehorn material or jokes in as they will stand out. You've got to be a lot more clever than that; so, sorry, but those 'comedy' ideas in the shoebox probably won't make the final cut.

My monster is not hungry enough: echo couples

The central protagonist of many classic sitcoms is a monster. They are recognisably of life but somehow larger. They're not a pantomime villain or a psychopath but they do have behavioural traits that make them outrageous, rude and taboo trampling and therefore funny. They have little or no threshold for embarrassment. They blunder into things without thought, or if they had considered the outcome it is either purely selfish or misguided in its intent. They are a character who creates drama and conflict wherever they go, be it from intransigence, pigheadedness, arrogance or rank stupidity. They see life askew – reacting to things in a way that we would not have thought of or expected. They bully or belittle others. They have traits that are irritating and annoying such as snobbery, pride or hubris. They have self-knowledge but precious little of it. They know who they are but they consider their faults to be positive attributes. They are Larry David. They are also seen in contrast to more 'normal' others – and it is from here that much of the comedy comes.

Sergeant Ernest G. Bilko needed his troop in *The Phil Silvers Show*, just as Mainwaring needed the platoon in *Dad's Army*. Del-Boy needs Rodney as Frasier needs Ros and Dad. Every Blackadder has his Baldrick, as Patsy needs her daughter Saffy (*Absolutely Fabulous*).

This is the straight man/funny man dynamic of sitcom and you mess with it at your peril (see also *Men Behaving Badly*, *Red Dwarf*, *The Likely Lads*, etc). It is this monster and their relationship to the world that will propel your creation into a second and third series and beyond ...

Some monster characters are less extreme, sometimes mere mouthpieces for stars: *Cosby*, for example, or Robert Lindsay in *My Family*, but they are there as a figurehead for the piece. Can you have two monster characters? Yes, but only to a degree. Frasier and Niles have monstrous elements, but are tempered by Dad and Daphne. Rik and Ade in *Bottom* were unrestrained children, but that was more slapstick than sitcom – whereas in their previous incarnation in *The Young Ones* there was the calming influence of Neil the Hippy and Mike the 'organiser'. Sheldon in *Big Bang Theory* is made acceptable by the fact that he is able (just) to retain his friends.

Often, when there is a sparky central relationship to the sitcom a trope is borrowed from romantic comedy films known as the 'echo couple'. For example *Will and Grace*, where we have Jack and Karen. The echo couple is a smaller, less dramatic evocation of the central conflict. One of the best movie examples of this is Bruno Kirby and Carrie Fisher as Marie and Jess in *When Harry Met Sally*. The echo couple mirrors the protagonists but in miniature. They are less attractive or successful, fatter, more clumsy or tongue-tied and often genuinely neurotic rather than amusingly ditzy. Adding echo couples can be a fantastic addition to your cast or it can be a danger. On the plus side it points up the humour and likeability of the main characters and on the minus, if the main characters are not strong enough to sustain the show, then they will take over.

Will and Grace was always going to be a brave show. It was the first to have an openly gay character in a leading role. You add to that your standard neurotic Jewish girlfriend and it seemed as though they had a hit. The trouble was that the relationship was non-sexual and his homosexuality precluded any chance that they would ever get together, which is perhaps what Middle America would ultimately have liked (Aw, she'll put him right!). In series six there was even talk of artificial insemination but despite the smoke and flames from redhead Grace and lawyer Will, there was not enough kindling to keep the show alight. Most of what we remember of that eight-season show was the sparring between Jack and Karen, whose outrageous behaviour, bitchy remarks and obtuse behaviour literally stole the show. A spin off series, mooted in 2008, never happened (perhaps put off by the failure of *Joey*, a spin off from *Friends*).

A British example of the echo couple is the BBC's *Gavin*

and Stacey. Series one concerned the difficult long distance relationship between the eponymous leads (geographically they were at opposite ends of the country). We had an interesting will-they/won't-they get together and a Romeo and Juliet for our times. The trouble was that the characters of Gavin and Stacey were entirely insipid. Other than their struggles to be together, to get time away from their families and ultimately to procreate, they had nothing to offer us. Their friends Neil 'Smithy' Smith (James Corden) and Vanessa 'Nessa' Jenkins (Ruth Jones) were the dynamic echo couple (they also co-authored the piece) who were larger than life in every sense. Smithy was proud of his appetites; Nessa was crass and rude to all. And Welsh. They became more popular and by series two they and their respective families – the Shipmans and the Wests – had hijacked the show. Having run out of steam it had nowhere to go and they wrapped up the series with a marriage and a proposal. The BBC started referring to it as a comedy-drama and the press and public questioned whether it was sitcom at all.

When you write your lead, you may by all means create someone outrageous to set up against them but watch out, if they start taking over, then you want to look again.

Are you sufficiently interested in your lead character? Perhaps you either need to graft some characteristics from the minor players onto them, combine two characters or explore more the strong secondary person. Maybe they're a real gift? Perhaps you have been too shy to see that this is the person that you really want to write about. If so, do so. You won't regret it.

My characters are so interesting all they have to do is talk

You have a brilliant idea for a sitcom. These two guys are so funny (they are based on me and my mate, Gary) that you can drop them in anywhere and they will crack you up. I'm sure Gary is hilarious. I'm sure you guys are great in the bar but transmuting that to the page and stage is going to take some serious comic alchemy.

Banter is the back and forth witty exchange between two or more characters. Banter is gentle joshing, teasing, Mickey-taking, the playing up of foibles and faults to the general derision of others. Good-natured banter was popular in music hall sketches a hundred year ago, and is sometimes used by stand-up comics with an unruly audience or if they have no material. It does not belong in sitcom because sitcom is all about character and plot. Sitcom may *seem* to be nothing more than comedy fluff but this is erroneous. In sitcom, nothing is wasted. Every line must reveal character, advance plot, be leading to or actually be a joke. And nothing else.

Character reveals itself through action. We are what we do when we are put under stress, be it emotional, verbal or physical. The catalyst is the inciting incident for the plot and this must kick in within the first two or three pages. The plot is the problem which the character must deal with and must resolve by the end of the half hour. Once the character is in a predicament they *must* act. Sitcom is not about chat. The writer in love with exchanges between their characters is learning their characters on the page. They are exploring them but have not reached the conclusions they need and have therefore not started the vital editing process to capture them better. The dramatic dynamic between any two characters in sitcom ought to be so constructed that the smallest piece of plot will have them exploding into argument and drama. The comedy comes as they bite at one another in their attempts to resolve the argument. This is where the love/hate comes in. They feel so much for one another that they have a genuine desire to sort out their problems but are endlessly frustrated when they are unable to. Their relationships are parental in this sense or at least a sibling rivalry. Like you and your family, they never *just talk* …

There's a lot more going on.

(How to speak every line)

BOB (*carefully*)
Shall I put it over here?

SARAH (*annoyed*)
I told you where you can stick it.

BOB (*threateningly*)
If he does that we'll never get to the clinic.

Some writers assume every line of dialogue must be accompanied by a strong adverb to show the actor how to read the line. Sometimes they will add two or three adverbs to further aid them and also several more in the action description to show that they ought to angrily slam the door or walk purposefully away from the burning building. Surprisingly, the actor rather resents being told how to do his job and on encountering such clumsy instructions will cross them out with his crossword pen. That is if he ever gets to read a script pockmarked with such things in the first place.

The actor's job is to interpret lines of dialogue. Having been selected from many desperate actors because they have the talent to fit the role and to bring something of it from their life and experiences, they are going to analyse in great detail every line given to them. They will also press for more lines of dialogue and if they are a comic actor, they will try to get as many laughs as possible. What ought to be clear from each line you write is its intention.

> DR MENACE (*evilly*)
> I am going to shoot you.

This does not need an adverb, as the intention is clear. He is not going to shoot someone gaily, regretfully or randomly. Here is another example.

> JANE
> We need to talk.

> JOHN
> Now?

> JANE
> Yes. Right now.

> JOHN
> Where's that going to get us?

> JANE
> I don't know. You tell me.

JOHN

... Divorced?

I hope the underlying emotions are not open to interpretation. She has a desire. He is blocking it. Writing arguments between couples is fun firstly because most of us have been a part of a couple and we know the territory and secondly, in essence there is only one argument, which is played out in myriad ways. One of them is unhappy and the perceived victim wants the other to love them back, or more, or at all.

The actress playing Jane has few choices with 'We need to talk.' She can be abrupt, petulant or angry, all of which are gradations of the same thing. She cannot say it lovingly, kindly or sexily. Likewise, 'Where's that going to get us?' Can be insouciant or sarcastic and not a lot in between. Most lines of dialogue do not need anything extra and are better written 'clean'.

It is the writer's job to give clear instruction on character, situation and plot. The actor interprets with the aid of the director. It is the director's job to decide how the scene will be played and to what degree of humour or pathos. This will be done during the blocking of the scenes in rehearsal where the actors may be given 'notes' if their vision of the performance differs to that of the director's.

The authorial role in the stage play is perhaps more prescriptive. Since it is hoped that a play will have a long life, one even beyond its author's demise, the playwright wants to be exacting when considering how the lines are to be said. A play does not always contain more adverbials or adjectives (modern folios are slender) but the comic playwright will often use more pauses and beats to clarify his position.

Read all your dialogue out loud. Have someone else do it cold or flatly and listen to their interpretation of it. Remove all unnecessary frippery from around the words and let the character breathe.

My characters talk just like real people. Boring

A dilemma. On the one hand you want your characterisation to be impeccable and to give a true flavour of regional dialect, slang and verisimilitude to character; on the other, the character may be dull and boorish and what they say is trivial, reactionary or plain mad. Whilst we do want to capture the former qualities, the latter are not going to sell a script to anyone until you make them funny. Real dialogue is dull.

F/X Phone dialing

GRAHAM (V/O)
All right Dave How's it going?

DAVE (V/O)
Not so bad. Yourself?

GRAHAM
Yeah, alright. Coming down the pub?

DAVE
Might do. When?

GRAHAM
Later?

DAVE
Shall I give you a bell then?

GRAHAM
Yeah.

In writing that I was slipping into a coma from which no number of Robbie Williams' songs could have reached me. Dave and Graham have nothing going for them as characters. Alfred Hitchcock said that drama is 'life with the dull bits cut out' and he was right. Think of the differences in how men and woman use the phone. A man uses it for arrangements and information and this is what Dave and Graham are doing. If they were women you can bet there would be much more going on, as well as the higher phone bill. Phone calls are anathema to the interesting script. Graham and Dave want to go to the pub but they have not yet reached a decision. The first thing you need to do to enliven this is to establish that one of them wants something and the other is going to deny them it. Secondly, there is no subtext to this exchange and so nothing for the viewer/reader to do. One of them needs a superior position. Thirdly, neither of them has any character signifiers at all. Nothing to interest us. Here is another version.

F/X Phone dialing

GRAHAM (V/O)
Alright Dave, How's it going?

Pause

DAVE (V/O)
Not so bad.

GRAHAM
Just wondering if you were coming out for quiz night?

DAVE (*sighing*)
What's the point?

GRAHAM
It's quiz night.

DAVE
We never win.

GRAHAM
We might win.

DAVE
Not with your mate Alex we won't.

GRAHAM
She's good on fashion and bands and that.

DAVE
Like I said. We won't win with her.

GRAHAM
You coming then?

DAVE
Look, I gotta go. Can you call me later?

Now Dave has something going on which is causing his chirpy friend to become stressed and needy. He won't commit to the arrangement, which means Graham will have to try harder. Dave clearly has a beef with Alexandra in their pub quiz team and has left Graham hanging on this point. It's not a comedic scene, but there is some momentum. Each line is driving us forwards. Push and pull. Are you coming? What is wrong? Why don't you like the woman? When will you decide?

Anything that is not driving forwards ought not to be there.

The sounding board

JOHN
I've had a brilliant idea. I'm going to write my sitcom about just one person.

JANE
Really?

JOHN
Yeah. Because all those other characters are just padding.

JANE
Oh yeah?

JOHN
They just bring them in to waste time when all we really want to hear about is the main guy.

JANE
Is that so?

JOHN

It will be just this one guy and his daily life, like a
kind of diary.

JANE

Of his day?

JOHN

Yeah and all the really funny things that happen to
him and that he thinks about. I could probably base
it on my life y'know, because things happen to me all
the time – I write a lot of them down in these diaries
and ... hey – are you listening to me?

Jane may as well not be there. She is no more than a sounding
board for John's rantings. This is a monologue and no matter
how much you may want to write them, you must break them
up with action or reaction. It is no good using mere interruption.
Always have an opponent, someone with a position, an opinion
and a voice. Allied to this is ...

The reactive protagonist

INT. BILL/SARAH'S APARTMENT. MORNING

BILL is reading the paper. SARAH is hovering behind him.

SARAH

When are you going to get started?

BILL

Soon as I finish the paper, hon.

SARAH

You've been using that excuse for weeks.

BILL

Have you seen the size of this Sunday paper? There's
half the rain forest here.

SARAH

I suppose I'm going to have to do it, aren't I?

BILL

I said I'd do it.

SARAH

When?

BILL

After I get through the Entertainment section.
Oh, hey, that movie's on. The one you wanted to see.
Look, at two pm.

SARAH

How about we go at five, give you a chance to get it
done?

BILL

OK. We'll go at five.

SARAH

… Bill?

BILL

Honey?

SARAH

I'm leaving you.

BILL

Hm. Before or after I get it done?

SARAH

Why?

BILL

'Cos if you leave now I won't need to do it.

The primary function of the lead character (protagonist) in a situation comedy is to drive the plot. The story is about them and them alone and if they do nothing then we are left with little going on. In this example, Bill's apathy has forced Sarah to do all the work, but if we keep having him evade any kind of real interaction then we'll lose interest.

A monster character can be obstructive, difficult, churlish, juvenile or contrary, but they are doing it in preparation for their next decision. Rightly or wrongly they have to affect change as they try to push towards order. Plots can be either internally or externally driven but either way motion must be created. In the external plot, an extra arrives with a letter or some other plot device, something which starts the clock ticking and unbalances the status quo. It will be something the lead wants. In an internal plot, a similar decision is made (I think I'll decorate/buy a new suit/ask that girl out) but from the inside – though again, there will have been an external catalyst, some recent moment of realisation just before the show started. Ask yourself:

- What if Basil Fawlty accepted the arrival of a hotel inspector and did nothing?
- What if the cast of *Friends* decided not to seek out a relationship that day?
- What if Earl put the list away?

I read scripts in which the story progresses but all the decision-making is taken up by minor or supporting characters. The writer believes that their lead is so amusing in firing off their witty barbs at all and sundry that they need do no more. In characterisation terms, the writer is too scared to let the main character run free and develop. Perhaps they are unsure of the depth of the character? Perhaps they have not seen that others are taking over? In both cases, the solution is to return to the lead and let them drive. If they stubbornly refuse to act then perhaps you are not convinced of them as a character? There are several signifiers in a script that indicate to me that we have a reactive character and these include:

- The character is doing lots of talking, making jokes all the time but is not involving themselves in the actual drama of the piece.
- Others are doing a lot of running about. There are more than three people in each scene. They talk about the character.
- There is no conflict between the lead and the others. They are just people in a room together, strangers at a party.
- It's all subplot.
- There are minor events happening of no consequence.

Mired in obfuscation

Dear Boy. It has come to our attention that in this year of our Lord two thousand and eleven, there are a growing number of conflagrations across the globe with seemingly no progress toward any diplomatic solution. At once, there is also a huge interest in matters of the sporting variety, in particular the World Cup football and sundry other completions of that ilk. May I be the first to suggest a solution that is both sensible and final, namely that opposing nations, for example, North and South Korea, Israel and Palestine simply play one another at the game and the winner, be it by golden goal or at final whistle, wins the country?

People in sitcom usually speak normally unless ornate verbiage is a quirk of their character and adds to their perceived realism. Sheldon in *Big Bang Theory* would be nothing if he did not belittle his friends with his superior geek knowledge. Tommy Saxondale (*Saxondale*, written by Neil MacLennan and Steve Coogan) mystifies his teenage helper Raymond with a wordy turn of phrase that is part rock journo and part pedantic history teacher.

We all have our verbal tics and idiosyncrasies. 'To be honest', 'I speak as I find', 'In my heart of hearts', 'I'm the kind of person who'. These are not willful ways of deceiving ourselves, rather, innocuous clichés upon which we have stumbled and taken hold. If you are going to use obscure speech mannerisms and patterns then you need to place them in context. We need someone from the real world to undermine them. A wife, boyfriend or best mate will usually do it.

Likewise, ornate prose scene description is unnecessary. Keep it simple and describe only what can be seen. If you introduce your main character as 'having a nose like a ship's figurehead' or 'a rotundity envious of a Greggs' employee', it may strike a chord with a script editor or it may not. Depends how otiose you are about it.

Long speeches are for politicians

KAYLEY

So I says to him. I'm going to lamp you one if you go on like that. I mean, they don't listen, men, do they? They go on and on pawing at you just cause you're got a skirt on and killer heels like that's a license to go at you. They won't hear a no. For them a no is yeah, have another go after you've had another pint. I'm sick of it. I'm thinking of swearing off men for good. Maybe I'll become a lezzer 'cos there's a lot of better looking ones out there now and that, what with Lilo and all. Trouble is the men would love that, me strolling into the club with a smashing bird on me arm. Maybe I'll go instigate, no, what's it called? Celebrate or summink. So, you wanna get a Bacardi Breezer and a cab out of here or what? What you mean your boyfriend's coming in ten? Well, alright. Any good-looking blokes in here tonight?

A rule of thumb is that no character in a sitcom ought to have more than five lines of uninterrupted dialogue at any one time. Monologues can work as voice over, so long as you are constantly seeing things as you receive the information, but in general they are to be avoided. Sitcom is deceptive in its long passages. They are almost always broken up on the page by the reactions of the other person who is being spoken to (desperately trying to get a word in) or by other events happening in the room. There are cutaways. Try recording a real conversation. It's fun and you can feel like an FBI guy with all the coffee and the sweat stains. You may find that we don't speak in a long dialogue unless it is a lecture. We are constantly being inter-

– rupted. Yes, thank you, the white wine. By other people. Some-
– What did you mean, dialogue? Surely monologue?
– Yes. Slip of the tongue. What are you?
– Oh this? It's a … um. A small device for killing …
– Well don't let it off in here!

This is how real speech looks. It is important to deconstruct what we say so as to understand natural rhythms. Sitcom is a reconstruction, a simulacrum, just as stand-up comedy apes real pub talk. It's not. It is artfully engineered to seem like the questions are open and the responses ad-libbed.

Also, time any long speeches you have written. You will discover that the short piece you envisaged actually comes in at thirty seconds or even a minute. On TV we cannot bear to see anyone speak directly to us for that length of time unless it is a particular dramatic device. It is always broken up with actions and movement.

Another word on timings. Never write in a script:

There is absolute silence for thirty seconds.

What are we supposed to be looking at for this time? Do the characters freeze as in some bizarre game of grandmother's footsteps? There are no ten, twenty or thirty-second pauses. If you need to stop then:

FREEZE FRAME

There is no need to say for how long. We will read it as about three seconds. THREE!

I can't find my character

This is a problem that crops up at the creation stage where a character refuses to come to life. Maybe you do not have enough knowledge about the life of this kind of person (a rodeo-loving chartered accountant with a predilection for lizards) having only known him fleetingly or having even (tut, tut) sourced the idea from TV or newspapers. Perhaps you just had an idea of a character and you can't get a hook on them. What then comes across on the page is a person saying the lines but with nothing underneath – like a politician.

Maybe it's the relationship between them and others that isn't working. Perhaps there is no contrast or they are diametric opposites who would never, in real life, speak? Perhaps you are too close to this person having based them on an ex-boss or backstabbing colleague? Are you too scared to let out your frustrations? Are you pulling back? Don't shy away. There can be therapeutic value in writing sitcoms as we mine characters from our own lives, and that can mean digging up the dirt.

The best sitcoms are about familial relationships – the desperation of Steptoe and Son or the awful apron string ties of *Sorry* (written by Peter Vincent and Ian Davidson) and *Everybody Loves Raymond* (created by Philip Rosenthal). This can be hard to go into and it takes bravery to convert raw experience and damaged memories to the gold of comedy. The best writing comes from an unflinching willingness to parcel up hurtful things and use them in your work. Where there is drama, go towards it rather than backing off. It will reap rewards. That or your therapy bills will be enormous.

❖ Character is at the heart of sitcom. Without a well-observed, resonant protagonist you have nothing.
❖ The lead character must be larger than life but *of* life.
❖ They must have a fatal flaw and a saving grace.
❖ The key to character is to find out what they want out of life and then not to give it to them.
❖ The character must act, make decisions, and drive the story forwards. It all centres around them.
❖ They need a foil, not an opposite, to play off: someone who is like them and knows them well, but who opposes them.
❖ If the character is truly monstrous you can create a worse monster to offset them.

5.

Plotting

> Will and Grace has three distinct stories. The A, B and C stories are even thematically linked. Most scripts that we reject don't have even have an A story, but consist of a bunch of people sitting around swapping one-liners. The trouble with these scripts is that nobody cares about what happens next. Stories involve us and keep us from reaching for the remote. Beginners avoid them, professionals embrace them.
>
> **D.H/S.W.**

> The most common mistake in script would be: nothing happens. People sitting around talking about something that happened the other day is not usually funny. Something happening, a comic drama unfolding in front of your eyes, that's what's funny.
>
> **Kev. F.**

> Write a sitcom script with a premise that has a clear narrative end in sight. Ideally you want to read the first script and believe in the world to the point where you can see it running and running – not just for six weeks. Remember you are writing a sitcom, not an episode of *Lost*.
>
> **M.M.**

Plotting is hell. Tortuous mind-numbing hell. A weak, ineffective or absent plot is one of the most common problems I encounter in script reading. I once held a workshop with thirty of the top writers and producers in Johannesburg at the SABC (South African Broadcasting Corporation). In four hours we were unable to unravel and reconstruct one single episode of a flawed sitcom to anyone's satisfaction.

Plotting is problems. We encounter problems all day, every day and in ninety nine per cent of cases we resolve them without undue drama or histrionics. Rarely do we act as sitcom characters do by making things worse. Most times we delegate, procrastinate or ignore the problem until it goes away. You cannot do this in sitcom. You must isolate and create a real issue for the lead character and have them act upon it. Their action has to be a catalyst in making the problem worse. For example, a neighbour asks you to clear the garbage from the shared passage between your houses. Most people would begrudgingly go ahead and do it but the sitcom character creates other choices. They may:

- Find that under the pile of rubbish there is a serious damp problem and blame it on someone else.
- Find things they have borrowed from their neighbour in the past and never returned and try to hide them.
- Refuse and add more rubbish to the pile.

These are provocations and will lead to an escalation. A sitcom plot needs to have at least a couple of escalations and a crisis, and from that crisis comes a resolution. No one gains from the resolution of the problem, least of all the lead character. Other interlopers in the sitcom may be brought down too, but any victory gained by our hero is a small one. There is no change to their fundamental being.

Plotting here is not about engagements or business ventures or making life decisions about elderly relatives. These may form the background to your narrative (if you really must have a narrative arc over the series) but plotting should concern itself with minutiae. If your lead is involved in getting married, you can easily get a whole episode around choosing a ring, deciding on the wedding list or making arrangements for the stag night. If your lead was to start up a business then base the whole thing around choosing the right name for it. If it is about an elderly relative, centre the whole show on who is going to sit next to granny's 'good ear'.

The escalation will come out of the wrong decision made.

- Our hero puts lots of 'male items' on the wedding list.
- He hires a cheap sign-writer whose grammar is not up to scratch.
- He places granny next to a hated rival.

These actions will make things worse and as a result others will impact on the protagonist's life. Before the mid-point there will come another crisis point in which (ideally) we put our head in our hands and say, No, no don't do that! Then, once our hero *does* then do exactly that, we are running on to the second escalation, which will lead to farce, public humiliation and a shameful climb-down. Things will get out of hand.

Plotting ought to be straightforward and simple, but it only gets that way by working long and hard until your head bleeds.

Here are some examples of how and when it all goes awry.

Seeding

INT. COL HUMPHRIES PALATIAL LIVING QUARTERS. DAY

COLONEL HUMPHRIES
You'll never get me to Brighton. The place is crawling with 'em.

HIS BUTLER
Really Sir?

CUT TO

EXT. BRIGHTON NUDE BEACH SEAFRONT. DAY – LATER

COLONEL HUMPHRIES
Gaaaaah!

A good plot will seed information early on. This means that although we do not necessarily become aware of it at the time, we are being given clues as to how the story is going to pan out.

The 'and-then-I-ended-up-in-Brighton' is a simple clash between what is said and what is seen, a cliché we can see coming a mile off. If the writer wants to illustrate the contradiction it might be better to have the character make the statement and then slyly show us the ways in which the trip to Brighton may become inevitable. Create friction and conflict and then have it happen at the end of the episode after having explored all the other avenues. This will hopefully reward us with a rich laugh.

Most seeding is reverse-engineered and it is often once you have completed the script that you start to see things you might bring in earlier. For this to happen you need to have a finished first draft. I suggest you do it quickly in no more than ten days. The speed and energy of this method brings many unexpected events and comic 'clues', which will be usable as comedic irony.

Don't give away the jokes too soon. Make the audience laugh but above all, make them wait.

We're so funny we don't need a plot

- Writer A creates a brace of sparkling funny characters, so hilarious that we are happy to see them toss insults and *bon mots* back and forth for page after page. This writer focuses on banter, ready wit and endless quips. It is a funny script.
- Writer B writes characters within a story that end up being hilarious because of their actions. It is an optioned script.

Aimless conversations are the province of plays like *Waiting for Godot*. Sitcom may seem like two people talking in a room, but it is much more than that. It is two people at odds, with differing needs and desires. It has substance, which is what Writer A lacks, the schlub. You can, in fact, set a sitcom episode entirely in one location: Tony Hancock in 'The Lift,' (*Hancock's Half Hour*) Fletcher and Godber in 'A Night In' (*Porridge*) and the episode in which the Meldrews' spent half hour in a traffic jam in 'The Beast in the Cage' (*One Foot in the Grave*) all managed to wring a great deal of comedy and drama out of these limitations.

Funny isn't enough. So how to go further if your characters are as slender as a supermodel? One exercise I try with my students is for them to imagine their two primary characters trapped in a room, a storeroom, elevator or a nuclear bunker. Somewhere uninspiring. You give them no means of escape and no TV or communication devices. There is no voice over or inner thoughts; all they must do is talk. Some stage directions are allowed but the idea is to produce dialogue and true character. After ten or so pages this ought to flesh out the burning issues between the characters and point up any problems in characterisation. If they run out of things to say, you haven't got enough emotion between them. If they try to kill one another then there are at least some *issues*. If the writer is still producing credible dialogue between them after ten pages, then I would consider the character 'proved.' They may find one character is more resilient (or credible) than the other so at least the imbalance is now clear. The writer can now rethink and restructure the weaker character (and if necessary the character dynamic) and return to the exercise, resulting in more fully formed people. Now you should be raring to go and all you need is to drop in a phial of plot. The room remains locked but you can introduce hidden information; say, a pressing appointment or a supposed medical issue. Maybe a body search throws up something unexpected, for example an avowed non-smoker still has an 'emergency cigarette.'

Characters cannot just 'be funny' in a sitcom. They are always funny with a direction, usually heading towards crisis and chaos. Imagine yourself at a party, stuck between two people you do not know, but who know each other well. Amusing through they may be, unless you are brought into the conversation by some point of reference or interest, your attention fades and you slip away muttering your excuses under your breath. Stupid party. Going home to cry. Stupid wedding.

Don't let that happen with your character.

Too scared to focus on my protagonist so I'd better give everybody else a plot

If you find your subsidiary characters taking over and running away with the plot, this is often less about them than an indication of a lack of faith in the lead character. Perhaps the character is too dislikeable (lacking a viable fatal flaw or saving grace) or you cannot get into their mind and see how they think. This sometimes happens when a writer bases a character on someone with whom they have had a single issue – a bully, an ex-boss or an old colleague. The writer, having put up with this abuse for too long, has decided that the monster is prime material for bringing down a peg or two in a sitcom. However, they still hate the person so much for whatever it is that they did that the anger is blocking their writing.

To create contrast the writer creates a simulacrum of themselves as the hapless victim/foil of the cruel schemes, a Rodney (*Only Fools and Horses*), a Tim (*The Office*) or a Milhouse (*The Simpsons*), and hopes that this will be enough to win the viewer's sympathy. The writer has a dynamic between the two – often master/slave or a sibling rivalry – but somehow the lead doesn't seem to be taking off so they create plots for the minor characters. They deal with the problem in their own way and you get an almost workable plot that does not concern the lead character. This is acceptable if it is a true ensemble piece such as *Seinfeld*, where Jerry often wisely stepped out of the limelight and let George, Elaine and Kramer have the lion's share of the troubles – but in general the lead ought to be right at the centre. A corollary to this is that once you are up and running (second or third series) then you will have bought some time to expand on the roles of the secondary characters.

If your main character is not leading the show in every episode (or in each one that you have plotted out so far) then you must go back and tinker with their basic makeup until they do. When I read plot synopses for the first series and find the lead is not driving every one I become enraged and petulant and start hurling crockery. A sitcom is not about the minor roles. *Cheers* did not produce 'Norm!' *Spaced* did not give way to 'Brian'. *Friends* produced *Joey*.

A caveat to this is crazy-neighbour-steals-show, in which a minor character is so strong that they walk away with every scene. Kramer (*Seinfeld*), Reverend Jim and Latka from *Taxi* did this, as well as the original concept for Roseanne (she was cast as the crazy neighbour). They have a good provenance. *I Love Lucy* had Ethel as the 'landlord next door' and that was way back in the nuclear 1950s. The crazy neighbour is most often a one-dimensional character with a catchphrase or a signature gesture.

You should not start with one of these characters. They tend to grow out of a show rather than form the centre of it. Their singular function is that of light relief. Yes, I know. In a comedy? In sitcom, as in romantic comedy, there must be dramatic elements undergone by the lead characters. A minor character should never have any real drama to their lives. It unbalances the show. Give the focus to your protagonist.

As ever there is an exception. In *The Good Life* neighbours Jerry and Margo Leadbetter were vital to the show. They were not mere opposition to Tom and Barbara, because that would have stymied the programme in its early days. They were friends who cared deeply about the reckless way in which Tom and Barbara had left the rat race and were now ploughing up their suburban lawn and seeding it with pigs. They fulfilled aptly the familial role as disapproving parents to the impulsive Goods. Margo often stole the show as the monster but Tom was not without his monstrous characteristics. The balance is hard to get right but you won't go far wrong if you focus on the lead.

When plots collide

Many sitcom episodes only have room for one main plot, which is fine: it absorbs the lead and minor characters and entertains us all. Any good plot has this potential. 'Christmas tipping' was one such for Larry David, as was 'The Contest' for Seinfeld. 'Redundancy – And Who Tells the Staff' was a big enough problem for David Brent in *The Office*. The subplot is the undercoat, subservient to the main action on the canvas.

Plots collide when there are two of equal weight. For example 'Giving up smoking' and 'Buying a used car' are both big events that may be used as plots. The writer must weigh the potential of each one before proceeding, as there is plenty of story in both. Let's look at each in turn. Giving up smoking offers some of the following options.

- Announcing your decision to the derision or approval of others.
- Getting rid of paraphernalia. Ashtrays, lighters, cigarettes.
- Avoiding social situations and walking past smokers.
- Choosing a replacement – gum, food, heroin.

- Managing the mood swings, which will affect those around you.
- Bargaining: the battle of wills against 'just one more'.
- Getting ill.
- Getting evangelical and stopping others.
- Relapsing, guilt and self-recrimination.
- Giving up giving up. Facing others and more lies ...

Breaking this habit is one of the hardest things that you can do and can propel you towards a life-changing series of events. You may, if successful, change who you hang out with and take up a whole new sporty regime. You might become another version of yourself. In a sitcom you might want to focus only on a part of this, and for maximum comic potential this will be the part in which you affect others. You might want to approach the challenge with a buddy, or do it for your loved one instead of yourself. Any of these starting points are enough for an episode. Let's look at the second. Buying a second hand car.

- Who is it for? You or your partner? Is it a gift?
- Sourcing the car. Do you trust the internet or person selling it?
- Verifying its condition (bringing in a mechanic or someone who 'knows cars').
- The test drive.
- Agreeing on a price. Barter.
- Obtaining the money.
- Getting it home.

Again, there is a lot here: a lot of exterior shooting and opportunities for visual jokes. How is this supposedly simple transaction played out? Where do you begin? With the decision to buy or – more interestingly – once you have bought the car and it all starts going wrong. Buyer beware is the rule, but what if you bought it and were convinced it was a bargain and nothing could persuade you otherwise? What if you attempt to get your money back from the bike club chapter president from whom you bought it? What if you discovered something in the car – the body in the trunk or a stash of hidden loot? What if it's stolen? The possibilities for drama and comedy are huge.

If two plots of this magnitude are placed alongside one another they will cancel each other out. They are too big to co-exist – plus they have no connection to one another. In conceiving your plot you need an event, which has enough energy to propel the lead character forwards, but not so much that it governs the whole story. Big plotting – and by this I mean life-changing events – is the preserve of the comedy drama. Sitcom must be kept small and emotive. Ask yourself, can I resolve this on the main set within the time frame of the half hour? Is there so much left over that the rest will spill out? You should not be trying to have two major catalysts when one will do. One good plot will always suffice.

Logic is not just for Vulcans

Another problem is logic holes; places where a viewer/script reader thinks 'they would never do that'. The difficulty is on the tightrope where you have to make the character act convincingly: not as one would in real life (which would just be dull) nor in the realm of the ludicrous, i.e. farcically, where vicars and bosses enter rooms just as trousers fall down. To this problem I apply Occam's razor, the theoretical principle that entities must not be multiplied beyond necessity, which is to say that the simplest solution is often the correct one.

The exasperated sigh is poison to the well-planned script. Some people have this reaction to slasher films, groaning when the cell phone fails to get a signal or when pursued by the axe-wielding maniac the heroine runs straight to the basement, only to find the remains of her friends in jars. They are missing the essential fact that the art of a good genre movie is to accept the tropes and limitations and work with them.

In sitcom this plays out as characters who behave as if they are in a sitcom rather than in real life. The problem here is that although they must be recognisably of life, they must be exaggerated. They do not have an embarrassment gene but they must act congruently. This does not mean they do the *opposite* of us, but they act almost in a parallel way.

When Brent is telling the joke about black people and gets halfway through just as a black guy arrives, he does not carry on blithely (because we need to see him squirm with shame), but tries to back-pedal. He is then encouraged to tell the joke anyway but then lets himself down by confusing the black guy with 'the other one'. He falls into the racist trap no matter how hard he tries to avoid it.

In one of my favorite moments in *Curb Your Enthusiasm*, Larry David thanks his friend for a meal. His friend's wife then asks to also be thanked. Larry refuses. She did not pay for the meal nor did she earn the money to do so. He disagrees that there ought to be any group thanking. The rest of us would, at this point, make a small apology and clamber down, believing that we are still in the right. We would expound upon this on the ride home to our exhausted and angry spouse. Larry David does not back down. Full of self-righteousness he tramples all over social convention. It is this, I believe, that makes him so attractive as a *character* (you wouldn't want to befriend someone like that in real life). He has no awareness of social conventions. He takes it too far, as does Basil Fawlty. Basil is at once in awe to class and aristocracy but appalled by anyone 'lower' class thinking they are his equal. Giving up or admitting you are wrong is never an option: this stubbornness is borne out of close observation of the blinkered among us.

You can't make characters do stuff just for the sake of it, 'seeming like a funny way to go'. This is leading by plot or comic idea rather than by character. We know that the story isn't real but we *want to believe* it is real. In real life we do not act out of character. If it's in us to do something daft or stupid then this is what we will do. If we are cautious then we will act with caution. Look closely at each plot point and escalation. There is nothing wrong with a funny idea and in trying to engineer a situation – even a crisis/calamity – but you need to have us on board all the way. There must be an internal logic, no matter how skewed.

This escalation is closed for repair

Sometimes the plot stalls. An interesting premise is set up: what if Frasier and Niles needed a top quality suit for an event? What if your balding lead character meets a bum who has long luxuriant hair because he never washes it and our man decides to stop washing his own? These catalysts are acted upon but nothing further happens. There is no complication, no gradual worsening of the situation and certainly no crisis. So what has gone wrong?

First, the comic premise may be limited. Students of mine once wrote a script based on the first idea. They created an exclusive English tailor to whom both brothers were in thrall. He played them off against one another, demanding ludicrous bespoke alterations to each suit until it was revealed he was a conman. The spiv then fleeced both, leaving them squabbling wearers of the emperor's new clothes. On paper this seemed intriguing but the idea was flawed. What event could possibly be so important that it demanded a 'special suit'? To a woman it is social death to arrive in the same dress but to a man, even if you're in Armani, a suit is a suit is a suit. Would either Frasier or Niles be blind enough to fall for dodgy schmutter? The premise spluttered and failed to get into second gear. If your initial idea will not bear scrutiny, then the resultant escalation won't either.

In order to correct this you must ensure that the character and the plot idea work together. Examine the plot idea and write down a number of possibilities as to where it might go. Take time on this. Think freely and don't tie it to character. Then whittle it down to those possibilities that are suitable for your lead. Once you have that, then look at the possible escalations (check out *Fawlty Towers* for just how this works). If there are a plethora of lead-outs then go for it, but if you start to question the logic, or find nothing dramatic happening as a result of the plot conceit, then drop the plot idea and start again.

Secondly, you may progress but it may be up a blind alley. What is leaking from your plot ship is drama. The idea promised a lot but cannot deliver. Let's look at example two. Your lead stops washing his hair (claiming like some hippy wastrel that after a week it washes itself). After three days he's looking awful and scratching his head, leading others to think he has nits. His spouse asks him to wash but he refuses, so she withholds sexual favours. Now he's sleeping on the couch where he picks up something from the dog. His hair starts coming out in clumps but he won't back down. He's going mad with the itching so he confronts the tramp and asks for the secret. The tramp is only twenty-five years old. Living rough just makes you look fifty.

A cute story but reactive. He would have to go several days

or weeks before people noticed his filthy hair and frankly, who is really all that bothered? He's dealing with the permutations of *not* doing something. It isn't as if he's cut all his hair off or coloured it. If there was more at stake at the start then we'd be hooked. What if he had a hot new girlfriend who was obsessed with hirsute men?

You have to work the simple plotline through as if you are kneading dough. You take the simplest idea and fold it, beat it, flatten it and roll it until the analogy is overworked. A simple through line must rely upon drama created by the protagonist.

When someone else solves the plot

'OhmiGod, we're going to die in here. Wait. Someone's left a rope just there ...'

Deus ex machina is Latin for god from the machine. The term relates to a situation whereby an inextricable problem is solved with the unexpected and contrived intervention of some new character, ability or object, say, a magic wand or Fairy Godmother. Horace told the poets that they must never resort to this to solve their plots, referring to the conventions of Greek tragedy where a device was used to lower the actors playing gods onto the stage. The machine could be either a crane (like a window cleaner's cradle) or a riser that brought the 'god' up from a trap door. Greek tragedian Euripides was often criticised for his frequent use of *deus ex machina*. Aristotle too, criticised the device in his *Poetics*, where he argued that the resolution of a plot must arise internally, following from the previous action of the play. The arrival of an external solution is anathema to dramatic writing. It is the cavalry, the God figure stepping in and solving it all. Children's bedtime stories are full of them. It was all a dream.

The key to writing good plots is to work, as Aristotle says, from the page. You must use the traits and abilities of your protagonist.

Coincidences happen in real life all the time. You are walking along thinking about your sixteen-year-old-childhood schoolboy crush and suddenly there she is right in front of you. 'Big world', you exclaim, marvelling at the tremendous coincidence that has brought you together (and making a huge *faux pas*, as you spot that she is nothing like the siren of your teenage dreams). In drama, it does not work like this. Life may be random but drama and sitcom are planned. We know it is artifice, no matter how much it tries to replicate real life. In sitcom, this is where plots are either clever or fortuitous. Your aim in the resolution to the story is to so construct an event – no matter how ridiculous – that it appears germane to the story. The best way to achieve this is to keep trawling through what you have written to find the solution. It will be there provided you have done the work.

What if your second in command, the foil, the minor character, solves the problem? It is better that he leads the main character to it. Baldrick's utter stupidity gives Blackadder an idea for a cunning plan, which is then often brought down by Baldrick because Blackadder hasn't thought it through. It is always Blackadder, or Frasier or Brent who engineers his own destruction. If the minor character effects the solution then they have acted as protagonist, thereby acting out of their role and position and the audience will be confused. We cannot stymie an audience in this way. It is Homer's plot not Bart's (*The Simpsons*). It is Mark's plot not Jeremy's (*Peep Show*). Make sure your main character is responsible for the denouement and that your minor one resolves only their subplot, otherwise you are creating chaos.

I cannot achieve climax

All writers at one time or another have this problem. You might be tired or stressed and I know it has never happened to you before, but it will. The plot is excited. Is escalates manfully, becoming engorged and praipic with comic potential. The laughs flow, the tension builds and then it all just … ebbs away.

The climax scene or single moment is the one we all remember. It is that revelation or public humiliation which the episode has been building towards. It is the biggest and best punch line. The trouble with life is that where it does have coincidences, it does *not* have punch lines. They are an artificial construct and as such you are trying to make something that is not credible, real. It's hard to do but not impossible. In plotting your episode, the ending will come one of two ways: either the Comedy Gods smile down upon you and deliver out of the heavens a gag/scene/climax so perfect that the whole thing writes itself, or they don't and you have to work at it. In this first instance you have a route map. You know where you are going and the fun is in getting there. The journey is assured and enjoyable. The other ninety per cent of the time you are working from a plot idea and plodding along hoping to get there in the end. There are, sadly, no easy answers, no comic Viagra. You just have to work at it. A sitcom need not have a hilarious gut-busting climax, but it helps if there are some great moments where the reader can at least visualise a broad comic scene. This will help it to sell.

Be memorable.

God made the world in seven days. Fawlty Towers took three months per episode

> I've finished. I'll send it straight out. Those production companies are all dying to read it and to commission me. The great thing is its fresh too. It only took a week. It's as ready as it wil ever be. My best wurk.

Presuming that you have at least scanned some parts of this book, you may have found that writing a sitcom episode is not as easy as you first thought. You have some fantastic characters trapped in a great emotional arena and you have conceived of some plots that explicate their situation, whilst being so funny that even to read them is to risk a hiatus hernia. You are wrong. You are wrong because not only is the plot probably not up to scratch but you haven't given it time.

There is hardly a piece of writing that does not benefit from either a second pair of eyes (objective viewpoint) or from putting in a drawer for a couple of weeks. Don't worry. The producers aren't going to go away. On the other hand, if they read something that is only half formed then they are not going to buy it. You get only one chance to make that vital first impression, so why blow it by being in a hurry and sending out something that isn't strong enough?

Plotting is grindingly hard to get right, which is why those *Fawlty Towers* episodes were so intricately planned. This is why there is a huge team of writers on every American sitcom. There is nothing wasted. Every single line contributes to the narrative thrust or revealing of character. Can you honestly say the same of your script?

How does each scene end? With an advance in the story? Every scene ought to be moving things forwards, whether through definite action by the protagonist or by a minor character, which will impact on the plot. Each page should be concerned only with the situation or an aspect of the situation that they are in. Sitcom must move forward like a shark.

Problem and solution

Life is full of problems. At their smallest they are the things-to-do lists which we carry around with us on a daily basis; writ large they are the more fearful issues, such as placing elderly parents in care or breaking up a marriage (don't do both on the same day). For every problem, looked at clinically, there is a range of solutions. In general we most times avoid the issue, procrastinating in the hope that someone else will deal with it or that it will go away. Sometimes it does. In sitcom this is not an option. In sitcom, your lead character (and in the subplot the minor characters too) must be faced with a problem that requires action. If they avoid it, then this apathy must in itself be a solution, an ineffective one because it will throw up another problem.

A way of garnering material for plots for your characters is to do the following: write down a problem that is bothering you on an A4 piece of paper. On the next line write a realistic solution. Then on the next write down the problem this then causes and so on.

The problem is a minus and the solution is a plus.

Have fun with it. Let your mind go free.

Continue doing this on each line until you get to the bottom of the page. It will often lead to the ridiculous. This is how farce is constructed; beginning with the sensible issues and letting the elements build to ludicrous endings. Out of this you will see that action breeds reaction. All writing is essentially problem and solution; how your character reacts to each one will define whether it is comedy or a tragedy.

Now do this exercise in the mind of your protagonist.

In order to be like Brent you have to think like Brent.

❖ Plotting is hell.

❖ Sitcom is narrative comedy. You are telling a story about a person who creates a plot.

❖ Sitcom plots are small, concerning the minutiae of life.

❖ Many scripts suffer from having no plot or too many plots.

❖ Plotting must proceed from a logical starting point. The character is faced with a dilemma – they must act congruently and believably. This is the inciting incident.

❖ Their actions, reactions and next moves will proceed in a problem and solution rotation.

❖ At the half way stage your character ought to make a decision that will have us covering our eyes – the 'oh no' moment.

❖ A further escalation will lead to the resolution. Ideally this is public humiliation.

❖ You can leave a character hanging in shame or embarrassment because next week they will be back at the start.

❖ Always resolve the plot from within the story. No *deus ex machina*.

❖ Write quickly, and then once you have a first draft, you can seed ideas from the end back to the beginning.

❖ Be very logical and take your time.

Nuts and bolts

6.

Scenes

" Show it don't tell it. Let's see the characters in action.
Massive coincidences that resolve plots are annoying and
insulting to the reader/viewer. You want to believe in these
characters and situations.

M.M.

Sitcom is composed of enough scenes to tell the story. A scene, as
Sid Field puts it so succinctly in his excellent book, *Screenplay*, is
a 'specific unit of action. The purpose of the scene is to move the
story forwards'.

Novice writers always want to know how many scenes to
include and as rough rule of thumb I suggest anywhere between
eight and fifteen per episode. This is because a scene may consist
of either a visual gag lasting no more than a page or an emotional
battle spreading across ten.

Certain episodes of *The Royle Family* seem to be a single
scene. As the family bicker and complain, the camera (situated
in the very place their TV would be in the living room) sits
mutely watching. People go in and out and we watch, appalled
and fascinated by their behaviour. Look more carefully. You will
see that there are cutaways, perhaps to a view of the hallway or
kitchen as someone arrives at the front or back door. There are
multiple scenes here and each one has its purpose.

A scene has a beginning, middle and end. At the beginning
we must establish where we are, who is peopling the scene and
where the action is going. The middle of the scene is when the
protagonist engages with the issue at hand. The end of the scene
is when they take some kind of action, thus thrusting us forwards
into the next scene, which will show us the result of their actions.
It is goal, conflict and disaster. The character wants something,

they are prevented from getting it and it gets worse. A scene has to have an inner momentum generated by the characters. It cannot be static even when it appears so. In *The Thick of It* or *The Office* are seemingly full of normal people in a pseudo documentary, but this is not the case. Everything is going on under the surface. In one US *Office* episode the characters are trapped overnight while Scott goes out on the tiles. They try to sort out a way of getting free by befriending a black security guard. This is event. Things go wrong and things move forwards. The ending must make us want to watch the next scene and so on until the show ends with a resolution. A scene is a unit of action based around a character.

Your opening scene

INT. PATTY'S LIVING ROOM – NIGHT
Patty has all her best friends around for a party. She hands out canapés.

PATTY
Hey, John, you know Nigel and Reece, and of course you heard about Susie?

JOHN
No – what about Susie? Who is Susie?

PATTY
Your sister silly. Hey. What's happening with you and Clarice?

JOHN
I think she's my girlfriend although I can't be sure. I was just introduced to Charlie and I'm not sure if he was a boy or a girl.

PATTY
Hey, Sam! This is John.

JOHN
What happened to Susie again? Should I be worried?

SAM

Hey, John. You one of the Fossborough Johns?

JOHN

I'm from Idaho.

SAM

Tom knows a great joke about Idaho, with the punch
line going I da Ho, like Hooker, hahahahaha.

PATTY

Clarice. This is Hannibal and Bill. You'll get on fine.

I think we can agree that the above is rubbish. We don't know
these people and there's nothing going on. The opening scene is
one of the hardest to write, especially if it is the pilot episode.
The writer panics. How did they get here? What is the situation?
I must put all of it in straightaway. If only I could have all the
exposition sliding off into space like in *Star Wars*. Can I? Can I
do that?

In the first scene you should never introduce the viewer to
more than three people. When you meet more than three people
at a party, you forget all of them unless they are wearing a low
cut blouse or have a devastating air of money about them. Instead
you go and hide in the kitchen and graze for food, which does
you no good.

Most production companies advise writers not to send in a
pilot script, but one a few episodes down the line. This is because
pilot scripts are stuffed with exposition and 'getting to know' the
characters – rather than telling a story. A good way to illuminate
the protagonist is through opposition. In the vignette above there
is confusion but no drama. If Patty and John are important to the
show then make John truculent and demanding. Make Patty a
cougar. Let us know within three lines that there is some kind of
tension.

Another way to open is to have a minor character arrive with
a message. This is the *only* function of the extra character and
if you can make them mute then all the better (the TV company

doesn't have to pay them so much). They are delivering the plot. They aren't involved in the story and their relationship to it is tangential. They are a messenger and that is all. Once they have delivered, the protagonist will react and then their foil will question or oppose the protagonist's action.

This is, or at least gives rise to, the inciting incident, which must come within the first five pages of the script. There is precious little time to hang around. *Seinfeld*, *Curb Your Enthusiasm* and *The Simpsons* tend to have a minor plotline up and running before the main event, but these are established shows. You have to intrigue us from page one. We have no time for anything irrelevant or for mere scene setting. Page one should introduce the plot idea so the protagonists can roll it around in their mouths, taste and savour it. The lead may register said plot and then go onto another tack, but they must have moved things forwards by the end of the scene.

An exception to opening with your lead is when the writer wants to get some comic mileage in building up just how horrible this monster is. There may be three or four minor characters talking about the new guy's arrival and telling tales about their past exploits. It is telling rather than showing but it is excusable as in this way the audience gets a sense of fear and anticipation along with the cast. The plot must nonetheless start the moment that he arrives. Think of how Jack Donaghy is portrayed in *30 Rock* or of how the Hotel Inspector is built up in *Fawlty Towers*.

Long action paragraphs

Stan breathes deeply to prepare himself. He grips the side of the passenger door and starts to push. Olly guns the engine but nothing happens. Stan gets the car moving and jumps in. Olly tries the key again. Nothing. The car is rolling down the hill toward the jetty. Stan suggests that he put the brake on. Olly discovers the brake is not working. Stan remembers the problem he had earlier in the shop and realises that that patch of oil had more significance than he at first thought. Olly tries to get out of the speeding car but Stan stops him. Olly tries to clamber into the back of the car but Stan pulls him back by his belt. The jetty looms near.

The water looks cool and inviting. Olly begins to pray. Stan lights a cigarette.

This is a long action scene more suited to screenwriting. There is a lot of 'business' here and also internal elements that cannot be shown other than by flashback. There is no room for prose description in television writing. Action and location descriptions should be so simple that a child or an agent can understand them. Any embellishment upon the basic facts is to give us a vital piece of information. For example, that the telescope found on the dresser once belonged to Admiral Nelson (because it is going to be later revealed that someone puts soot on it and then someone puts it – ho ho – to their eye). Otherwise, keep it simple.

Also, you do not need to direct. This is the director's job. 'Angle on, close up on. He moves with THE CAMERA to …' is just telling us that you went to a film school and therefore have to wait on even more tables to pay off your crippling student loan. If it is necessary to include a close up then use something short and characterful in the description. Let us imagine that a girl named Natalie notices that her friend Jane is wearing the necklace that Simon, her boyfriend, gave to her. You may put:

Close up. Jane's necklace. As she fingers it, Natalie's eyes bore into her.

When it comes to physical objects and rooms, it is the job of the set designer is to furnish the set and they will know what a living room looks like or even, God forbid, a student apartment. All you need are a few graceful touches.

INT. APARTMENT. NIGHT
A loser's apartment – the kind a writer lives in.

There is no need to give instructions on how a person leaves a room, what they are wearing or how they are doing something. Just write an engaging argument between two people and leave the director to place them in the scene and the actors to do their business with the props and pipes etc. Your job is to make that scene work as a piece of rip-roaring comedy and that's hard enough in itself without describing all the furniture that they are going to trip up over.

Show not tell – how to avoid exposition

> VILLAIN
> So, we meet again, but this time I think the advantage is mine.

> HERO
> Sorry, I don't think we have been introduced.

> VILLAIN
> Oh. Good. Let me give you the tour of the evil headquarters before I kill you.

> HERO
> Splendid.

The nadir of bad writing is exposition (showing your working), and the only people allowed to do this are James Bond villains. They always seem to take the time to explain just how they set up the whole plan and how they are going to 'feed Mr Bont to ze chelly feeesh'. Meantime, Mr Bond is loosening the ropes and preparing the tactical nuclear missile he has secreted in his underpants.

In film, theatre and television writing, you *show* the story. We judge by actions, which happen in the present tense. You are not a journalist. You are not reporting what happens, you are living the moment. You write as if the action were unfolding in front of you on screen. If you are used to writing prose you will have learnt that there is no *telling*. Try writing fast – leaving yourself no time to put in any description or to qualify anything.

Exposition is clumsy. Telling us the plot or back-story impedes the flow. Like a speed camera, exposition is an irritant that serves no useful purpose and slows you down so that you are likely to crash. It's not important to know what led this pair to be living together and how they became trapped in their lives. It is enough to know that it simply *is*. Readers and viewers care little for what happened before. They like to feel that they are doing the work themselves and are not being spoon fed acres of gibberish. If your lead is a cynical man, then let him adopt that pose. We'll pick up fast that he's been wounded in love or by life or by failure because he'll allude to it. It will be in his bones, his sense memory. If you want to show that someone broke his heart and busted his jaw, then have him react to someone *inappropriately*. As soon as he shows us that he distrusts women we pick up that he's been hurt, or that he's a psychopath. Essentially, once your character homework is done, never apologise and never explain.

Too long and too short

Some scenes go on with no sign of an end and the reader starts flicking pages in the hope that they can one day take a breath or contemplate suicide, murder or a career change. The opposite of a scene stuffed with exposition and over plotting is when there is nothing happening but aimless banter. The scene may simply be too short, cutting away after the first gag or interchange and scurrying off. You read it and think – nothing *happened*. It is the mere exchange of information. There is no plot or discussion or engagement at all.

A scene must end either comedically with a laugh or dramatically with an exciting decision or twist. A disaster or a decision. A scene must build a bridge to the next scene. In film there is often a transition, which is a visual connection to the next scene: say, for example, a detective looking for clues uses a magnifying glass to examine an old black and white 8x10 photograph. We close in on his face as he realises something. The frame freezes on the glass, which is then matched to the bumper of a car. The murderer's car. In this way we have linked one scene to another in the mind of the viewer through visual synthesis.

Sitcom does not work in this way, as the camera is not used in the same way. We can wipe or freeze but most often, the sitcom scene simply cuts to the next. The early episodes of *Frasier* were smart and cute in that they used old-fashioned title boards to bookmark each scene. These were witty and added branding to what was already a sophisticated show. With the advance of computer graphics, the tricks of CGI are becoming commonplace and it cannot be long before a sitcom uses myriad interfacing graphics and comic book tropes. However exciting these may be, the truth of the scene must remain sacrosanct. We must be left wanting more.

Comedic and dramatic scenes

Drama

A dramatic scene introduces jeopardy. It makes things hard for the main character. It is predicated on the goal/conflict/disaster model where it begins with the character stating a goal. They are placed in and opposed by conflict and this ends in disaster. Put simply, it ends in someone saying no. It is even stronger if that no is given with an additional set of conditions. Essentially, 'No – and furthermore ...'

This kind of dramatic plotting makes it hard for the protagonist, so we empathise more and are glued to our seats. The classic way of introducing intrigue and jeopardy is to have someone walk in with a gun. Another is to introduce hidden information of which the lead was unaware. This shifts everything around so that whatever course of action had been decided on before is now null and void. You can also have the ticking clock. You see variations of this in almost any action/thriller/cop movie, in which there is a limited time to 'defuse' the situation. It's the old ...

CHIEF

Kowalski – you got twenty-four hours to solve the case. I don't care if you are retiring soon or that it's your last case or you have a family to feed. I want. It. Done. Now.

Kowalski does not then say ...

KOWALSKI

Sounds like a lot of pressure. How 'bout I do three hours on the case Tuesday then pick it up next – wait – I got some annual leave coming. Say I do five out the twenty-four hours tomorrow then we see what we got next week? Chief? Chief, you're turning kind of blue there ...

119

The ticking clock does not have to be known to the protagonist but it does have to be seen by the audience. However, this kind of dramatic device is not suited to sitcom. You can set a deadline in an episode but it would be more concerned about how they fail to complete it than the deadline itself, ie, the deadline is not bigger than they are – which *is* the case in a movie where there is a bomb under the table.

A dramatic scene can end on a cliffhanger. The stakes are high in a TV drama or movie, life or death, but sitcom cliffhangers are based on life decisions. Will Sam leave Diane? Will Niles and Daphne get together? The sitcom cliffhanger is only used at the end of a series to hook us in for the next season and is more a decision brought about by the show-runner (the executive producer/creator or co-creator of the show) and ought not to concern us here.

Comedy

The comedic scene introduces incongruity. Some characters (Kramer in *Seinfeld* or Homer in *The Simpsons*) are so off the wall that they operate a stream of illogic that bedazzles from the start. The coffee table book that is a coffee table is one such idea, or when Homer the inventor creates the makeup gun for a woman who needs to be ready to go out in fifteen seconds. We are happy to go with any number of Del-Boy's crazy schemes or Victor Meldrew's ways of combating social unease because they are believable within the frame of reference of that character.

You make the rules using a degree of probability. You decide what your characters will and will not do given the circumstances. Even though it is not a 'real situation' there must still be consistency. Give us funny and random once and it's amusement, but repeat it again and again without logic and we are bemused and no sitcom can run on mere bemusement. It becomes trying, no matter how warped the 'genius' behind it.

Instead of introducing a gun to the comedy scene, you bring in a man with a water pistol. He may be a figure of authority who pees on the bonfire. It's always good to have this kind of outsider to act as an anchor for the show. Great comedy works well when there is enough of a reminder of the boundaries of the real world to fight against. Of course comedy policemen are ultimately powerless against the forces of Dionysus, but having them there will provide a good laugh. For police you can read fathers, wardens or any figure of authority.

As I have mentioned guns, a note about death. One important thing about comedy is that no one dies; at least no one ever dies for real (this is a constant). Comedy does not involve itself in mortality and if the comedy is about death, it is usually about someone already dead or quasi dead, which is one reason for the current popularity of zombie/undead films, most of which have comedy elements to them. Death is treated flippantly in comedy.

Introducing new information in a comedic scene will cause fresh conflict. This is most often done in two ways; either have the character realise that the person who they have just insulted is standing behind them, or reveal that the person to whom they are talking is a spouse/direct relative/boss/co-worker of the person they have insulted. It is based on public humiliation and embarrassment is most effective in making us squirm. Abrupt changes of behaviour too are amusing but this must be connected to character and congruent with their *modus operandi*. Sudden volte-faces are funny because we do them in real life.

Finally, a comedic scene should end on a big laugh. The culmination of the seeded set up. A visual gag is always better than a verbal one and there is nothing to beat that great 'out' moment.

A wonderful example of combining both drama and comedy was a scene in *Frasier* where Niles Crane visited a sperm bank to discover whether his 'boys' were responsible (as he would expect) for a genius child only to discover that his boys had been found to be of substandard quality. It was played straight, without a single laugh until – appraised of the information – Niles leaves. He gets the wrong door. As he opens it we hear the muffled cry of a man interrupted as he makes his 'donation'. Cue shock and quick exit from Niles and a huge laugh to end on. This took nothing from the scene nor did it cheapen it. And there's nothing like a good knob gag.

How to end a scene

Once the plot point has been delivered and action is decided upon the scene is over. Once the public humiliation has been meted out, the scene is over unless you can wring any additional lines or shame out of it. Once the joke has been told, the scene is over. Comedians, when they are wise, save their best for last and while they are telling the joke, move the mike stand to centre stage and place the microphone on it. They deliver the gag, say goodnight and leave.

Tell your joke and get off.

You're leaving a party. Yes, I love my party analogies. You are standing in the cramped cold hallway giving your fulsome drunken goodbyes to the host and hostess. She is wearing rubber dishwashing gloves (it may have been *that* kind of party) and he is slapping you on the back and ushering you towards the door. You have half remembered something important that you need to tell him and he tells you to call tomorrow. Your spouse is holding you by your expanding waist and tugging at your shirttails. You clap your friend on the arms and kiss his wife too amorously and say that you must do this again soon. You are halfway out of the door when you remember what it was that you had to tell him: you launch into it and later you stumble out to the car with your frosty wife. A week later you wonder why they haven't called you and why your wife has instigated divorce proceedings. It's because you kept everybody waiting for nothing and you deserve what you got. Don't do this with your scenes. Once it's over, get out. Storm, flounce, skip if you must, but get out.

Pathos

The *Oxford English Dictionary* describes pathos as a quality in speech, writing or events that excites pity or sadness. It is very relevant to comedy and especially to sitcom and to its monsters. Think of Basil Fawlty, Mark in *Peep Show* or George Costanza in *Seinfeld*. All can be resolutely awful in thought, manner and behaviour but where do you stop? You have thrown everything but the kitchen sink at your protagonist. You have humiliated him publicly, ridiculed his opinions and dress sense, and torn his dreams to shreds. The monster is defeated and has lost all, so what do you do now? Do you leave him as a pathetic creature crawling in abject failure or offer him some morsel of humanity?

The use of pathos has its benefits. The saving grace or ray of hope that makes us understand the character is a good thing. A sense of pity enables us to appreciate their humanity, which is important if we are to follow them over several years. It is rare to find any sitcom in which the character is resolutely awful. You might say it of Larry David in *Curb Your Enthusiasm* but he frequently gets his comeuppance from wife Cheryl or manager Jeff, from his staff or from his showbiz friends.

Jill (Julia Davies) in *Nighty Night* was a brilliant creation, a narcissistic sociopath without a single redeeming feature. *The Times* described the show as 'a blistering wall of superbly unredeemed cruelty that manages to trample over every social convention in a pair of cheap stilettos'. It was pulled after two series. The Bluth family in *Arrested Development* managed just three. In the main, and against their worse judgements, most of our sitcom monsters end up doing the right thing. Larry Sanders is vain and amoral (who isn't?) but he gets shamed into making amends. Homer always comes good and on occasion so does Mr Burns.

We must offer some sympathy for the devil. Every serial killer has a mother (and they often dress in her clothes to prove it) but resolute awfulness is not in the bailiwick of sitcom, it's in the horror film. Give them something. Once you have nearly drowned them, offer a helping hand up out of the mire. Crass though it may be sometimes – and yes, sitcoms do sometimes descend into mawkish sentiment – a crumb of redemption brings warmth and rewards.

Memorable scenes. Visual punches

The most memorable scenes in sitcom are generally visual. Del-Boy falling through the open bar flap; the chandelier falling in the same show; anything Homer Simpson does; David Brent's 'dance'; Basil Fawlty beating his car; Edina Monsoon tumbling into the flowerbed. Many of these share the simple idea of hubris. Frankenstein is toppled from his tower, King Kong falls, and truth is laid bare and revealed. The visual is seared onto our retinas. It's much easier to remember than a punch line. Did you see that moment when … is a far more common reaction than reeling off lines of dialogue. This is annoying for writers who have toiled for months on a script full of witty apercu's and hilarious rib-tickers, but bear in mind that one visual gag is worth ten killer lines. Be sparing though. The big set up gag should come at the end. Allow the idea to build. If there is an opportunity to bring about a visual resolve then use it. Describe it simply on the page with lots of space.

Enjoy it.

+ Show not tell is the most important rule of writing.
+ Every scene has a beginning, middle and end.
+ That ending may be comedic or dramatic.
+ Do not overdo your scene descriptions. Leave the work to the set builders.
+ Write in as many entrances and exits as possible. Once a character has delivered exposition or plot, get him out.
+ Always try to write visually.
+ Give your character pathos.
+ Scenes should not run longer than three or four pages.
+ A scene can be as short as a few lines.
+ Try to end on a sight gag.

7.

Jokes and dialogue

> Honestly, we just want to read something that makes you laugh. If you care about the characters and the script makes you laugh then we'll take things from there. Don't spend too long worrying about what broadcasters want and how you can target certain markets. Write the script you want to write, make sure it makes you laugh and you've got the best starting point possible.
>
> **M.M.**

> Please don't write 'jokes'. Jokes have no place in sitcom because sitcom is all about characters in a situation not people firing off witty one-liners. Also don't write things that will only make your friends laugh – you have to reach a broad audience. Make sure that everything you write is relevant to the story, the character and the plot.
>
> **M.J.**

It ought to be clear by now that the humour in sitcom is the result of fine characterisation and plotting. Once you know how to construct a funny scene and have harnessed your comedic gifts to a compelling couple in a deeply emotive relationship then it's time to add the funny. All this is a long way away from sketch comedy, which comes out of the simple comic idea, and from stand-up too, which is more polemic and observational. The comedy of sitcom comes in the interchanges, the nuances between people. The funniest times happen in life with our mates, in pubs and bars and clubs and restaurants. They are off the cuff, unscripted, based upon teasing or repetition or inventive insults. We take an idea and stretch it to its furthest. Now we have to take the essence of all this and use it in our script.

Can comedy be taught? Having been a stand-up for twenty years and having taught hundreds of people (including many who are now gracing our screens) I have to say this. Yes, the nuts and bolts can be passed on, as the forms and functions of comedy have not changed in essence since Greek and Roman times. However, it takes an aptitude for it. The combination of the gift for comedy and comedy writing, plus the dedication to master the craft is what will bring success. Untutored comic skills will flare up but die down as quickly. The journeyman writer, if he has an iron will to succeed, will do so – and remember that comedy writing is a team effort. A script can and always will be polished. Anything you submit may be your last draft but it is the first to the reader. Keep writing and looking for the funny stuff and please try to avoid the following.

Pedantic dialogue

BOB
Steve, I am gonna market your idea for self-heating gloves all over America and even Canada.

STEVE
That is great Bob. You know that has always been my dream.

BOB
I didn't know that. Well, we can discuss the finer points later. Are you interested?

STEVE
Of course. Can you really do this?

BOB
I can and I will. I am the premier glove manufacturer on the Western Seaboard and I have already drawn up a contract that will make you a millionaire. Do you want to read it?

STEVE

Heck no. Where do I sign?

This scene takes no account of business formalities or technicalities and leaves credibility behind at the start. The comedy, because it is so ineptly written, is accidental and naïve. Dialogue must pay homage to the real. Listen to people, how they speak. Above all, read your dialogue out loud or arrange a reading with some actors. A good rule of thumb, which applies to words and grammar, as well as unconvincing dialogue, is that if it doesn't feel quite right then it probably isn't. Trust your instincts. Is this really how people speak? Huh?

Please excuse the pun

BOB

This is a nice plaice.

BRIAN

Yes, thank cod.

BOB

Shall we call salmon over?

BRIAN

A mermaid?

No, I will not excuse the pun. Why would you want to offer a joke that asks for an apology instead of a laugh? What are the adjectives appended to puns? Here's a clue. It's not brilliant, wonderful or hilarious. It's awful, cheesy or terrible – a groaner, a poor play on words that insults our intelligence. In isolating the pun, I am not damning all wordplay, as this is the solid basis for much of the humour in the English language. Puns are a subset of this, wherein one letter or syllable of a word is altered to change meaning. Newspapers delight in them and the average commuter must face them every day (which may explain their grim demeanour).

The trouble with puns is that we could have got there first had we had time to think about it. Puns are often painful rather than playful. They are written to be read. If I see one in a script I know that the writer is thinking more about how his script looks on the page rather than how it will be performed. Puns are also old school, the product of another generation. If you have a propensity for punning, do realise that this has nothing to do with character, that is, unless you create a character who likes to pun – and if they do we will probably want to kill them, or zap to another channel.

One caveat to this is that puns can work in aggregate: the hilarious British comedian Tim Vine blitzes his audience with groaners but his stage persona is so buffoonish that it works. In the sitcom in which he stars (*Not Going Out*) he wisely drops them. Puntastic.

'Jokes' you heard or found on the Net and must include

Sitcom is not about jokes. No one in sitcom tells a joke *per se*. They also do not spout the funny thing they just read on the Net or received in a text or heard in a bar unless it has a direct bearing on the story at hand. Jokes draw attention to themselves, as they are the staple of barroom wits and stand-up comics but not of fully-fledged sitcom characters. John Cleese of *Fawlty Towers* fame once had a job as a script editor and spent his tenure removing jokes from scripts. Think of how you react when someone starts to tell you a long drawn-out joke. Put aside the inevitable hesitations and corrections and endless embroidering of said joke and instead concentrate on the fact that you want it to be over. You staple on that rictus grin and nod and look around for a baseball bat. Jokes in sitcom are part and parcel of the action and character interaction and must never be shoehorned in. Look at what happens when David Brent tries to tell a joke in *The Office*. Yes. That bad. Every time.

Poo, wee and man-fat are not always funny

Scatological humour has its place in sitcom and that is in *South Park* or *Bottom*. One barrel-scraping exercise was *Gimme, Gimme, Gimme*, which concerned an overweight woman and a gay man who were both obsessed with finding a man. It had its camp followers, but many found it trashy, pointless and repetitive.

A knob or dick joke is a staple of comedy and is almost always guaranteed to raise a laugh when told by second-rate stand-ups. The shock value of bodily parts will offend the sensitive and bring out the gutter-snipe in all of us, for there's a part (snicker) of humanity that revels in the crude and the lewd, just look at Chaucer (filth) and Shakespeare (poor jokes, murder and more filth). It is not 'polite' to talk about our genitalia or bodily functions and to do so is to cross into the territory of the *abject*. This is an area discussed at length by philosopher Julia Kristeva, author of *Powers of Horror: An Essay on Abjection*, who claims that we are obsessed with that which is simultaneously of our body and yet *not* of our body, ie, that which is both alive and dead.

Children, at what Freud calls the anal-retentive stage (age 1–3), are fascinated by their own excreta. Come puberty and our bodies start rebelling against us, producing nocturnal emissions and nasty purulent facial breakouts, which are funny but only once they are over. What remains as a source of humour is bodily functions and waste. Jokes about semen can be hilarious and alluding to male gloop as man fat, boy joy, man glue, pee paste or white wee-wee is puerile and funny, but mainly only to students.

On the US networks, there are stringent rules about what you can and cannot say on network television. The UK is more lax, especially on Channel 4, which is why many shows on that station are more adventurous (*Peep Show*, *Ali G*, *Catterick*). The BBC too has become more forgiving (*The Thick of It* is particularly good on insult), but on primetime the shit is not going to hit the fan. The BBC uses its younger sibling channel, BBC3, for those with broader tastes.

Subtlety should never be undervalued. Think of the *Seinfeld* episode 'The Contest', which was entirely about the impossibility of both men and women to restrain from onanism and was a masterpiece of hilarity without once referring to a pork sword or beef curtains. Remember that most sitcoms are broadcast when people are relaxing and they don't necessarily want your dick jokes thrust down their throats at eight o'cock at night. Jokes about defecation, urination and sex have their place but just be aware that a reader is hoping to sell your idea to a broadcaster and fifty jokes about smegma isn't going to help.

Be inventive – 'smeg' became a great catchphrase in *Red Dwarf*. Be smart, because we will tire of rolling around in the gutter after a while. Likewise, constant drunkenness or alcoholism is a hard trick to pull off. *Never Better* was a BBC1 sitcom about a recovering alcoholic (Stephen Mangan) that never took off, but one about a drunk that has succeeded is the long-running BBC2 sitcom *Rab C. Nesbitt*, who is a dirty, lazy, foul-mouthed, sexist alcoholic. It is due to record its tenth series in 2011. I guess it's the excretion that proves the rule.

Although repetition is

Repetition is a stalwart of comedy. At its most simple, a catchphrase cements a character in our mind and gives children something to shout at one another in the playground. It is interesting to point out that most American sitcoms don't have catchphrases in the way that UK ones do; they often make do with shouting the person's name. 'Norm!', 'Hello *New*man'. 'Niles!', 'Bilko!' The most glorious exception to this is of course *The Simpsons*, which has a million of 'em. Haa haa.

In Britain we are awash with repeated phrases, from the lugubrious 'Stone me' of Tony Hancock to the petulant 'Stupid boy' of Mainwaring, the abandoned 'I'm free' of Mr Humphries, to 'Sweetie Darling' of Edina Monsoon and 'I. Don't. Believe it' of Victor Meldrew – the list is endless. It must be noted that these are organic and often grow out of the character's performance on the night rather than being manufactured, except in the plethora of repeated verbal tics in the classic *The Fall and Rise of Reginald Perrin*.

Repetition robs a word or phrase of its meaning. We come to look upon it as a sound or mere combination of phonemes. The *Garlic. Bread. Garlic?* [beat] *Bread*, routine is a wonderful demonstration of this by UK comedian Peter Kay. The target was his less than urbane father, who considered the combination of the two food items to be totally incredulous. No matter that the meaning has gone – the word has done its work in expressing anger, indignation or plain old lunacy. It has become totemic. An emergent catchphrase defines a character, in some ways reducing them to caricature, but also helping to stamp their persona into the common cultural commerce and helping to achieve longevity for the show.

What repetition does, broadly, is to flatter the audience, making us feel that we are all part of the joke. In stand-up comedy it is known as the callback. British comedian Eddie Izzard is the master of this, as he seamlessly links and loops ideas around one another in a bolus of mental knitting. The callbacks act as punctuation and as markers, pulling us back from his distant comedic worlds. Nearer to home, we use repetition and callbacks all the time. It's the night with your buddies writ large. The night where you mention each other's embarrassments and conquests and failures and repeatedly go on and on about them long after the comedy has gone ... and then ... incredibly, it becomes funny all over again.

There is a deep hole here. Simply saying something over and over again is not in itself funny. It is the antithesis of funny. There is a long nasty pause where if you repeat the phrase once more then you will be embroiled in a bar/gun fight, but after this has passed, then you are out of the woods and it's time to laugh again. Who can judge the right moment? One who does is British comedian Stewart Lee, who mines this expertly and excruciatingly. In one routine, he dwells at length on the Del-Boy falling through the bar scene that is supposedly the funniest in all British comedy, deconstructing it and leaving the bits on the floor. So it goes. The snake eats its tail. The key is timing. It is knowing exactly when and how often to reheat something and this only comes with years and years of practice.

Cheap misdirection

ARTHUR
Is this the mind reading course?

DEAN
Shouldn't you know that already?

ARTHUR
OK, who wants to start? You have your hand up?

DEAN

Yes. Can I go toilet please?

ARTHUR

No. So here we are in Dorset.

DEAN

Yes I do.

ARTHUR

What?

DEAN

Endorse it. I think the course is great.

And so on. The trouble with this tortuous wordplay is that it is obstructive. I once knew a philosophy teacher (yes, I *know*) who spoke in nothing but riddles and wordplay of this nature and it was impossible to have any kind of sensible conversation with him. Wilful misunderstanding or misdirection is a barring device that speaks more about the insecurity of the speaker than any attempt to be amusing. Of course there are funny misunderstandings – try teaching English as a foreign language and you may be invited to a weeding or to keep your pens in a pencil house or to lie on the bitches in summer – but these are perfectly understandable mangling of the English language as spoken by non-native speakers. Purposeful misdirection based on the *play* of words rather than the visual gag is simply tiring and is best avoided.

Rubbish set-ups

INT. MUSEUM. MORNING

HEALTH AND SAFETY OFFICER

I would like to welcome you to the Museum of Valuable Things and to remind you that flash photography is not permitted. We are going through to the jewel room in which the main exhibits stand. Please remember that these are the only two in existence and they are irreplaceable, so please do not let anything happen to them.

ENTER KOKO the clown, riding a small bike.

The utterly predictable sometimes works in a surreal sitcom, in which we are expecting the rules of time and logic to be broken, but in general this kind of set up is something anyone can see a mile off. There is no delicious anticipation or clever misdirection here. What would be funny is if the two priceless objects were to *avoid* destruction, but Koko destroyed everything else with his huge clown shoes and tiny tricycle, in short thwarting the expectation. All comedy is based on surprise and a pedantic and obvious set up will cancel this out. Be surprising.

Murder your darlings

You have a scene in mind, a great joke, a wonderful exchange, a *bon mot* unparalleled. You have written the scene into your script and it's really funny; it matters not that it doesn't quite dovetail with the piece you started with and you had to hammer it home, breaking a few edges as you did, but it's there – a shining example of your brilliance and well done you.

You are going to have to cut it.

OK. Put the gun down.

You cannot hang a whole sitcom episode on one line, joke or set piece. It will stand out – yes, as a brilliant piece of writing, but that is what it is – something shining and wonderful but extraneous. New writers collect, often for years, all the funny things they wish they had said (all those *l'esprits de l'escalier*), the things they did hear, the funny things that 'happened in our office' and in their relationships, for further use in sitcom.

This is all well and good and yes, much of this kind of material *has* made it into sitcoms, but there is a kind of radar you develop when reading scripts that spots something incongruous. It is your call on this. Is your sitcom a seamless piece of comedic writing where we meet dysfunctional characters in an intriguing relationship, trapped by their own foibles – or an excuse to sling in a bunch of stuff you thought would be good in a comedy?

Yeah. Thought so.

Your f *$@ing profanity count

Along with excretion and sex comes blasphemy and profanity (and what a party that is). There are sitcoms that thrive on it and there are those that steer clear altogether. In the US, direct blasphemy is frowned upon in a country with a ninety-five per cent Christian population. The UK is more secular and multicultural and has some degree of freedom of speech. The first time 'fuck' was said on British television was on 13 November 1965 by theatre critic Kenneth Tynan as he participated in a live TV debate as part of the BBC's late-night satirical show *BBC3*. Asked whether he would allow a play to be staged in which sexual intercourse was represented on the stage, he replied: 'I think so, certainly. I doubt if there are any rational people to whom the word "fuck" would be particularly diabolical, revolting or totally forbidden'. His biographer, Paul Johnson, later called Tynan's use of the word a 'masterpiece of calculated self-publicity', adding 'for a time it made him the most notorious man in the country'.

Good times.

Profanity and blasphemy get many complaints from the moral majority and broadcasters are careful to note where the line is. Sitcom is not by its nature topical and so in general avoids offence over aspects of current celebrity or tragedy. As sitcom is recorded and closely overseen before it is broadcast most issues of current taste tend to be removed, but you cannot legislate for those with finer sensibilities. I suggest you think carefully about the nature of your sitcom and about which network you are aiming at. If it is intended for Channel 4 in the UK or HBO in the US then you will get away with plenty of naturalistic swearing (eg, the restaurant Tourette's scene in *Curb Your Enthusiasm*) but the bigger broadcasters will be less accommodating, though there are exceptions. At present, *The Thick of It* is making much creative use of swearing with its spin doctor character Malcolm Tucker. There is reportedly a scriptwriter paid to come up with the inventive cussing. Nice work if you can f***ing get it.

Swearing and rudeness are not new, of course. *Till Death*

Us Do Part (written by Johnny Speight) featured a true East End monster, one Alf Garnett (Warren Mitchell), a racist foul-mouthed Tory based on Speight's father. It ran for seven series from 1965 to 1975 and inspired the US version, *All in the Family*. Alf was renamed Archie Bunker and this too was successful, running for some nine seasons. *Till Death* was groundbreaking, smashed social taboos and was unfailingly insulting to the womenfolk appearing in it but today's sitcom has lost its power to shock. Perhaps it cannot serve that function anymore in a multi-platform digital world.

Having said that, the judicious use of swearing is a weapon in your armory. Husband it. One of the best uses of swearing in a sitcom I have ever seen was at the climax of *The Office* (UK) series two Christmas finale, when David Brent finally stood up to his nemesis Finchy and told him quite simply to fuck off. The power of this was immense. In an instant, Brent matured. How ironic that it took a profanity to do it.

On the other side of the coin, using weak euphemisms like 'sugar' or 'gosh' instead of swear words smacks of being prissy unless the idiom is germane to that (elderly or Christian) person. If you are a bit of a sweary person then it's best to rake through the script and take them all out. They are extraneous and serve no real function save emphasis.

How did you guess I wrote that part for myself?

Many sitcoms are written by stand-up comedians looking to extend their range. Most British and Irish stand-ups are not actors (in contrast to their counterparts in the US) but they still see sitcom as the logical extension of their career. Hancock did it. Seinfeld did it. Chris Rock did it. Larry David dabbled. Jack Dee (*Lead Balloon*), Lee Mack (*Not Going Out*) and Al Murray (*Time Gentlemen Please*) have all done it, as has Peter Kay (*Phoenix Nights*) and Dylan Moran with Bill Bailey (*Black Books*). It seems a no-brainer. The comic is a proven commodity. They know how to get a laugh, they can write comedy, they have comic timing and a pre-existing fan base.

The trouble is, it doesn't always work. Ray Galton and Alan Simpson made comedian Tony Hancock a household name in the classic BBC sitcom *Hancock's Half Hour* (watched by over half the UK population) but when it came to their next show *Steptoe and Son* (in the US: *Sanford and Son*), they preferred to hire comic actors Harry H. Corbett and Wilfred Brambell. Why? They knew how to conceive a depth of dramatic characterisation and did not need to get a laugh every ten seconds. An actor can play pathos and pain and anguish as well as comedy, giving them a huge advantage when it comes to portraying three-dimensional characters.

This may make actors sound like geniuses but there is a further problem. There is little comedy training for an actor. It's easy to go to drama school with the desire to be Cate Blanchett or Christian Bale but where do you go if you want to be Ricky Gervais? (Don't answer that.)

In the US they have improv, but in the UK the old repertory theatre has all but disappeared. Rep was the proving ground in which actors would be performing one play at night, whilst rehearsing and learning two more during the day. In this way both drama and comedy were learned and you soon found out if you had a gift for either. There is a lot more Fringe theatre now (most of it unpaid or on a risible profit-share) plus the Edinburgh Festival, but there are nothing like as many opportunities as in stand up. Currently many putative comedy actors in Britain are testing their mettle in this way. They work hard: three hundred gigs a year is a fair number, with doubling up (performing at two venues in the same night) being common. You learn on your feet and die on your arse. However, it doesn't teach you to be a team player or to riff off others (more on this in 'Casting').

If you make it through this ordeal and then write a sitcom, you will perhaps inevitably write a part for yourself. At worst, it shows and in an uneven script the lead character hogs the lines. The script apes the worst of the US style where every line is a set up and the script is too gaggy at the expense of characterisation. What is missing is sharing the laughs. It is all about you. The smart stand-up will go the *Seinfeld* route. Put yourself in it, but be on the side. Be the sidekick instead.

Frobishers

BARRY

What the hell did you think you were doing?

NICK

Doing? I was doing what I was told to do by you.

BARRY

By me? It was you who suggested this whole stupid plan.

NICK

Stupid plan. Now it's a stupid plan? When you came up with it, I might remind you, you said it was a work of genius.

BARRY

Genius? Genius!

NICK

Genius. Ow.

There is no other reason for calling this a Frobisher other than we once happened to conjure up this name in a class of mine and it's stuck. Stuck? Is this getting irritating yet? You will still find examples of people talking in this way but in general we haven't had this kind of 'comic' repetition since the 1970s. No one actually talks like this. We might kind of half-say something back to somebody to achieve clarification, but we do not automatically repeat their last words. To show how cardboard it is, try having a conversation in this way with a friend, but please remember not to have any baseball bats in the vicinity. It is one of those tics that creep in without the writer noticing it and a simple read through ought to iron it out.

Iron it out?

Gaahh!

❖ Sitcom is not about jokes.

❖ Jokes are the last thing you will put into your sitcom, after character, relationships, trap and plots.

❖ Avoid puns, scatological humour, profanity, fey observations or anything that draws attention to itself as 'comedy' rather than sitcom.

❖ The laughs in sitcom arise out of the characters' behaviour; that is, their creation of and reaction to situations, plus their inappropriate behaviour whilst in them.

❖ Watch out for writing that is not germane to character. Those precious *bon mots* and observations you have made will have to go. It is sitcom not stand-up comedy.

8.

Your first episode

"About twenty-five per cent of entrants [to Sitcom Mission] send us the first episode, even though we state quite specifically not to. Industry has told us they don't want to see episode one, so we're not going to put it on. And if it's not funny on page one, why should I turn the page? We've got five hundred of these to get through. Make it easy for us to put it in the yes pile; don't make it easy for us to move onto the next one.

S.W.

"More often than not the first script is an introduction. Proof you can write. Ten funny pages of script is the best way to say, 'hello'. There are only so many places a script can go – so taking on twenty projects and sending them all to the same broadcaster isn't going to help anyone.

M.M.

"Don't try to reinvent the wheel, just create one with a nice new chrome hubcap.

M.J.

Although I am going to consider the 'first' episode in this chapter, in trying to sell your sitcom most production companies would rather you sent them an episode from the middle of the series instead of the opener. They want to see what its going to be like 'on its feet' – as if they were a viewer tuning in for the first time. I mentioned this earlier in the character section and I return to it unashamedly. In practice, you should dispense with the tedious exposition and set up and get straight on with telling a funny story that explains in plain terms who these people are, why they

139

are here and why we ought to stop watching re-runs of *30Rock* or *Spaced* and watch this instead.

Don't ever call it a pilot show. Let the production company do that. Do not give the episode an amusing title. *Friends* was 'The one with the amusing titles' and that is now a hackneyed device. On the front page of your script put the name of the show, your name and a contact address only. There is no need for any other explanation other than a short one-paragraph pitch in your covering letter. As to character and plot breakdowns, write them by all means but do it for your own benefit. I don't read them and nor do other script editors. If you must include this information (one page for each please) then attach it to the *back* of the script so that if the reader is champing at the bit to read more then they can see how it will progress. A reader needs no more than the script to learn all they need about the show.

It is an especially bad idea for the novice writer to conceive of a high concept sitcom with a strong narrative element. TV drama (*24*, *Lost*, *Desperate Housewives*, *Shameless*) does this and sitcom does not. Compared to them it is a deceptively simple *amuse bouche*, a *canapé*, a bonbon or some other French word. There are examples of successful sitcoms that do have a continuing narrative but you will not write these. They will have been devised by those already on the inside track with a network or production company or who own their own production company or those who have in other ways the confidence of a broadcaster. You do not. So why make it hard on yourself and break your mother's heart? Again.

Even those who did succeed with a continuing narrative had it hard. *Seinfeld* was broadcast on BBC2 in the UK where it struggled to find an audience. *Gavin and Stacey* ran out of steam after two series. *My Worst Week* (written by Mark Bussell and Justin Sbresni) and *Bedtime* (written and directed by Andy Hamilton) were stripped across the week, meaning they went out on the same time slot each night. They were not huge hits. An ITV experiment, *Moving Wallpaper* (created and written by Tony Jordan – who has also written over two hundred and fifty episodes of *EastEnders*) halved its audience, and as a result they called it comedy drama, which is what you do when sitcom fails.

A script reader can tell from the first ten pages of a script whether or not it fits the remit of sitcom. Most scripts fall before this fence, so here are some less than glorious ways of getting it wrong.

I moved back in with dad/mum/some sheep

On page one our hero stomps upstairs to his old room, lights a cigarette out of the bathroom window then has a long sulk. *Home Time* was about a woman in her late twenties who moved back in with her parents in Coventry, but it did not go to second series. Being a phenomenon of the current recession, there will inevitably be more sitcoms about boomerang kids, so how is yours going to set the world of comedy alight? The obvious tropes are there. Mum and Dad haven't changed, and you, their failure son or luckless spinster daughter, are home with tail between legs. The cuckoo has returned to its nest. You will be expected to perform some menial duties in exchange for your bed and board. Mum and Dad still see you as the errant teenage son/daughter. There will be screaming and fighting and no one has ever thought of this one before. Yes, they have. Ronnie Corbett never even left his domineering mother in *Sorry* and it ran to seven series.

So where will it go as a story? How will we feel about your central protagonist? That they have failed in life? Does this engender sympathy or not? This idea *is* probably going to happen and be broadcast sometime and this will depend on the best script that nails the idea. The set up is simple but it all depends on character. Make sure, if you want to do this, that you have created something universal.

Sybil has lots of story lines

> **BOB**
> I'll cook her a meal. Women like that. Or shoes. Or chocolate. I could cook her a chocolate shoe?

> **TERRY**
> You can't cook – you haven't got anything in.

BOB

I'll make do with what I've got in.

TERRY

By the way, can I borrow your motorbike?

BOB

Why – are you going to the match?

TERRY

Yeah – it's a crucial one.

BOB

So where do you want to meet on Friday?

TERRY

The Go-go club?

BOB

I can't go there. I owe money.

I have mentioned before the problem of introducing too many characters in the first few pages. Allied to this is starting up a number of potential storyline threads, none of which go anywhere. All it serves to do is confuse the reader because they are looking for one story and are faced with lots of them. Start with one storyline and one only. Not everybody needs to have a story. The supporting cast can quite happily back up the lead or add other opinions, disagreements and opposition to them. As for the lead character, they only need one thing to deal with and this will amply fill the slot that a sitcom requires.

But my narrative is in episode five

The obverse to the above is when you read page after page of banter and talk and even possibly good character interaction, but there is no plot. The writer wants to set things up for later (a comedy drama trope, incidentally), and 'hold off on the information' to keep us interested. Sorry. We aren't. Every episode must start telling us a story about these people from the word go. You will not be invited in to a meeting to explain that in three episode's time something is going to happen – because you won't ever get that far. Begin your narrative straightaway.

This sitcom vehicle has no engine

Sometimes I come across a great idea, which is simply that – a great idea – but there is little under the surface. Many new writers try to come up with something that has never been done before and, although noble in intent, it is a reactive way of working rather than mining your own experiences for comedy and drama. The attempt to devise something fresh is a false trail as it *has* all been done before. Honestly. It's all been tried and yet slightly new things appear all the time. The trick is they aren't new. They are re-packaged re-imaginings of ideas which have been around forever. It is said that there are only seven (sometimes ten) basic plots and the rest is all derivation. A new sitcom succeeds by replicating and updating a formula that was a hit before but pushes the boundaries a bit further, just as *Peep Show* updates what was once done in *The Likely Lads* and *Birds of a Feather* was an updated version of *I Love Lucy*. *Friends* spawned *Coupling* and *How I Met Your Mother*. *Curb Your Enthusiasm* is a pimped up *Seinfeld*, and bears a passing resemblance to the UK sitcom *Lead Balloon*.

However, nothing has been done in the unique way that you would do it. You don't have to reach. The novice writer comes up with a sitcom about ...

- An oil rig/the moon/a lighthouse.
- A disgraced politician goes back to the country.
- A pub quiz team
- Twin sisters trying to get dates.

There has been no sitcom set in a lighthouse or on the moon or on an oil rig to date and maybe there is a good reason for this. It's not in our communal experience to know what it would be like to live in those places and writers have not yet come up with a convincing way of getting a will-they-won't-they romance, a bromance or a familial story to work there. Maybe places that rely on a diet of fish and mermaids just don't have enough to them. Having said that, a comedy set on a distant island concerning a disgraced parish priest doesn't seem a sensible idea (*Father Ted*) nor does a family of aliens living as humans (*Third Rock from the Sun*).

Another problem is when a writer conceives a culture clash say, between Muslim and Jew. Sure, it's radical and provocative, but beyond the differing customs and religious beliefs you have to go to all the trouble of explaining why they have come together and what the problems are. It's not entirely credible. It is another idea-based sitcom, like pairing black and white in the 1970s (*Love Thy Neighbour*) or gay and lesbian (hasn't happened yet). A reader will sense that this will run out of steam in a few episodes.

This can also happen to the fish-out-of-water sitcom where your lead character is placed in a new environment. The move is usually urban to rural where they struggle with curmudgeonly locals, customs and difficult geography. Sure, the character is in difficulty, but what is happening internally? They are going to have to go on a journey where they will be accepted into the new community. Let's posit the disgraced politician who returns to the country. It could work but only if the central character is larger than life with plenty of people to react against. The politician must win our trust with more than simply losing their position. We are not predisposed to this profession and you would have to go a long way to win our sympathy. A week is a long time in sitcom. An illustration of how the urban–rural move *can* work is in Simon Nye's sitcom *How Do You Want Me?*, the opening of which is transcribed in the following chapter.

Another example of a successful fish-out-of-water sitcom is *The Vicar of Dibley*, which played to old-fashioned sitcom strengths of strong characterisation, a limited setting and people trapped by their dogmatic lives and attitudes, written by Richard Curtis, who also wrote *Blackadder*, *Four Weddings and a Funeral* and *Notting Hill*.

A pub quiz team has the problem of being set in a pub (more on this later). How are we to get enough out of a bunch of mates who meet up once a week to answer trivial questions whilst eating pork scratchings and marinating themselves in lager and a glass of Pinot for the lady? Sure it pulls them together but the quiz is no more than a hook. It is at present being mooted as a stand-up sketch hybrid for British character comedian Al Murray, and perhaps this is where it may flourish.

Another engine that runs out of steam, as exemplified by the 'twin sisters and dating' is the one-off idea. This was done effectively in the 'Principal Charming' episode of *The Simpsons*. Dating is limited as an element that we wish to see repeated again and again, as it is the same thing with permutations until you pair bond or give up. Sure, *Friends*, *Seinfeld*, *Peep Show* and *Two Pints of Lager* have a lot of dating in them, but it does not overbalance the shows. The datee is always going to be a peripheral character. Likewise, a dating agency (where, oh irony of ironies, the workers are all unable to find dates either) is too focused on a singular aspect. *Agony*, starring Maureen Lipman, was a successful show about an agony aunt, but it hasn't been replicated since.

When writing a first episode you must think your way through the series to the end of season one at least. Can we really get six episodes out of dating without it becoming repetitive? A script editor can tell when an idea has not been thought through. Do the work yourself and beat them at their own game.

Referencing other sitcoms and TV

Good sitcoms create their own world and to barge in on another's creation is comedy Kryptonite. You will have noticed that in most soaps and sitcoms people do not watch TV or if they do they don't make a big thing of it unless they are being all post modern and ironic, which is also a tired trope. This is because the camera is where their TV ought to be (front and centre in the living room) and because unlike us they have lives. The only point of having a TV on is to fleetingly catch that all-important news broadcast.

> BROADCASTER
> Up next, the vital piece of exposition you've been
> waiting for. Stay tuned, after these messages.

Other than that, leave it alone. There are sitcoms that pay homage to films or other TV genres (*Spaced* was successful in this, and *The Royle Family* made a virtue of it) but television is such an easy target to make jokes about. It also dates your show. Jokes or spoof episodes about reality TV will lose meaning once we have lost patience will the drooling morons who appear on them. This is the same with current celebrities. Lady Gaga, LL Cool J or Fifty Cent are going to mean as little to future generations as Lucille Ball or Frankie Abbot does to the current one. This is not to deny that cultural references are useful hooks and we do live in a world saturated in them, but do try to be judicious.

Referencing other famous sitcoms is a bad idea, too: it draws attention to the fact that yours is a poor imitation of what was once great. It's like being reminded of the heroic boyfriend your sexy Goth girlfriend dated before you. Why reference that? Why bring that up again? You want your new sexy script editor to love your brand new script not to pine over the older better ones, so help them to forget it by not mentioning it ever.

Watching TV is a passive experience and your characters must at all times be active. There is no time for them to reference TV unless it is a catalyst for something else. As to referencing movies, there is a broader scope. Film is global, a unit which has cultural currency. It also has so many genres that anyone can relate to. We all know what a James Bond film is or a rom com or a courtroom drama. The tropes within this are so easily recognisable (and clichéd for a good reason – they *work*) that they can be lifted wholesale for use in another form. For example, in any courtroom we know there will always be a wise black judge and a hotshot lawyer who will ask to approach the bench. There will be objections! Sustains! Overruled. There will be, 'If you object one mo' time councillor I will *cle*-arr the cawt'. Bang, bang. There will be a surprise witness, a grilling, a Jimmy Stewart figure who implores the jury to see common sense and finally the verdict (cue press interview on steps of courtroom).

Use them and twist them.

(Lucille Ball was the star of *I Love Lucy* and Frankie Abbott was a teenage tearaway in the ITV sitcom *Please Sir!* I don't know who Fifty Cent is.)

146

Actors and acting

If you are lucky enough to garner interest in your sitcom, perhaps from one of the dedicated live performance groups or via a production company which has arranged a read-through, then you will come across those sensitive flowers known as actors. Skittish creatures all, they tend to hide in places where people still smoke and wear cheap footwear. Having not worked or eaten for a while they will be only too glad of the chance to be in your showcase for their talents. Most young actors and performers will work for free: a sad fact, but no more unrealistic than starting up a new business where you would not expect to turn a profit in the first years. We all have to invest, to learn our trade, to perfect what we are offering. The difficulty for actors (more on this in the casting section) is they have to hit the ground running. No one expects to pay to see a musician who cannot play his instrument and yet stand-ups and actors are supposed somehow to just be able to do it. This is a fallacy. They endure hundreds of open spots, humiliating auditions, TIE (Theatre in Education) productions and miserable runs at the Edinburgh Festival Fringe (I could fill another book with Edinburgh horror stories and never touch on Burke and Hare). The fact is *work makes work* and a can-do attitude makes all the difference between the amateur and the semi-professional. Make a noise. Show them you are there. The fruit does not fall far from the tree. Get nearer the tree.

Most likely there will be a director between you and them and the director will absorb much of the flak. It is the director who will question you concerning the punctuation of and the reading of your lines. It is they who will suggest any cuts or changes. The actors will work their magic with what you have put on the page.

It may all go wrong. Sometimes through miscasting, fluffing, nerves or a poor performance on the night, it flops. A character and a performance are something you feel for like a blind man catching eels.

Actors must undergo several stages to achieve a performance. First, ignorance. They have no knowledge of the piece. This can serve them well, as they may sight-read well, performing naturally at the read-through, an innocence that is hard to capture again. Next there is learning the role. They move into the hard part

147

where the mist has burnt off and they must work hard to find the character, the vocal and physical mannerisms and make them work in conjunction with the other actors. They must then get up to speed for the first performance and they must do this all at the same time. It can mesh perfectly or it can fall apart. They have learned as much as they can and must hit their marks and not fall over the scenery. In a televised sitcom, they may have less than a week to rehearse a show, two if they are lucky. If it is live in a TV studio, they have few chances to fluff. In most sitcom recordings I have attended, it is not the actors who make mistakes, but props and technical difficulties which demand re-takes.

The pressure is immense. Say they come out of the gate badly. The laughs aren't there and they dry up. Every stand-up knows the feeling of beginning to die. Your gag flops so your timing goes. Fear sets in and hangs over the audience's heads like a shroud. No one is able to laugh no matter how much they may want to. They feel too inhibited. In stand-up you can 'call' the situation, defusing your mistake and re-booting the act. In a sitcom recording, though I couldn't possibly advocate this, it might be a good idea to screw up the take so as to release the pressure on the cast and audience, but it's a high-risk strategy. Sometimes actors add a lot of business to what they do – visual gags or noises that are riotously funny the first time they do it, but when repeated somehow fall flat. Performing sitcom is faking spontaneity so feel for them. It is not rocket science, but it is hard. This is why the best ones get paid a lot of money and as much sex as they can eat.

Casting

Casting is often seen as one of the dark arts. Esta Charkham, a leading UK casting director (also former producer of Alomos' *Birds of a Feather* and *Nightingales*) says:

> The real casting is when you hear the character in your head. Dick Clement (co-writer with Ian La Frenais of numerous hit sitcoms including *The Likely Lads*, *Porridge* and *Auf Wiedersehen, Pet*) could be every single character in his sitcoms.

It is another matter to find the right actor to play them. It's Charkham's belief that a comedy actor needs precision, a sense of rhythm and of comedy punctuation, as well as being able to understand the character. Comedians are of little use to her as they are too fond of prowling the stage and do not know how to earn the laugh. Casting is a sense of who would be 'right' for a role. This means that a director must trust the casting director implicitly. Comedy history is littered with examples of shows that failed or struggled because of the wrong casting. *Men Behaving Badly* began with UK character comic Harry Enfield as Dermot, but when he stood down after the first series, actor Neil Morrissey picked up the baton. The chemistry between him and Martin Clunes made more sense and the clash of personalities and character traits bedded in much better.

Charkham says that the best actors have a 'twinkle' about them (citing Alec Baldwin as the magnificent Jack Donaghy in *30Rock* as one example) and that when casting it's a gut feeling. She looks for an actor with truth, honesty, stillness and a little sadness to them. Much as this sounds like an augur pawing through entrails to make the right prediction, it points up just how hard the business can be. The writer may toil for months or even years on a script before selling it; they may be subjected to fifteen or twenty re-writes before the casting, the read through, the performance, the scheduling and the fickle fancy of the audience – all of which can scupper it. This seems depressing but hope springs eternal: great sitcoms do get through and they get through despite all the vagaries of the business.

It also demonstrates the subjective nature of comedy. You may not go for *Alan Partridge* or *How I Met Your Mother*, but millions do. There are a lot of people who like *My Family* and *The Last of the Summer Wine* and *Everybody Loves Raymond*. There are many prime time sitcoms in the US and in the UK that are derided by the cognoscenti, but who have huge followings, just as there are guilty favourites. Charkham produced Channel 4's *Nightingales*, a hidden gem.

> The lesson is that once you have learned the rules you must go your own way, trust in your own sense of what is funny and stick to it regardless.

Overnight success, as we know, is a short decade or so to the top. Make a plan, a long plan and never give up the day job (sorry).

First, second and third drafts

After the work has been done on conceiving your concept, characters, dysfunctional emotional relationships and plotting, it is time to bang out your first draft. As mentioned before, I believe this ought to be done quickly in order to capture the heat and passion of the show. You should not pause if you cannot think of just the right joke; it will come and if not then maybe you were just trying too hard anyway. By all means write long if you want to, and leave in notes to yourself – perhaps ideas that might broaden the character, or even modify your initial idea of them. Try for at least five pages or a scene a day. Don't re-write either.

Allow yourself to only go back one page before pushing on, otherwise you will criticise all you have done before and it will never get finished. Remember, it's not a whole screenplay or a novel. If you cannot finish it in a fortnight then perhaps there is something wrong in its conception, but let us assume that you reach those wonderful words 'the end'. You are breathless, exhausted, moist even. There are coffee cup rings and pizza crusts in abundance. Good, now put the file in a folder and go clear up.

Leave the first draft alone for at least a week. It needs time to settle and you need to view it with a pair of objective eyes. The opinion of many people in TV is that the first draft of anything is rubbish. Whilst I disagree with this, it is a truism that there is not a single script that has been produced without it first being tampered with. After this time has elapsed you may return to it. I suggest you print it out and read the hard copy. When on screen it is easy to work into it without seeing the wood for the trees.

The second draft is often worse than the first. Sometimes after having prepared an in-depth report for a writer client, I receive a second draft, which has lost all the spark of the original. They have tried to incorporate all the notes and changes. They may have had objections to some of them and there is some shoehorning going on. They have done what was required but have not had enough time to be objective. As a result the second draft is a mish-mash of changes and compromises, more like a first-and-a-half draft. This is common. It is hard to take criticism when you feel you *know* the characters and the world. Who is this upstart scrawling all over my child in bright red pen? What right do they have to fiddle with my plot? Others are more gracious, taking on board the opinion of an experienced eye and taking their time over making the necessary changes. Don't worry. Second Draft Syndrome is also common in commissioned work too. You are not alone.

In the third draft, plot and characters are integrated and the jokes flow. All extraneous dialogue, reactive characters and unnecessary banter have been excised. From page one we are clear whose story this is and what this episode is going to be about. The first ten pages flow smoothly, introducing us to living, breathing people. There are laugh-out-loud moments. There is sympathy for the monster character, some pathos or at least a way into the world. There is an element of recognition. The reader reaches the end satisfied and composes an email to the writer to congratulate him on a great first draft.

Writing for radio

Jane Berthoud is head of Radio Light Entertainment and Katie Taylor is her counterpart in TV Entertainment. They are well integrated with the ideas of passing projects through from radio to TV. Both *Miranda* and *Not Going Out* began on radio. The two radio sketch shows with a open submission policy are *Newsjack* and *Recorded for Training Purposes*. These are the main entry points for the new writer.

M.J.

As mentioned in the introduction, writing for BBC radio is an excellent testing ground for a comedy writer and one of the best ways into the business. There have been a number of open submission topical sketch shows from *Weekending* and *The News Huddlines* (which ran for many years) to the current Radio 7 show, *Newsjack*. When on air, the deadline for jokes and sketches is Monday mornings, after which the script editor and producers

151

select the best and then table read them with the cast. The show is recorded live on a Wednesday night and broadcast on Thursday evenings at 11pm (repeated on Sundays). Anyone can submit by email to newsjack@bbc.co.uk but please first Google newsjack + submissions to check requirements (three sketch maximum, word documents only, etc). Not only does learning how to write fast and funny help to nourish your comedy bones but also, if successful, it will get you noticed by the producers (which, as you will have figured out, is the name of the game). Simon Blackwell, a former student of mine, began this way in 1996 and went on to write for sitcoms *The Old Guys*, *Peep Show*, and *The Thick of It* and has been Oscar nominated for *In the Loop*. Not that I'm jealous.

Your real aim here is to get known by producers at the BBC. In order to do this you must be successful in getting stuff on the show, which in turn will lead to you being offered a commission, meaning you continue to offer up several minutes worth of sketches a week, but are now guaranteed payment. Once you have created a dialogue with your producer and started to gain access to others around you, now is the time to offer up your sitcom ideas. The BBC has regular offers rounds, which are an internal market for comedy and drama pitches and occur every six months, annually or even bi-annually. If you are in with your BBC producer, they will guide you through.

However, if you wish to go via one of the fifty 'preferred' independent production suppliers, you will need to contact them directly. The BBC Radio 4 website has this information in a pdf file. You can also find them in the *Writers' and Artists' Yearbook* (A&C Black), which is searchable online.

When cold calling a production company you will be expected to have developed your idea to spec script level, unless you are a produced writer with a track record. In addition to this you will need to have a brief outline (essentially, the pitch), which can be expressed in half a page, in fact, the fewer words the better. This outline must give a sense of the characters and situation, and express the story within the pilot episode. You may request that they read the outline. You should have a calling card script as well, one that demonstrates your ability to write dialogue for radio (scenes, not merely a sketch).

The scale of the commissioning process is vast. There are up to three thousand proposals at the pre-offers stage (this is inclusive of drama proposals). At this stage, your producer will place your idea on a large database and you have a maximum of one hundred words to sell the idea. The producer has two hundred extra words to sell the project as a whole and you as a writer. Do also try to make your title as attention grabbing as possible.

If you pass through this then the next stage is the final offers round, for which you would need a two-page outline. Here you can break it down into the six episodes, describe characters and any narrative element. This is followed by an agonisingly long wait and then it's feast or famine.

Where radio differs from TV writing is that you are not bound by the visual or by budget constraints. This is not to say that you ought to set scenes in the frozen tundra or amidst herds of teeming wildebeest in the South African veldt, but it does free you up. It enables you to learn to write clearly defined characters. Before attempting this, I suggest listening to some sitcoms which have been adapted for radio. *Yes, Minister*, *Dad's Army* and *Hancock* are all particularly good on characterisation and have superb plotting, plus of course they are written by the best in the business: Jonathan Lynn and Anthony Jay, Jimmy Perry and David Croft and the great Ray Galton and Alan Simpson.

Voice

When setting up a character for radio you have no visual clues so it must all be in the voice. A voice will convey age, class, race and gender but in addition to this, it is the clearest signifier of emotion and temperament. Happiness and sadness, optimism and pessimism are carried across in upward or downward intonation (lilting or soporific) but also in the dialogue itself.

What did she do?

This simple question can be asked in a number of ways. It can be caring or disinterested, accusatory or furious. It is the actor's job to interpret the emotion behind the line but it is your job to ensure that the context in which it is placed is as clear as possible. In comedy there isn't a huge dramatic range as all is subservient ultimately to the laugh, however, pathos and sympathy are important. In your first radio attempt it is a good idea to write for a broad age range. Try to have a good balance of males and females both young and old. Too many 'blokes trying to be stand-ups' gets irritating and is the preserve of the panel shows not your sitcom. Two men or women of a similar age, class and/or profession will need specific characteristics to differentiate them.

Dialect is one. Look at Stephen Merchant's wistful Bristolian as set against Ricky Gervais' sly Estuarine English, with its rising nasal inflection and sarcastic turns of phrase. The difference between Johnny Vegas and Alan Davies is vast, both culturally and in every cadence. The clash of posh and poor is a common device, as heard in *Miranda Hart's Joke Shop*, another successful radio to TV crossover. Miranda's posh tones are usurped by her more posh mother (Patricia Hodge) but brought to earth by her friend Stevie (Sarah Hadland). *Dad's Army* was possibly one of the clearest examples of the class divisions in English society (and ought to be a set text in sociology classes), pitting a pompous, jumped up bank manager (Mainwaring) against his subordinate (Sergeant Wilson) who was, if not landed gentry, then certainly made of 'the right stuff.'

A person who speaks quickly and at great length will always come across as more needy than the one who takes their time and utters their statements with great import. A person who snipes from the sidelines may not want to engage with the argument, whereas the blowhard who rolls up their sleeves loves the cut and thrust of the fight. Someone with a naturally high voice will find it hard to be taken seriously whereas mellifluous sonorous tones are considered warm and affable.

Your characters might have certain tics, turns of phrase, mannerisms or even speech defects (Michael Palin has used a stutter on more than one occasion). You only need give a flavour of this, as in Ronnie Barker's Arkwright in *Open All Hours*, for it to become a defining characteristic: one in this case which the hapless and bullied Granville (David Jason) had little option but to try to belittle.

A simple way of helping the listener to tell who is speaking is to borrow a trick from *The Archers*. In this long-running radio show, the character will often say the name of the person they are speaking to ('What's that, Dan? Susie's come a cropper in the lower field?'). Ah. The listener thinks. He's speaking to Dan. It must be Dan. This is a device also employed in news interviews and after a while we don't notice it.

> PRESENTER
> ... a valid point, Minister, but let me turn to you,
> Joseph Fritzl, for a comment on childcare provision
> in Austria?

Scenes

Scenes in radio can be as short as a couple of lines or as long as several pages of dialogue. So long as you break up the action with sounds (written as FX, which is short for effects) then a scene can stretch as long as you like. A fade in and fade out is also a common to break up the passage of time and it operates ...

> FADE OUT
>
> FADE IN

... like this. One of the most important things to remember in a scene is to try not to have more than two people speaking at any one time. If you must have a third, be clear that their function is as an 'interrupter' or bringer of exposition. This is also true of TV sitcom. Without walls, doors or exits there is not clearly defined way of ending a scene or exiting a room unless you write:

> FX: DOOR SLAMS SHUT. FOOTSTEPS FADING
> AWAY

The great advantage of radio, of course, is that you can trick the listener, such as in the following example.

> BUNNY
> I have never been so insulted in all my life. I'm
> going to take this slander to the highest court in the
> land and then see what you think. Ha!

FX: WALKING OFF. DOOR KNOB FUMBLES

SIR MAYHEW
(*whispering*)
But he *did* take poor Sally Hawkins up the V&A.
She couldn't sit down for a month.

BUNNY
I am still here you know.

Music/grams

The use of music 'stings' or 'stabs' are short bursts of music to counterpoint the spoken word. They, too, will act as a scene break, much as the flash of an outside building does in *Seinfeld*.

STING: ROLLING BASS RIFF

Grams is the term used for all other title, credit or incidental music. Remember that most recorded music is under copyright. There is an international standard for this, which states that the copyright lasts for between fifty and one hundred years after the composer's death and a shorter period for anonymous or corporate ownership. This means that using any recorded music from the last forty years or so (therefore all the best known rock and pop) is going to incur cost. It is best therefore to write in a generic instruction, for example:

GRAMS: BRIT POP ANTHEM, THRASHING
GUITARS, ETC ...

You can also use music as background, in which case you write

GRAMS: FLIGHT OF THE BUMBLEBEE (HELD UNDER)

BUNNY
There a bee trapped in here somewhere?

Where radio also succeeds is in creating atmosphere. Simple sounds can indicate a windy day, a storm at sea, a crowded shopping mall, a dungeon or the attack of one thousand camels.

It works brilliantly when creating aural slapstick. Any radio fan should have listened to, if not memorised, the entire output of the *Goon Show*. The sheer range and inventiveness of Spike Milligan's stage directions were a monumental challenge for producer and sound effects man Peter Eton.

A short or long pause in radio is more eloquent than on TV, as it is left up to our imagination as to the facial and physical reactions of the characters. In this way, the listener will create the comedy so long as the pre-requisite setting up has been done. Sound can too transport us instantly back in time (all you need write is FX: FLASH BACK IN TIME) or forward, or to any location you require. In order to confirm the destination, the character only need to state where they are – and it's funnier if it does not correspond to the sounds we have heard ...

FX: HARSH HOWLING WIND, WAVES LASHING A SEA WALL

FRIMLEY
Ah, the French Riviera in June. Magnifique.

The great thing about radio is its cosiness. The one-to-one relationship with the listener flatters them and its inclusivity makes it an intimate relationship – something which is vital if a sitcom is to connect with its audience. It may be true to say that the majority of BBC radio sitcoms are resolutely middle class, but that is its main target audience. Few of the success stories listed previously have many working class characters in them, and the whole clubbable BBC Radio panel/parlour game ethos does rather bleed through to its sitcoms, which are fairly bourgeois. The time slots too define its audience; being in the main 6.30pm (pre-watershed) and at 11 or 11.30 at night, with a weekend lunchtime repeat. Long gone are the days when the whole family would gather to listen to *Worker's Playtime* or *Hancock's Half Hour* so radio comedy tends to be for those who are driving home, preparing food or nodding off. Having said that, there are a lot of truck driving fans of BBC radio comedy and let's hope they aren't being put to sleep by it.

If you are considering writing for radio, you need to listen to as much of the output as possible, get a feel for the use of music and effects, the styles of comedy on offer. Note that you should keep your cast to about five characters maximum, and if you have extras, consider writing a part for a voice actor with the versatility of Kenneth Williams or Paul Whitehouse. Plotting can sometimes be more extreme on this medium, eg, *The Hitchhiker's Guide to the Galaxy*. The listener will go with you on your aural journey anywhere you wish, but not at the expense of poor characterisation. The ludicrous, as with farce, must always come from a credible premise. Establish that, and then you have won your freedom.

Record or at least read your script out loud, with all its sound effects in place. One page is equal to between forty and fifty seconds of radio, and the shows last twenty-eight minutes, leaving time for credits. The radio format is available to download for free on the BBC Writersroom website and is called ScriptSmart.

Try to get work (sketches) onto the topical comedy shows so that you get known and remembered, but this will all take time. Bear in mind that although BBC Radio will not furnish you with riches or sex, it may well transfer to TV, although it is not a good idea to tell your producer this at the start, as that would belittle the good work they are doing in radio. Of course you want a crossover hit, it's just better that you keep this to yourself. Phil Bowker, my former producer on BBC Radio 2's *News Huddlines*, is now the writer, creator and director of Channel 4's *Phoneshop*. It only took him twenty years.

A final word on releasing your own material on the Net. This is a great way of establishing your brand and with no interference. Home recording equipment and computer capacity has advanced so fast that broadcast quality material can be produced (as with music) in your seedy bedroom. Put it out there. Create webisodes. My Space and YouTube are currently the best delivery systems, but by the time this book is published I am sure that there will be more. Many people are making their own podcasts and, once you have established a brand, this seems like a great way to go. Cut out the middleman. Go guerrilla as with live sitcom.

❖ Never send out the first (pilot) episode.

❖ Your episode must have a self-contained plot.

❖ Everything you need to know about the sitcom and its cast ought to be in the first script.

❖ Avoid cheesy 'set-up' opening episodes, such as moving back in or the inheritance.

❖ Don't reference other TV. You make your own world.

❖ You have no control over casting, but write great characters and a great script and make it actor-proof.

❖ You can perform a great script badly, but you can't do anything with a bad script.

❖ Radio makes great demands of the form but will teach you well.

❖ Expect to write several drafts before yours is ready to go out.

❖ No matter how complete your script, it will always be a first draft to the reader.

9.

Case studies

Simon Nye is one of the most prolific and successful sitcom writers of the last two decades. I asked how he got into sitcom writing.

I considered myself a novelist, and had two novels published. Legendary agent and producer Beryl Vertue heard about the novel *Men Behaving Badly*, knew Harry Enfield was looking for a sitcom role and put us together. I'd never even thought about writing a sitcom. I actually thought the actors made most of it up themselves. They don't.

What was the process in getting *Men Behaving Badly* to screen?

The producer asked me to write half a script on spec, which I did, mainly by copying out chunks of my novel. Not the best approach, but then Thames TV commissioned a script, then a second. The whole thing went pretty quickly because Harry Enfield was attached. We shot a pilot, which wasn't great, but was good enough to get a series commissioned. Thames TV, the broadcaster, did some market research – which is always hilariously unhelpful – and I think the only thing we changed was to put a more boring fridge in the kitchen.

Harry Enfield famously stood down to make way for Neil Morrissey. Can you explain about that, and the subsequent BBC input?

Harry tried to get out of the show after the pilot but Beryl referred him to his contract and he went ahead with the series, but reluctantly. I don't blame him – he was at the height of his fame and wasn't really right for the part. ITV were shocked when he left but were happy with Neil Morrissey, who had a big following in the drama *Boon* – mainly because women liked his long hair, apparently. He knew Martin Clunes and was an inspired and rather easy choice – we didn't see anyone else for the part. But the series didn't hit ten million viewers so ITV dropped it. I'm still not sure why the BBC picked it up, because the scripts were still a little underpowered, although I was learning a lot.

When did you get a sense that it was becoming a hit?

There's no moment when you know you're a hit, at least not for writers. Nobody shouts out of a white van at us. I suppose one way you know is that you all start to have more arguments on the show because the pressure gets to everyone. That happened to us, but nothing too serious – the odd slapping from actors if my gags weren't up to snuff, that sort of thing. And, as every writer who's had a success complains – the reviews tend to go straight from 'I don't like this sitcom at all' to 'This sitcom's not as good as it was' without the nice bit in between.

How much were you involved personally in the directing and casting?

I was involved in the casting, which can be a rare privilege for a writer – Hartswood Films is a very writer-friendly company. I have no interest in the directing or theories of how to shoot comedy, personally, but it's great if you can form a creative bond with the director. TV directors are severely undervalued. Martin Dennis has directed most of my sitcoms and he was always good at telling me when a joke was forced, or not something people would ever say, or simply not good.

Was it easy to get subsequent projects made after MBB?

A hit sitcom is the Holy Grail for the BBC – endlessly repeatable – so the writer and actors get a bit of carte blanche for a few years. Which is probably why I was allowed to write and make *How Do You Want Me?* (probably my favourite show) and have a very free hand. But it's never easy to get shows made, there's always broadcaster interference on casting, whether there's an audience for it, etc. It often goes down to the wire on budget too. *Wild West* was made because Dawn French was in it, for example. Attaching a star is always the quickest way of getting a show made. Which is why any old rubbish with Nicholas Lyndhurst in it will always get waved through.

When did you give up the day job?

I gave up full time work (I was a translator) during the second series of *Men Behaving Badly*, but the key moment was when I was commissioned to write a different project (*Frank Stubbs Promotes*, a drama) because I felt then that I was not just a one trick pony. I'm a bit conservative on this – the day-to-day contact with people in a job often feeds the writing. My advice to wannabe writers is get a part-time job and write in the mornings, if you can. Or shack up with someone wealthy.

What are the most important skills you need to be a sitcom writer?

Love of language helps, if I may be so pretentious. The difference between a boring line and a funny one is often an interesting adjective or an unusual turn of phrase. Ability to sit in a chair for hours at a stretch, that's always trotted out, and it's true. A sense of ownership and craftsmanship helps – you put in the extra effort because a sitcom episode can be a beautifully wrought thing, plot strands interweaving etc, and you made it.

What problems do you encounter in dealing with indy prods, commissioners and with broadcasting companies?

I've been lucky and never had huge problems with indy prods. You have to see it from their perspective: they're often in a desperate position, gagging for a commission or everyone will be out of a job etc. So if they ask I'll almost always do a two or three page outline for free. Broadcasters are more complicated because the people who commission scripts are usually on your side but it goes wrong further up the food chain when they throw weird preferences at you: 'We're only looking for raucous edgy fun shows' turns overnight into 'Have you got any delicate warm family sitcoms?' But if you think comedy departments are maddening or opaque or simply bastards, you should experience drama departments …

What is the daily/weekly routine of a successful writer?

Miss deadline again. Apologise to producer. Delay writing by answering questionnaire about sitcoms. Have perfectly good idea rejected by the powers that be. Have lesser idea accepted and proceed to write it. Go to cafe to write; see a whole bunch of other writers with their Macbooks; check IMDB profile; wonder why someone has added 'fuck' at random in your Wikipedia profile. Finally get into The Zone, write happily and successfully, and wonder why the hell you didn't do that earlier in the week.

What advice would you give to the putative writer?

Don't talk about it, just do it. Don't linger too long on cherished projects and get destroyed when they are rejected – immediately move onto another one. Try writing in a variety of genres: if the sitcom isn't working, have a go at a short story, or a radio comedy-drama, or a novel, or an article, or even a diary – it's all writing and it's all ultimately useful or usable. If you're really stuck, have one large glass of wine and write for two hours without thinking too much about it, just enjoying it, then leave it a day and see what you've got. It may not be useable but you never know. The mornings are the best time to write, if you can.

How do you want me?

This sitcom is Simon Nye's favourite, though it did not gain a wide audience and only ran for two series. It starred Dylan Moran and Charlotte Coleman, who played Ian and Lisa Lyons, a newlywed couple who leave London to return to the countryside where Lisa grew up. Ian does not fit in with rural life or with her family, in particular her boorish brother (Peter Serafinowicz) or her turkey-breeding father (Frank Finlay).

How Do You Want Me? is a double meaning. Ian is a photographer so this is the kind of line a casting couch ingénue might use. It's coquettish and submissive, but also aptly describes how lost and naïve he is in this new world. It helped that comedian Dylan Moran brought his dark Irish insouciance to the role and Charlotte Colman as Lisa reprieved elements of the kooky character Scarlett, which she had played in the film *Four Weddings and a Funeral*.

What follows are the first two scenes from episode one, series one, showing how the characters are introduced …

HOW DO YOU WANT ME

By SIMON NYE

Episode one - "A Stranger In Paradise"

4th (final) draft

1/1 EXT.   **CHURCH**   **DAY**   **DAY 1**

Wedding photographs are being taken outside an old rural church. The impressive line-up includes the YARDLEY FAMILY, a host of village worthies, quite a few children and on the fringes one or two slightly odder villagers. There is a strangely low-key, almost surreal air about the proceedings. Apart from the odd buzz of conversation people don't seem to be having much fun.

> **Comment:** Sitcoms usually take place in a limited number of days. On a shooting script these are numbered.

The photographer MR WEBB, a sweet elderly man, gently directs operations.

> **Comment:** A simple unfussy scene description, telling us the principal characters and the mood.

> **Comment:** Two adjectives is quite enough.

                    MR WEBB
          We're being happy. Lips all
          wide.

We focus on the main protagonists. LISA YARDLEY, the bride in full regalia, is attractive, cheerful, in her mid-20s. She is flanked by her groom IAN LYONS – a little older, his expression long-suffering and faintly disbelieving – and her father ASTLEY YARDLEY, dapper and rather brutal-faced, a force to be reckoned with. HELEN YARDLEY is the bridesmaid, too old for comfort in the role.

> **Comment:** A nice quirky thing for a photographer to say. He is telling them how to behave, thus intimating to us, the audience that something is wrong already.

> **Comment:** The wise choice of descriptors are a great way to introduce the hero. Faintly disbelieving is ironic and detached,

                    ASTLEY
          Bride and immediate family.

> **Comment:** All these are valuable clues to the casting director and to us, the readers.

The Yardley family convene in a group. The others disperse, hovering. Ian hovers the most awkwardly of all, alone, while the others chat easily amongst themselves.

                    MR WEBB
          Lips plump and wide. Very
          lovely.

We CUT to a little later. Another photographic set-up, this time all the women. Lisa's voice drifts over, comfortable in the limelight.

                    LISA
          Wait, wait, my mouth's gone.

Ian finds himself standing next to his father-in-law Astley, surrounded by gravestones. Astley realises he is there and stiffens, his body language oozing aggression. Ian forces himself. He puts his hand on an old gravestone.

> IAN
> Are you a funerals man or more
> of a cremations –

> ASTLEY
> Apologise or piss off.

Astley walks off. Ian watches him go, then calls after him.

> IAN
> How d'you mean?

> MR WEBB
> Right, well. Do we think that's
> enough?

The photos taken, everyone instantly undoes their ties and makes a desultory exit.

1/2 EXT.   **COUNTRY LANE**   **DAY**   **DAY 1**

Minutes later. Ian and Lisa are walking along a pretty, deserted lane. As they talk, Lisa loosens the many buttons and clips of her wedding garb.

> IAN
> No, no, it was lovely.

> LISA
> Well, thanks for doing it.

> IAN
> Of course, as an empty, self-
> defeating ritual it was up there
> with the Eurovision Song
> Contest.

> LISA
> (pointing casually to a
> tree)
> Sycamore.

> IAN
> We've already got photographs
> of our wedding.

Comment: Here we are introduced to the main emotional tension in the sitcom, Father and Son-in-law. Old man and young buck.

Comment: An unexpected reaction, which intrigues us. Rather than just throw jokes at us, we are being given a whole relationship – with all it's uneasy struggles – in one simple insult.

Comment: This tells us that this is no ordinary wedding. It's not a particularly comedic scene, but there are notes of humour to show that it's not all dramatic. This first scene has introduced us to all the main players.

Comment: Already apologetic, which is a good way for both men and women to feel sympathetic towards him.

Comment: This confirms that Ian is the comedic centre of this, and that he is dry and sardonic. The first 'joke' of the show it makes a simple comic comparison. Yes it *is* a TV reference, but to an outdated institution that all can laugh at

Comment: Nice way of deflecting the pointed comment. This later becomes a running gag.

LISA
Yes, weirdly, my parents don't
think two grainy polaroids of us
outside a registry office in
Budapest count as –

IAN
I think I'll do the same to them:
'I'm afraid as you didn't invite
me on holiday with you to
Wookey Hole I want you to
restage it so I can get some
snaps' –

Comment: This tells us what is going on. Exposition yes, but clear and effective in answer to the question posed in the first scene, which is 'Why is this wedding so odd?'

LISA
I warned you how they'd react.
            (indicating another tree)
Elm.

IAN
I'm not doing trees today.

Comment: The running gag. This tells us that they have an easygoing relationship.

LISA
What's that one?

IAN
Pussy willow.

LISA
Cedar.
      (a beat)
You had to say 'pussy' didn't
you.

They smile wryly. Lisa has almost freed herself from her voluminous dress.

Comment: A shared joke. A nice moment between them.

IAN
Your Dad still expects me to
apologise.

LISA
He just wants you to go to him
and be nice. Why won't you?

Comment: More tension here...

IAN
Because I've got principles too.

LISA
No you haven't.

Comment: This is typical of what women say to men and also of the writer, whose style is often to allow his male characters to self-aggrandise, before being brought down to earth by a more sensible female partner.

Lisa dumps her bulky wedding dress in Ian's arms. Underneath she is wearing a skirt and T-shirt. She kisses him and heads off.

> LISA
> I won't be long, I've got
> shopping to do.

Comment: Nicely irreverent. After all those British films about sumptuous weddings it is nice to be glib, flippant and disrespectful of the ritual.

> IAN
> But it's our wedding day. I'm
> supposed to carry you across the
> thing.

Lisa carries on walking. Ian looks disappointed.

Comment: Funnier to *not* say 'threshold'.

A wide, high shot of Ian and Lisa, dwarfed by the gorgeous country-side around them. Ian, struggling to control the yards of white material in the breeze, chases after Lisa. They giggle. Finally Ian catches her and holds her. She squeals.

> LISA
> Leave me alone! I'm a virgin!

1/3 EXT.   FOOTBALL PITCH   DAY   DAY 2

The thud of a heavy, illegal tackle. The culprit is Lisa's brother DEAN – wild, impetuous, charismatic. The referee blows for a foul. Dean spreads his arms in innocence.

Comment: And out on a comedy moment. The wide high shot will be expensive but this was shot on film and its a nice way to go. We have established that these characters like one another, are great friends and share their attitude to life - and the antagonist, her Father, is seething in the background.

> DEAN
> What did I do!?

A wider shot reveals that the match is being watched by a handful of people, on a pitch which slopes alarmingly.

Comment: Three fantastic adjectives. In the right hands, this would make a fabulous anti-hero, a D'arcy or an *'Alfie'* – but as we have already met the lover, this is unlikely to be the case. It's playing with the stock characters, reshuffling the pack.

Dean continues to protest his innocence with operatic gestures, re-enacting the incident in mime. The victim of his tackle has got up and, unseen by Dean, advances on him. He jumps on Dean, dragging him to the ground. An unseemly scuffle ensues, with more players joining in the fracas.

Comment: This introduces a second antagonist, DEAN, her brother. He's thuggish to her father's outward rudeness. This places IAN as being the fey intellectual and thus the rules of war are drawn up. Brawn vs brains.

The Sunshine Brigade, Marc Blake

The following is a script for a sitcom I adapted from my published novel *Sunstroke*. It concerns four ex-pat Londoners living in Mijas, Southern Spain. JOHN and JACQUI DRAKE live next to KEITH and THERESA BEASLEY. John and Keith are former cabbies and their wives are sisters. The nub of *The Sunshine Brigade* is that John is bored. He's made his pile and now they're all 'living the dream'.

The trouble is a dream that becomes real is no longer a dream. With nothing to aspire to, his frustrations and bad habits have come to the fore and must continually be tempered by his wife and pals. Although this is a pilot, it could be any episode. It did get some good feedback from producers and in particular Mark Freeland (then Head of BBC Comedy) but this one was scuppered by the arrival of *Benidorm*, which happened before I could get this one sold.

Though it shares a location, the styles are very different. Whilst my script was intended as a traditional studio-bound audience sitcom, *Benidorm* was shot on location and on film. It also had an arcing narrative in its studies of poolside behaviour and dysfunctional holidaymakers, and is more reminiscent of *Duty Free* in that respect, not that I'm bitter.

Sadly, as with many others (the circus one, the wannabees one) I put it in a drawer, only to bring it out occasionally and tinker with it. I include it here to show another way of setting up your characters and their emotional arena.

1. EXT. POOLSIDE. MIDDAY. THE BEASLEY'S. MIJAS, SPAIN

Three ex-pats lie by the pool.

North London ex-cabbie KEITH BEASLEY is spark out on a lounger with a baseball cap over his face. He's tall, tanned and gaunt.

His wife THERESA 'Tee' is the colour of walnut whip. She flicks through Hola! *There's a copy of* Puzzler *beside her.*

Her sister/neighbour JACQUI DRAKE (John's short-suffering wife) is a slender Caramac. She's allergic to flat shoes.

JOHN DRAKE comes out carrying a tray of tinkly drinks, flip-flops smacking on the tiles. He's every woman's dream so long as the dream is a retired Teletubby. Bald, fat and sweaty.

JOHN
Mango up yer bum? Who wants it?

Tee raises an arm. He hands her the drink.

JOHN
Jap's eye juice?

KEITH
Mine. John-john

JACQUI
What about mine?

JOHN
Thought you said you didn't want nothing?

JACQUI
Before you went in. I do now.

JOHN
How'm I supposed to know?

JACQUI
Same way as you're supposed to remember things like wedding anniversaries.

JOHN
Mind reading. What'm I thinking now?

JACQUI
That's illegal in this country.

They all laugh. She slaps him playfully. John sips his drink. Theresa reads. Jacqui applies lotion. John examines the area under his armpit.

JOHN
Never tan under here. It's like between your fingers. If there was a colour chart for tans I'd be 'Umber log' or 'Burnt Fust'... 'Malteser garnish' ... 'Coffee enema'.

JACQUI
Belt up will you.

JOHN
Year of this and we'll look like scrotums.

THERESA
Speak for yourself.

JOHN
Shrivelled up ball-bags. Bunch of shrivelled up ball bags –

KEITH
(*singing*)
Sitting on a wall. And if one shrivelled
(*JOHN joins in*)
... ball-bag should accidentally fall ...

JACQUI
(*to Theresa*)
It's the quality of the conversation I like best.

John exhales meaningfully. Theresa goes back to Hola!

170

JOHN

What you reading that for?

THERESA

Why d'you read about Germans who died in a war sixty years ago?

JOHN

Culture. That stuff is a load of –

Jacqui shoots him a look. He sips his drink.

JOHN

I read everything in the house. All that Stig Larson. All that Dan Brown stuff. Anti pasta in the Vatican. Rubbish.
(*Pause*)
Jeffrey Archer was alright though, for kindling.

JACQUI

Drink your custard fountain like a man.

JOHN

It's not. It's a fizzy bung.

He sucks it through a straw. Sighs.

KEITH

"I can't settle"

THERESA

"There's nothing to do"

JACQUI

Someone look up retirement in the dictionary and see if it says 'Buy a villa in Spain then spend every day boring the arse off everyone.'

JOHN

We get legless every night. Daytime its cancer roulette.

KEITH

This is the life.

JOHN

I'm *bored*.

KEITH

Want to go back to driving round Russell Square in the pissing rain, John, do you?

JOHN lies back. They relax. John sits up. Opens his mouth –

JACQUI

If you suggest calling the kids back home one more time I'll lamp you. We're doing all right.

JOHN

I s'pose. There's others suffering worse. War, famine, SuDuko …

JACQUI

You want to be useful get us a VAT, heavy on the voddy.

JOHN

I'll make up something else. Man fat mountain. Back door burrito? Spunk monkey?

JACQUI

I think you've got Tourettes. You got the symptoms.

JOHN

Yeah. They're on Sky.

He stomps off inside.

INT. NIGHT. IRISH SAM'S BAR. COSTA DEL SOL

A British pub. San Miguel and Pride on tap. SKY TV, dartboard. The four sit waiting for their meal.

> JOHN
>
> Thing is, you have to have some sort of structure to occupy your time, make it meaningful. It's a philosophtical issue. Man cannot live by bread alone.

KEITH eyes the meagre remains of the garlic bread starters.

> KEITH
>
> When it says 'Service not included' they mean it.

> JOHN
>
> Know what happens to most blokes once they retire? Dead as a doornail in a few months.

> JACQUI
>
> We aren't exactly queuing up for the walk-in bath. What's your point?

> JOHN
>
> I'll go off my trolley if I don't start doing something soon.

> JACQUI
>
> How about housework?

> JOHN
>
> Not that.

> JACQUI
>
> You mean another hobby. Like that one you got now that uses up so much toilet roll?

IRISH SAM (50s) hoves into view with their meals. This tall Saturnine Scot is still smarting over Bannockburn but has learned to semi-please his English regulars.

IRISH SAM

Alright John? There you go.

JOHN

The Atkinson's yeah? Onion rings.

IRISH SAM

Yeah. (*to Jacqui*) All right Late?

He exits. Theresa turns to Jacqui.

THERESA

He's still calling you that then.

KEITH

What?

THERESA

Late.

KEITH

What?

JACQUI

Late. A joke on my name. Jacqui. Jacqui Late. Har har har.

John and Keith laugh. Keith stops abruptly.

KEITH

Don't get it.

THERESA

Never mind love.

JOHN

In north Spain there's a procession to Santiago de
Compostela – every year thousands of pilgrims
walk hundreds of miles on foot in search of
something meaningful.

KEITH

Blisters?

JOHN

What do we do all day? Sod all. We're lemmings.

JACQUI
(*raising her glass*)
Bon appeteet then.

*John takes a mouthful, pushes his plate away and downs
half his pint. Keith struggles with his steak. John eyes it.*

JOHN

That'll go down in the fifth. (*To Jacqui*) Fish OK?

She removes a bone.

JACQUI

Jesus wouldn't give his mates this.

JOHN

Sam won't have the lemon wedge.

THERESA

But it's the only place round here. What was last
weeks special?

KEITH

Gravy.

JACQUI

There is that Spanish bar up the road.

175

They all stare at her.

KEITH

Sam's got the urbanisation sown up.

JOHN

It's a lomopoly. (*to Keith*) Mind you – he did blow up all them balloons for your birthday.

KEITH

Out the condom machine. Kids went home with ready ribbed.

THERESA

We should stop coming here.

JACQUI

And go down the coast? It's always you or me ends up being designated driver.

KEITH

You should learn to drink quicker.

JACQUI

Or it's paying the earth for a cab home.

KEITH

Rip-off merchants.

JOHN

Ought to be properly licensed. Bloody immigrants.

THERESA

What was it these two used to do for a living again? – Oh, yeah cabbying. Who'd have thought?

JACQUI

And *we're* the immigrants – or hadn't you clocked that?

Irish Sam approaches.

> IRISH SAM
> Enjoying your meal there folks?

They respond effusively.

> IRISH SAM
> Only, I have to ask 'cos they passed some
> European directive. Bastards. It's this or some
> effin' questionnaire.

> JOHN
> Jax reckoned her fish was a bit ...

> IRISH SAM
> A bit what?

> JOHN
> Bit, bit off? No, it was all right, wasn't it?

*IRISH SAM stares at the plate murderously then whisks
it away. John stares glassy-eyed into the distance. Jacqui
waves her hand in front of his face.*

> JACQUI
> Earth to planet John.

> JOHN
> I've had a revelation. An epitome. I'm gonna run a
> bar.

> JACQUI
> You?

> JOHN
> Couldn't do worse than this.

JACQUI

All right then. Go on.

JOHN

Yeah?

JACQUI

Yeah and Kate Moss eats chips.

IRISH SAM reappears with the plate, which he puts in front of Jacqui. They eye it suspiciously. There is a bunch of parsley on it.

IRISH SAM

Garnish.

JOHN

Sam, settle an argument?

IRISH SAM

Just let me get the bat.

JOHN

No, no. How hard would it be to run a bar round here?

IRISH SAM

Piece of pish. Watch your profit margin, watch the stock control, keep the brewery sweet. Keep the punters happy. That's no hard, you can feed them scraps and they'd still come back like a dog to its vomit. Enjoy.

Jacqui stares at her food. Irish Sam exits.

JOHN

I'll do a recce tomorrow.

JACQUI

You're not serious.

JOHN

I need a challenge Jax.

JACQUI

You are a challenge.

JOHN

Back in the smoke there was challenges every day. Livingstone. Despatch riders, roadworks, rickshaws, congestion charge, East End scribbled all over so it looks like Abu Dabi, Ken fuc-

JACQUI

You don't know the first thing about becoming a publican, other than the drinking part.

JOHN
(*getting up*)
I'm gonna get down Fuengirola, check out the estate agents. Who's up for it?

No one moves. He reaches for his wallet.

JOHN

All right. Well – this my treat.

THERESA

Treat as in what – botulism?

KEITH

S'all right John-john. I'll get it.

JOHN

No it's my shout.

KEITH

It's our turn.

JOHN

I'm not arguing.

KEITH

Nor me.

JOHN

So I'll get this.

KEITH

No mate.

JOHN

But it's on me.

KEITH

Don't have to.

JOHN

I want to.

KEITH

No, I got it.

JOHN

No, you're all right.

KEITH

Well let me get the drinks then.

JOHN
(*A friendly hand on his shoulder*)
Alright then mate. Laters.

He exits. Keith has not figured it out yet.

THERESA

He didn't ...

JACQUI

Here we go again.

KEITH
(*getting it*)

Ejaculate!

END of SCENE

❖ Read as many scripts as you can. Learn the form and rhythm.
❖ A good layout makes you want to read a script.
❖ Note how sparse they are on the page.
❖ Remove all adverbs and as many adjectives as you can. Be sparing and judicious at all times.
❖ Don't tell actors how to say the lines; it ought to be clear from the text.
❖ Make each scene word hard, setting up the plot and characters and introducing any back-story we need.

10.

What production companies put in their shredders

> " I can't think of a time when a script has just been binned without reading but please never put in the covering letter that your script is 'better than *The Office*' or 'the most original thing you've seen since *Monty Python*'. That's just arrogant. Let the person reading make their own mind up about how good you are.
>
> **M.M.**

The chapter heading may read as crass, but there are ideas that have been tried time and time again and which have no chance of success. Unlike the film world where the William Goldman maxim 'Nobody knows anything' allows for amazing turnarounds, sitcom is a business in which everyone seems to know everything. Comedy people will wax lyrical for hour upon hour on comedy and timing and what works and what doesn't. A lot of this is of course after the fact. Sitcom, like anything creative, is a lot harder to build than it is to tear down. However, and I hope I can make each example clear here, there are certain things which don't work. Here they are.

I won the lottery and inherited a mansion

INT. ELEGANT DRAWING ROOM. DAY

Sitting at a large oak desk is an FUSTY OLD LEGAL RETAINER. He holds a ribbon-wrapped file as he peers over his glasses. Opposite him, illuminated by a shaft of

uncomfortable morning sun, is DAVE SWARTHY, an
unshaven man in a suit he last wore in the dock.

FOLR

So Mr Swarthy, your Aunt Selina, of whom
you hitherto had no knowledge, has it seems,
bequeathed you her entire estate.

DAVE

What, like a motor?

FOLR

Her country estate, Mr Swarthy, comprising a
thousand hectares of land, fifty head of cattle,
sundry other livestock, the village pub, a grouse
moor and the ancestral home; Blackstone Hall
– a twenty room mansion which comes with six
permanent staff and *droit de seigneur* as regards the
hot and cold running maids.

DAVE

Did you say a pub?

FOLR

I did. But the cellar in Blackstone Hall is one of the
finest in all of England.

DAVE

What do I want a cellar for? You saying I'm a serial
killer?

FOLR

No, Mr Swarthy, but you are rich. So obscenely
rich that even King Midas would wish to shake
your hand.

DAVE

Blimey.

FOLR

Is that all you have to say?

DAVE

A pub you say? Blinding.

The inheritance sitcom and its sister concept the lottery winner, seemingly has legs. The fish-out-of-water story of a poor person being thrust into another world is one you would think might reap comedy gold: there's the class clash, the comedy of all those pesky new manners (oh, which fork to use *now*?) and a bunch of moral questions that arise when someone not born to money is given access to spend beyond his wildest teenage fantasies. *The Beverley Hillbillies*, which spurned other comedies such as *Green Acres* and *Fresh Prince of Bel Air* was a great example of this. A family of hillbillies discover oil on their Ozark Swampland and move in next door to their banker in swanky Beverley Hills. They are moral and unsophisticated in contrast to the vain, superficial self-obsessed community. It ran forever.

Today it looks like hokum, because this kind of thing doesn't happen. Yes, there are feckless lottery winners every week and they have been seen in many documentaries. We get one of two versions. Either they cope and invest well and are the deserving newly rich (no story) or baboon-like criminal reprobates who will lose every goddam cent within a year (satisfying story). Either way we don't like hearing about sudden winners, especially not in the UK. There was one successful comedy drama on this idea, which skewed it wonderfully. *At Home with the Braithwaites* was about a woman who won £36 million on the lottery but whose family deserved not one penny. Therefore she didn't tell them and instead became a kind of charity fairy godmother. This was drama, not comedy. Another aspect of the 'change of life' sitcom is the shift in social standing. In sitcoms where people suddenly become rich you get:

- The newly rich person lords it over the locals and comes a cropper to the old country ways.
- The newly rich person lords it over their former friends.
- They spend recklessly and must learn the value of money

before the windfall is gone.
* He tries to win a woman with his new money and fails.

This is all rather predictable and to make something convincing out of it is a tall order. A reverse example was *To the Manor Born*, starring Penelope Keith and Peter Bowles) in which aristocratic snob Audrey Fforbes-Hamilton loses her family seat due to widowhood. It is purchased by nouveau-rich Richard De Vere who allows her to remain in the tied cottage on the estate. What was so impressive here was that it was about money brought down, which engendered our sympathy. The widowhood idea is impeccable as she is blameless. Despite her outward snobberies she learnt to eat humble pie, accept humiliation and became more human. It helped also that there was a budding romance between them. It spoke eloquently about new and old money in England.

Usually with inheritance comedy idea there is a catch. You can have the castle but with it you take the butler/groundskeeper/ghost too.

These are contrivances and come across as such unless well planted in advance. Ideas like this are the preserve of the comedy movie (*The Ghost Goes West*, *The Ghost and Mrs Muir*) – as they are high concept and can only be explored comedically for a short length of time. Think of body swap comedies like *Freaky Friday*, *Big* or *Trading Places*. The idea sustains ninety minutes, but won't work being revisited each week.

In terms of comedy butlers, once you get the joke (the class clash of high status butler mixed with low status client), we are repeating it over and over again. Unless the butler and his charge have real depth to their relationship – for example in the film *Arthur* or P.G. Wodehouse's *Jeeves and Wooster*. These two pretty much mine every seam of that comedy gold and what you have left are two character traits clashing and little more.

It's set in a pub

The pub. That great British institution stretching back to time immemorial, wherein the humble ploughman to the landed gentry may gather together in convivial company to sup their ale from a straight glass or pewter tankard and pass the time smoking a small clay pipe and making comments in the snug. The pub is the social hub of British culture, whether it's a local boozer, working man's club bar, corporate gastropub, a Harvester or Ye Olde Country Inne – and this location features in all our soaps from *EastEnders* to *Coronation Street*.

Successful sitcoms are not set in pubs or bars, except for *Cheers*.

The exceptions, *Time Gentlemen Please*, acted as a vehicle for character comic Al Murray as the Pub Landlord, and *Early Doors*, its Northern counterpart, written by and starring Craig Cash – a winsome look at a deserted Mancunian boozer with a gullible and inept landlord. Neither went beyond two series.

The pub set may feature in sitcom (mandatory in any lad com) or as a second set (*Two Pints of Lager*) as it offers contrast and gives an opportunity to showcase the supporting characters: *Only Fools and Horses* had the Nag's Head; *Phoenix Nights* was set in a nightclub – which is different as its clientele, opening hours and function are different to that of the local boozer.

The trouble with the local is that it's a big arena. This is why the soaps have so much going on in them, a lot of drama and more importantly a lot of comedy. *Coronation Street* has consistently had some of its funniest moments in the Rover's Return. These are characters people get to know three times a week over twenty-five years. Can you compete with that? *Cheers* ran for over two hundred and fifty episodes and spawned *Frasier* and proved that in the US you could set a sitcom in a bar. US soap operas are not set in bars. US soap is aspirational, glossy, super rich. It says these people are better, richer and far more beautiful than you could ever dream of, but hey, they have problems too. *Desperate Housewives* is a hair flick away from *Dallas*. They don't go to bars. Americans are rather shy and puritanical about drinking alcohol (unless they are writers) and don't like to dwell on it. Rarely do you ever see anyone inebriated in *Cheers* or even in *My Name is Earl*, which often features bar scenes. We in Britain are steeped in it.

Also, *Cheers* was set around a compelling story line, that of Sam, the ex-baseball player and Lothario. Would he finally be tamed by ice maiden Diane or later by mouthy Rebecca Howe? Around him you had characters like vituperative Carla and stalwart backups like Norm and Cliffy. US bars seem somehow more egalitarian; the place where everyone knows your name (in the UK that would be 'Oi – Wanker!') – a place where Frasier can rub shoulders with and give advice to Woody.

In the UK, there are local pubs and posh pubs, inner city boozers full of lager fuelled hooligans, and snooty country inns. There are dead places and busy bars. Perhaps a Scottish or Welsh bar might work, or even one set abroad – but it's a tough call. A pub or bar is a secondary setting.

Colonels, butlers and ghosts

What these three have in common is that they are dated. They belong to the black and white era. Butlers, as mentioned, are a product of the waning British class system. Colonels or other military folk are also the product of a by-gone age (unless you are planning to update them). Ghosts are tricky to carry off (*My Dead Dad*) but a sitcom about a butler a colonel *and* a ghost might be brilliant.

And a pirate.

Heaven and hell

Sometimes a writer thinks outside the box and conceives a sitcom in some unearthly paradise or fettered hell. They reason that they are able to people it with any hero or anti-hero they like and can play with time or bizarre combinations of people and physical laws. This does not work. Why? Because they are metaphorical places and metaphor cannot sustain a sitcom.

Sitcom is a genre and as such plays by genre rules, the art being to bend and not break them. Once you depart from genre you are lost. All stories fall into a pattern, whether you recognise the two, three, five or seven act structure. Campfire tales do not begin, 'It was a fine day in hell ...' unless you live in Croydon. Also, religion is a sensitive subject with broadcasters and networks and in order to avoid minority sensibilities they would rather not go there. It is hard enough getting a sitcom off the ground in this life, let alone the afterlife. Heaven and hell can be used in animation, both *South Park* and *The Simpsons* have done it several times, but in essence, it does not work because if you look at most sitcom characters, they are already in purgatory.

It's about therapy

Frasier was a huge success: one of the all time great sitcoms. *Dr Katz*, ran for six series of animated shows about a psychotherapist with famous patients. Shrinks pop up everywhere in US shows from Dr Jennifer Melfi in *The Sopranos* to Dr Charles Kroger in *Monk*: Dr Linda Freeman in *Two and a Half Men* and even Dr Marvin Monroe in *The Simpsons*. They are part of the landscape, a facet of the introspective nature of the American citizen. The head doctor is confessor, ally, nemesis or parental figure, as well as being an excellent way of delivering necessary exposition.

This is not the case in British sitcom, where talking about one's inner demons has not caught on. For a country with fifty ways of saying sorry, we are too reticent and portraying the talking cure on TV is usually left to criminal psychologists such as *Cracker*. *Help* was a short-lived comedy drama about a psychotherapist in which actor/comedian Paul Whitehouse played twenty-five patients. It lasted one series. *The Life and Times of Vivienne Vyle* contained a shrink, was co-created by one and it too lasted one series.

Writing about therapy, hypnotherapy, alternative practises and the like is becoming more popular in the scripts I receive and to date, nothing has reached the screen. I suspect these scripts are written by frustrated therapists (bang goes their patient confidentiality clauses) and serve some kind of therapeutic value. This area has so far resolutely failed to interest the commissioning people. Is it too middle class? Too rarefied? Too self-indulgent? There is perhaps an element of all three but in the main, mental health is something that is usually avoided in sitcom (despite its focus on neuroses rather than psychoses).

Furthermore, psychoanalysis is internalised and therefore does not make for a dramatic or visual plot. If you are poking fun at things people can't help, it is also perhaps a bit churlish. Psychotherapy is relatively new in the UK and, though the profession encompasses many interesting offshoots (some of which are easy to spoof as plain quackery) there just isn't a hard target here. Besides, all those neuroses can be evinced in your lead characters without putting them into analysis. Would we really derive laughter from putting David Brent (*The Office*) or Mark (*Peep Show*) on the couch?

In the episode of *Fawlty Towers* in which a psychiatrist came to stay he had his hands full with Basil's insane behaviour. The laughs came from our empathy for Basil being caught like a bedlam inmate. We laughed *at* the psychiatrist and this, I fear, is still somewhat the case.

No one has ever written about the media before

INT. TV SET. DAY
A daytime shopping channel. The PRESENTER has too many white teeth for his wide mouth.

PRESENTER
Thanks for six hours of top quality chat about
the multi-peeler vegetable slicer. Now welcome
to the China clay figurine hour with me, Derek
Nonce. It's all crap and we've got a million of them
at knock down prices in the back but you're too
stupid to turn away ... aren't you?

Making observations about trash TV is an idea that comes easily; after all, it's all rubbish, isn't it? These morons are making TV for morons in an annoying and moronic way. Only I, the genius writer, have seen that the Emperor is wearing a diaphanous nylon gown made of zilch. I am going to expose their shallowness by writing a spoof show about a cable station, perhaps a shopping channel (because all the things they sell are crap?) or a rolling news-style programme (because the presenters are so fake and full of their own importance). I will show the crass stupidity of these scum-sucking overpaid morons as they spew their vile filth upon our nation. I'll take the piss out of the actors and presenters because they are vapid idiots. Did I say they were all morons? I'm sticking it to the man. I'm a cut above all the other idiot writers. My parody of their pathetic shallow world will really get under their skin. I've never been to a recording of a TV show, and I

189

have no experience of what it is like to work in TV or radio – but you don't need that. We can see it all the time on TV and anyway what's wrong with using your imagination? It's amazing no one has seen it before. Those bastards will be beating a path to my door. Ha.

Here is the rule for writing about the media in any form or fashion. No. Not under any circumstances unless you are already a proven media success, of which more later. Television people spend their time stuck in airless committee rooms, undergoing strategic and budgetary meetings, managing resentful employees, being managed from above, soothing the egos of overbearing directors, ego-maniacal and/or depressive actors and trying to get their job done. Do they want to read more about it? No.

No, because you know nothing of their world.

No, because they want to see something fresh from the real world, from your life, something *of* life, something that shouts authenticity and real human interaction. The script that interests them is the one that does not fall back on the clichés of the modern media, which is that it does not try to be any good. No one goes into making a million dollar programme with the intention of lowering standards. Below par programming is just as much of an accident as the good stuff, but the actors, crew and production team are all on the same side. Anyone not pulling their weight will eventually lose their contract. Just because you think that the orange-faced, white toothed silicon-implanted presenter garbling on about zircon encrusted tweezers is the nadir of human existence doesn't mean someone somewhere isn't pleased to see them on their screens. TV is made for everyone: it's egalitarian like that.

People inside the business don't want their failures paraded before them. Would you want to watch a show about your first day at work? Do you want to see a show about the tedium of your day-to-day existence, with all the lame in-jokes and not-at-all-amusing references to personal hygiene? Well yes, but only if you can make it funny. Really funny, like in *The Office*.

Otherwise, falling back on TV parody will not bear up over even a single episode let alone a series. This and spoof are affectionate devices, a weaker sibling to the more powerful satire. Satire has a better defined and yes, *worthy*, target: government or bureaucracy, for instance (*Yes, Minister, The Thick of It*), or an institution such as the armed forces (*M*A*S*H*), or even the more pompous and self-regarding of the chat shows (*The Larry Sanders Show*). Parody runs out of steam once it has made its jokes about form and format whereas satire goes in for a good kicking and keeps going.

You will notice from the examples given here that each of these has great character roles. Malcolm Tucker in *The Thick of It*, Jim Hacker and Sir Humphrey in *Yes, Minister*, Hawkeye Pierce in *M*A*S*H*, and Artie, Hank and Larry in *The Larry Sanders Show*. They are complex characterisations, monsters yes, but human ones. The media sitcom, as written by a novice, takes the outsider view instead of the insider one.

The caveat is that once you are 'in', biting the hand that feeds you tends to be the first thing you do. Given carte blanche by the powers that be, you now turn your jaundiced comedic eye to the new world you now inhabit. This can be done with great success such as in *Extras* or *The Larry Sanders Show* (his previous postmodern outing was the wonderful, crazed: *It's Garry Shandlings' Show*) but there are many that flounder. The point is that there are already lots of people far more famous than you who are going to be doing their media spoof first, so there is no point. Don't write telly about telly until you are on telly.

This also applies to the slightly off-piste media ideas such as the perennial local newspaper-in-trouble sitcom (unsuitable girl or boy is relegated from the city or promoted to the cub reporter's desk, only to encounter fusty sexist dinosaur) or local-radio-in-trouble sitcom (unsuitable girl or boy is placed in charge of late night or hospital radio slot, only to encounter crazed callers/patients).

The audition

This is more of a comment about a recurring scene. Any sitcom pilot with an audition scene in it is likely to attract flies. They usually revolve around a new person invited into the hornet's nest. It is usually a presenter or band member or, as in this example, the new flatmate.

INT. FLAT. DAY

The first FLATMATE sits on the chair. She has a mop of curly ginger hair. She looks like she dressed in the dark.

VERONICA
I hope you like pets? I really like pets. I got like a hamster and a guinea pig. People say they smell but I never notice it. I guess that's because I lived with them for sooo long.

CUT TO: *In the chair now is a slender girl in a long black dress. She seems like a stunner until ...*

KATY
I hope you'll fit in with me. I'm tidy. Really tidy. Do you run? I run. Just ten miles a day – nothing obsessive.

CUT TO: *A guy who looks like a roadie. Long greasy hair, black leathers, badly spelled tattoos, crooked teeth (one gold). He picks his teeth with a blade. Before he can speak we.*

CUT TO

And so on. We have repeatedly seen the flash cut to the next unsuitable candidate, and it no longer adds anything to characterisation or plot. It is a repository for a joke that we are over familiar with. Twist it, make it fresh or lose it. The flipside of media and celebrity is ...

The comeback kid

The idea of a story about an ageing actor, celebrity, comic, singer or even an *X Factor* or reality show contestant seems to have potential. After all, they are down on their luck, they have the smell of failure about them but they have had a degree of success before, so they are not beyond redemption. They may even exhibit many of the qualities of the classic sitcom monster: a dab of vanity, arrogance, a sense of entitlement and perhaps some delusions of grandeur. They have most likely trodden on people on their way up and are now going to have to eat a large slice of humble pie. They have a strong desire: to regain their fame, almost like a dispossessed prince. There is one simple flaw and let me make this as un-technical as possible. Here we go. Who gives a shit? Who really cares about any of the people who have clung to fame in the mud pit of TV getting another chance? What more do they have to offer anyway? More crass karaoke? More cookery programmes? More crying on TV?

There is a reason why the rags-to-riches story is such an enduring myth and that is we are rooting for the underdog. The film *Rocky* is a great example of this. When he realised he could not physically win against Apollo Creed, has-been Rocky accepted that he was going to have to compromise. He changed his goal. He changed it to going the distance. This was not only memorable but also infused with nobility. If you want to write about someone who tries to come back and fails spectacularly that would be either *The Wrestler* or *Raging Bull*, both deeply human tragic stories – and neither of them sitcom.

Rock bands making their comeback has also been well served in film and comedy drama, as in *Anvil* (documentary), *Spinal Tap*, *Still Crazy* (written Clement and La Frenais) and *Bad News* (The Comic Strip). It has been done with great poignancy in *The League of Gentlemen* when it featured Les Macqueen, the hapless Crème Brulee guitarist. What can you say that has not been said? What can you add to the canon? Go younger perhaps? A boy band back on the comeback trail. The trouble here is that a boy band's audience are teenage girls and teenage girls are following a fad. Afterwards they discard it, scorn it even. It is a rite of passage. A period of about ten years would have to pass for them to see it with irony. There is sadness here too. Following boy bands is about burgeoning sexuality and unattainable love and to look back on this with nostalgia or yearning implies something is missing from your life. How would you feel about a man or woman who persistently followed a band into their 20s, 30s and onwards? That they needed a restraining order maybe? What was and what will never be again is a sad fact of life and hard to inject with humour. Regaining past glories is never going to be the same.

The great thing about sitcom is that it lives in the here and now. Secondly, even though you know Homer is dumb and Mark and Jeremy are total wipe-outs with women, you think that maybe, just maybe, they might grow out of it. Del-Boy was great so long as he was struggling; Frasier was superb as he tried to attain love, status and position.

In writing about lost fame and its companion, fortune, we are again sliding away from sitcom territory. Let it go. They had their moment in the sun.

Copying

Homage is not an ugly word but plagiarism is. Surprisingly, outright theft of material is rare in sitcom: this is perhaps because the skill set is so complex to learn and the combinations of character, relationship and situation are almost infinite. Any obviously lifted material, say, from an existing show, is pretty easy to spot. In my experience I have never come across any direct borrowing, but what I do come across are sitcoms that ape others.

It is fine to be influenced by *Spaced*, *Seinfeld* or *Curb Your Enthusiasm* but showing your working in the margins has its problems. Firstly, these shows are so well known that they leave a long shadow. They have also created their own unique style so that the show becomes branded. This is a *30Rock* show or a *Peep Show*, show. Some sitcoms, such as *Spaced*, have a look to them which is all their own. The writer and director (Simon Pegg and Edgar Wright) both love movies and included many subtle references to their favourites in that sitcom. One joke they employed to the max was the saying-one-thing and then showing-us-another trick. Likewise, in *Peep Show*, there are small cameras placed the heads of the lead actors which shoot their POV. This allied with voice over means we get to hear their thoughts then see an alternate reality. These devices are so successful that, when done by newer writers, it just comes across as a milder copy. That is not to say you cannot employ these devices, but if you too try to make it the central branding idea for your show, then you are likely to fail.

Admittedly, once a sitcom is a hit there are sometimes offshoots that are variations on a theme. *Men Behaving Badly* bred no fewer than three lady-coms (*Dressing for Breakfast*, *Life After Birth* and *Babes in the Wood*, but none of them did huge business.

Search for your own original idea.

Northern soft

Northern soft refers here to UK sitcom. In the disunited Queendom, there is a long-standing rivalry between north and south, just as there was between Yankees and Confederates. America's televisual geography is mapped out in terms of West and East coast. Californians are laid back, obsessed with body modification and with being 'kewl', whereas New Yorkers are rude, arrogant go-getters. Rubbish of course, just as the UK's equivalent clichés that Southerners are soft, moneyed and posh and Northerners are workshy, poor and miserable. They can't all be Liverpudlians. Britain is a land, seemingly, where everyone is in conflict with everyone else. The Scots hate the English. Northerners distrust Southerners. The Welsh are universally derided and when you get to the urban metropolis, North and South Londoners are divided against one another. Perhaps there is one person stood on the international dateline at Greenwich wondering why everyone hates him? He's probably from Croydon.

If you are writing about Southern England, unless it is generic West Country or laddish Essex, then there is little need to make note of dialect. Estuarine English has spread all across the South. Del-Boy (*Only Fools and Horses*) was distinctly South London because its writer John Sullivan was from Balham and used his direct experience in writing it, likewise Johnny Speight used his first hand knowledge of the East End to write *Till Death Do Us Part*. *The Office*, set in Slough, mirrors life in the M4 corridor. Gervais is from Reading and knows well the dormitory towns and the vacuum that is the Winnersh Triangle, but *The Office* could have been set anywhere. The most recent UK sitcom to make play of regional difference was *Gavin and Stacey* (Essex and Wales). However, when you get 'oop North' things are not the same.

There is a different pace and rhythm to Northern-based sitcom. The word order can be different; and stress, colloquialism and pronunciation will all change if they are particular to Lancashire, Yorkshire and all points north – and woe betide those who get it wrong. Can you locate the following?

The Royle Family. Early Doors. Ideal. Dinnerladies.
Phoenix Nights. The Likely Lads. Catterick.
Bread. The Liver Birds. Two Pints of Lager and a Packet of Crisps.
Last of the Summer Wine. Brass.

Many sitcoms set in the north of England are working class and concern the family unit. In earlier times the working classes were inclusive, keeping their young to themselves and not wanting to let them go. Escaping 'down south' was seen as betraying your roots. Marrying out or above your station was also frowned upon, as was succeeding enough to be able to buy your own home. You were expected to live and die with your family, to muck in, to know your place. This is a limited and patronising view – after all, the merchant (middle) classes began in the mill towns and the idea of individual as opposed to inherited wealth and social mobility came out of the North, and yet, see how traditional *The Royle Family* is? Daughter Denise was accepted as she had brought her lazy fiancée right into the bosom of the family and to the confines of its sofa – but as soon as 'our Antony' made any attempt to get away it was met with derision – not only by his sister but also by both parents. Stick to what you know. Know your place. Northern soft. We're right friendly and we help us selves out.

Northern *hard* is the province of comedy drama. *Our Friends in the North, Shameless, Queer as Folk* are all taboo-busting foul-mouthed examinations of poverty and social issues. When they stray over to drama, they enter 'gritty' Bafta territory. There are no soft comfy cadences of mam and party cakes and tea at six and chips wi' gravy here. Northern soft plays on nostalgia for safety and there is always an audience (those who are not watching 'Corrie') for this and a big one too as a lot more 'telly' is watched in the North. The BBC has finally acknowledged this and is due to move its production base to Manchester. If you are from the North of England, use your roots and the clichés to your advantage. Don't mek it bobbins.

Old people's homes are intrinsically funny

They can't leave. They are old and weak and incontinent. There's a tyrant ruling the old folk's home but the cheeky old folk who still have a lot of life in 'em yet are going to run rings around them. There's even a naughty sexual relationship because crumblies are randy too. They repeat themselves and make old jokes and they're a funny bunch and they wee themselves.

Waiting for God worked in the UK, Grandpa Simpson is permanently retired in *The Simpsons*. *The Golden Girls* was a hit in the US for several years (although they were not in a care home) – so why not dig it up and try that one again? OK, here are some pointers. They are all going to die.

Care and rest homes are not full of witty brave old soldiers and this tired trope has been trotted out in movies too. It's a lie. These places are in general more tragic than comedic and attempting to inject several series of humour into it is going to be a tough call. This is why Britain's longest running sitcom about the elderly (*The Last of the Summer Wine*) never went there but stayed in the sunshine of the Yorkshire hills and Dales.

If the old 'uns are feisty it's for a short period every day (pre-nap) and they aren't trying to escape – escape to what? If they were put there by caring relatives it was for their own good. If it was against their will, it was because they are a danger to themselves. There is comic mileage to be gained out of the silver surfer generation (*The Old Guys* on BBC is trying it right now) but a retirement home is too sad. This may change as health care providers, drugs and the quality of life changes for senior citizens. Perhaps there will be whole retirement towns like most of Florida or the Cotswolds in the UK. Perhaps not.

The danger is that it has no contemporary relevance. As we age our frame of reference shrinks. In a few years your iPod Nano will contain most of the music you liked in your teens and twenties. We become more conservative and less radical, less open to change. The great Victor Meldrew in *One Foot in the Grave* was the last sitcom character to stab at ageing in the UK, but look at its targets. It was the world conspiring against Victor. The outside world. *Getting On*, a new BBC sitcom, is dealing with the sick in hospital. It is too early to see how it will fare. The problem with the old folk's home is very little filters in. Plus, sitcom is always about a recognisable place or people, and the elderly, like the very young can often seem to be very much the same.

My work, my relationship, my life is a sitcom

Do you say any of the following on a regular basis?

- It really happened, honest.
- We're all mad around here/in our office/on this wing.
- You should meet my mate Kevin – he's totally bonkers.
- You wouldn't believe the things that happen to me.

If people tell you that your life is hilarious and wacky and tragic and you should turn it into a sitcom then don't. Sure, it's far funnier than most of the shows you see on primetime, but it is not going to become a sitcom unless your name is Simpson (Homer) or Cosby, Fawlty or Blackadder. Why is this? It is because unless you can forge this into comedy gold, we're not going to get it. You know intimately the quirks and foibles and the back history of all your friends and family but to us you are strangers and weird strangers at that. 'Because it really happened' is not a reason in itself to commit something to paper. This is also true of biography and autobiography. Think of your reasons. Why do you want to turn your life into a sitcom? Is it because …

- You and your best mate have a set of catchphrases and running jokes that make you wee yourselves.
- An elderly relative or child is funny because they 'don't get it'.
- You are very lucky/unlucky.
- You just think they are funny *in their own way*.
- You or a family member/friend is a *classic* practical joker.

If so then I would think again. Let us approach these in reverse order. First, practical jokes are a good indicator of nascent socio-pathic behaviour. Are practical jokes funny? Rarely. They are acts of cruelty aimed at embarrassment, hurt and public humiliation. This works in isolated moments on TV clip shows but when taken further is the act of a clinically disturbed person. Your local practical joker is practising for when they become a serial killer.

You think they are funny in their own way. OK, but you are going to have to convince us. There are two main groups of stand-up comedians: those who are high status and who fire out their anger at others and at the state of the world, and those of low status who poke fun at themselves. This second classification (Woody Allen, Eddie Izzard, Harry Hill, Emo Philips) is much harder to do because you need to create your own world. You are inviting people to laugh *at* you rather than *with* you, and that takes guts. To understand a mind like this is difficult, and to transcribe and re-create it for another actor to play the role strikes me as asking for trouble.

Luck and bad luck. It is often said that we create our own luck, that some people are born lucky or unlucky or that we cannot control our fate and a bunch of other sayings of no real consequence. Luck or the lack of it is out of our hands, which is anathema to sitcom, as it is always plotted. There is no room for contrivance and any chance element that occurs (often the last minute discovery of the lost or long sought after object) was planted at the start of the episode. Luck is not an element that should be employed in sitcom.

People who 'don't get it' are fine as supporting cast. Trigger and Granddad in *Only Fools and Horses*, Alice in *The Vicar of Dibley*, Latka in *Taxi*, Gareth in *The Office*, Hank in *The Larry Sanders Show*. The list is long and honourable. However, they are the support and not the prop or main pillar. They are icing, parsley, Parmesan.

Catchphrases have been mentioned before but let's return to them for a moment. They are a strong way of branding a show but are rarely contrived or reverse-engineered and tend to be organic. One line is said in a certain way in a show and it strikes a chord. Mainwaring says, 'Stupid boy' twice and it begins to stick. It has relevance. Victor Meldrew, in thrall to another example of the utter stupidity of local council petty bureaucracy, says, 'I don't believe it' and we take up the chant. There are some sitcoms which have contrived catchphrases, most notably BBC TV's *The Fall and Rise of Reginald Perrin* (I didn't get where I am today by ... Great. Super). But David Nobbs was commenting on the vacuous nature of the rat race in contrast to Reggie's attempts to escape it.

In the US the most catchphrase-stuffed show is *The Simpsons*. 'D'Oh!', 'Why you little ...', 'Excellent', 'Ha Haa', 'Hi! I'm actor Troy McClure. You might remember me from ...', 'Mmm, donuts' ... all work because when there is such a large cast there is little room for characterisation, therefore it is expedient to create verbal signifiers for minor players. This is also true of the work of British writers Jimmy Perry and David Croft. Their most notable success, *Dad's Army*, produced 'We're doomed', 'Might I be excused', and 'They don't like it up 'em'.

If you are going to create an ensemble workplace sitcom (most sitcoms with catchphrases are based in the public arena) then by all means try to create a catchphrase – but how are we going to know this from the first episode? When David Brent in *The Office* did a comedy turn about the catchphrase of a fellow office worker 'I don't believe that's appropriate in the workplace' it bombed. You need to create a memorable person first before you can tear them down. It can't just be you.

Students

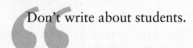

Don't write about students.

M.J.

There are hundreds of sitcoms about students chugging through producer's shredders as I write. This is because students do not get a good press. I will admit this is a particularly UK thing but even students seem to hate other students. Being naïve, self-centred, oversexed and slothful ought to make them ideal fodder for sitcom but sadly it doesn't.

Student-life is a transitional phase. It is a time of huge change and supposed drive toward maturity. *The Young Ones* succeeded not because it was about students *per se*, but because it nailed tribal youth cultures like the hippy, the punk and the anarchist. It was the first New Wave 'Alternative'* comedy sitcom and its groundbreaking anarchy superseded any faults it may have had. In retrospect, a lot of the comedy and slapstick has paled and it looks more like a period piece than a classic show, but it was the only student-centred sitcom to date that has worked.

Can lightning strike twice? After all it's thirty years on. Are there identifiable student archetypes nowadays? The PC game nerd? The self-harming Goth, the comix nut, gap year girl, the student Tory or skunk smoking trustafarian? Sure they exist but until someone very observant comes along to properly define the new breed then we are still waiting, and not in excitement either. Traffic jam waiting.

In my teaching at university I can, at time of writing, define no real burgeoning subcultures other than the above. Youth culture used to be musically defined with a branded uniform. Politically, the student body was traditionally Left Wing but this has dissi-pated. Radicalism in any form seems to have disappeared. John Sullivan (*Only Fools and Horses*) created a great suburban rebel in 'Wolfie' Smith with his cry of 'Freedom for Tooting' (in *Citizen Smith*) but he was a student of Life rather than a college boy.

The trouble with students is that they are not fully formed; they are trying on personalities, poses and attitudes. College is about experimentation whereas sitcom is about stasis. You can do it in comedy drama (*Campus*) and you can do it on film (*Animal House*) but you cannot do it in sitcom. There is too much change and precious little empathy.

You might get away with one of your characters being a student (for contrast or to focus on one area of life) or even a mature or perennial student, but if you set your sitcom entirely in halls or on campus you are going to fail your comedy degree.

---

* Alternative comedy was a term widely used by the British press in the early 1980s to describe the new breed of non-sexist, non-racist comedians who wrote all their own material – a principle that holds true to this day. The progenitors were stand-ups Alexei Sayle and later Ben Elton, actors Rik Mayall and Adrian Edmondson, Tony Allen, poet John Hegley, Glaswegian comic Arnold Brown and the late great Malcolm Hardee.

I'm so surreal I should be sectioned. No, really

This is a distanced, backwoods hillbilly cousin of the 'my life is a sitcom' segment, in which you – yeah, crazy, funny, you – have such a unique comic sensibility that you have decided to transfer it to thirty-five sheets of A4 paper and put your name on it. What are we to make of this and can we get hold of some of your medication for a party I have coming up? Do you even know the extent of your *idiot savant* abilities? Has your work been turned down before or has it come back with question marks in the margins? If this is true and those selfsame question marks and comments peter out after a few pages, then this might be the time to think of some gainful employment.

Sitcom is a specific and complex skill set that rewards those with a spark of creativity and with great application to learning the craft. I don't receive all that many scripts postmarked 'Isolation Ward' or c/o a health professional or in green ink but just because you think all the people in your head are funny doesn't mean they will reach an audience. Let's reiterate what sitcom is.

- A flawed but interesting central character who interacts in an emotional way, with a small coterie of people around them.
- Supporting characters that prop the central character up and in their own dysfunctional way, need them around.
- A static situation and location in which multiple emotional dramas can occur.
- Funny stories rounded out, which bring us back to the start.
- Character-driven plots and great jokes.
- Half an hour (twenty-two mins in the US).

If you have written sixty pages of rambling please check with your carer before you send it out and keep away from sharp objects. Thank you.

This sitcom in space will cost you your company

He pushes open the doors of the courthouse. Two armed policemen with machine guns throw him to the ground. Seven more officers surround him, shouting, bellowing orders. A tank appears around the corner, and behind it GENERAL SNARGIT riding a white stallion. He is followed by the entire Army of North Korea. Riding turtles.

There are certain settings that will ensure your masterwork does not see the light of day. Arctic/Antarctic research stations, post-apocalyptic or climate changed environments, space, submarines, and all the other places you find listed on the warning on a DVD.

The trouble with the above is that, although they are remote and provide an interesting 'trapped' environment in which disparate characters might play out some comic adventures, they are profoundly limited.

Porridge was a successful sitcom with a high concept. It was brave to set a sitcom around the criminal fraternity, but without its stellar cast (Ronnie Barker and Richard Beckinsale) it would not have stood a chance. *Porridge* was in fact just one of a series of six pilots starring Barker (*Seven of One*) and it wasn't even Barker's favourite. Towards the end of the 1970s it was still just about possible to believe in the 'old lag' and the cheery young thief – after all, the UK had a filmic history of glamorising crime, from Flash Harry (*St Trinian's*) to Mr Bridger (Noel Coward in *The Italian Job*) to *The League of Gentlemen*, to Arthur Daley in *Minder*. The character of Fletcher was paternal but fond of sticking two fingers up to the system. He looked after number one but reluctantly took the fledgling Godber under his wing when they became cellmates. Added to this were motherly warden Mr Barrowclough and officious tyrant Mr Mackay. The world portrayed was an idealised one where the truly malevolent criminal (Grout) represented only a token threat to the day-to-day running of what was essentially a British boarding school for miscreants. For twenty-seven episodes (three seasons) it worked. Today we cannot sustain the illusion that prison is place for the luckless chancer.

Basing a sitcom on a remote location seems like a great ideological leap but what do you do when the characters have run out of jokes about their situation? Having been lead by the concept, you are now trying to get the characters to inhabit it, rather than finding your characters and an emotive situation and writing that.

The locus for the sitcom ought to be simple. *Taxi* was almost entirely set in a greasy dirty garage or rec room, and managed to play out over one hundred editions. Setting a sitcom on a space ship or on a different planet is hard to do. Cost is the first factor. Each set is going to have to be built and the horizons of Jupiter don't come cheap. The most notable sitcoms, in space have been *Red Dwarf* (a lad com in space) and *The Hitchhiker's Guide to the Galaxy*. The BBC recently tried *Hyperdrive*, but it did not survive more than two series. *Red Dwarf* obtained a huge cult following. Its writers, Rob Grant and Doug Naylor, played fast and loose with the time and space continuum even before Stephen Hawking arrived on the scene. Its central set was a living area with bunk beds and a command module – rather like the original *Star Trek* and about as cheap. *The Hitchhiker's Guide* came from a BBC Radio 4 series written by Douglas Adams and was not strictly sitcom at all.

In the US, aliens are as common in sitcom as they are in their Government but to date they have all been aliens who have landed here and are fish-out-of-water stories. The lineage goes from *My Favourite Martian* to *Mork and Mindy* to *ALF* to *Third Rock from the Sun* (with *Futurama* being a notable exception – and animated). In the main, the alien character is a simulacrum for the outsider or foreigner in society and could as easily have been replaced by the immigrant, for example Latka Gravas (Andy Kaufman) from *Taxi* or Balki Bartokomous (Bronson Pichot) from *Perfect Strangers*. The wonderful Borat, as depicted by Sacha Baron-Cohen, could easily fit into sitcom.

Ye olde sitcomme doth protest methinks

Writing about the past is as fraught with difficulty as trying to create the future. In the US, other than a nostalgic look at the recent past of the 1970s (*The Wonder Years*) and the 1950s

(*Happy Days*) there is no period sitcom. This may be because the US is a forward-looking country or because they have so little history. *The Simpsons* sometimes uses snapshots – going back to the Salem witch-hunts or aping American historical tableaux (George Washington, the Native Indians, the discovery of the Wild West) but there is precious little retrospection.

The UK has more history to trawl through, so why not plunder the heritage? *Dad's Army*, set in the Second World War on the Home Front, was a huge hit. Then there's *Up Pompeii* in which Lurcio (Frankie Howerd) played fast and loose with Roman history. Staying with Rome but coming across to Britain there was *Chelmsford 123* but overall the most successful period sitcom by far is *Blackadder*, which skipped through Tudor, Elizabethan and Regency times then leapt to the First World War, ending on a poignant note as the entire cast went over the top of the sodden trenches. Its success has to date almost single-handedly stymied other period sitcoms. One attempt, *Hippies*, concerning an alternative newspaper in the mid-sixties was cancelled after one season. It was felt among TV producers that history had been done.

Great sitcoms leave long shadows.

A novice sitcom writer must therefore trawl round for a period or a group of people which is not only somehow relevant to today, but also has not been done or has not been seen to have been done. This means you are working from a lot of negatives. I get a lot of Victorian ones.

Another problem is cost. Correct period costume, sets and fittings must be sourced, which means hiring carriages and dressing street scenes to look old. This is expensive. Most complaints to TV stations are received about period drama/comedy – admittedly from pedants and historians – but nonetheless, it is an invitation for the press to say 'you got it wrong. That was a King George pedestal brush and not a Queen Anne. You poltroons!'

Do you know your history? If you are to set your sitcom on a pirate ship or during the Blitz, have you at least a smattering of knowledge about the period? Have you read around the subject gaining a sense of the vernacular, the sanitary conditions of the times and how people thought politically? You cannot rely on anachronism jokes – they wear thin like the britches and you end up repeating the same joke time after time. Where *Blackadder* succeeded was in its apparent congruency to the times in which it was set. The over-the-top acting of those playing the royals (Queenie, Lord Melchett) harked back to Sheridan.

Radio is a good way of getting around much of this; however, you must choose a suitable time period that is in some way relevant to today. Guy Fawkes was a 'terrorist', but could you stretch the 5th November plotters out to a whole series? Henry VIII was the first to divorce but again, as TV drama has so comprehensively covered his life, what can you add? What about Boadicea? Shakespeare? The Boer War? The Empire?

The 1950s through to the 1980s are currently being mined in TV drama. The last few decades allow for nostalgia and a comforting sense of 'how funny we were all back then with our silly clothes and hairstyles'. In a few years we will nail the 1990s and the Noughties but at present we're too close. Maybe you'll be the one to get it spot on. Good luck.

Laters.

❖ There are good reasons why some ideas are unlikely to succeed. Think like a producer and understand them.

❖ Contrived ideas will not sustain a series.

❖ Sitcom is conservative.

❖ Avoid high concept, at least in the UK.

❖ Do not set your sitcom in places more suited to dramatic areas.

❖ Do not write about the media until you are in the media.

❖ Period is hard to do, so is science fiction.

❖ Northern and regional sitcom will often find an audience.

❖ Make your flat-share sitcom stand out via character or interesting relationships.

❖ Break the rules but know them first.

11.

Team-writing

> There is no real team writing being done in British sitcom except perhaps for *Two Pints*, which attempts to produce volume. Channel 4 has money set aside for comedy following the end of *Big Brother*, and they are putting it into developing comedy and drama.
>
> **M.J.**

The above quote refers to team writing as opposed to writing in pairs, which is as fundamentally British as toast and Marmite. Mmm. This chapter concerns that happy accident when you meet someone of like mind and temperament and are able to spend a long time procrastinating with them to a point where some work does actually get done.

The pacer and the writer

Most American sitcoms, once devised by a pair of creator/writer or writer-producers, are farmed out to a stable of writers who work in parallel, one on the first episode, the next on the second until they run out of episodes or writers and the first writer begins again. Sometimes they work as a team and sometimes they develop story lines individually and pitch them to the show's creator who re-writes them. 'The room' is an office full of embittered men with hygiene and dietary issues who fight tooth and claw to get their storylines and gags on the page and more importantly their name on the script. Watch *30Rock* to see this, or read Rob Long's excellent *Conversations With My Agent*. In the UK, it is more often the lone depressive or the brace of writers (team writing only having been done in the last decades on *Birds of a Feather* and *My Family*). It does seem as though the pair is a natural formation for sitcom writing, as witness

    Galton & Simpson
    Perry & Croft
    Clement & La Frenais
    Esmonde & Larbey
    Curtis & Elton
    Grant & Naylor
    Jay & Lynn
    Linehan & Matthews
    Gervais & Merchant
    Bain & Armstrong

The received wisdom is that one is the thinker/pacer and one is the scribe. In the time of typewriters (for younger readers these were machines that didn't crash or lose all your material in one key stro) it was necessary to have one good typist, but today both are likely to be as pro-active in bashing out a first draft. *Blackadder* was written where both Ben Elton and Richard Curtis would separately write a draft, exchange copies and improve on the other's until the funniest script was reached.

Some writers think best on their feet, walking, playing, talking it out; others are more introspective and need to digest ideas, maybe working them out on the page or on a whiteboard. The joy of the combination is that it plays to both strengths. It also means that the sum of the parts can be greater than the whole and this explains the American hiring and firing method. In the US, it is understood that there are differing skill sets and you may be brought in because you are good at one particular aspect, be it jokes, story-lining, problem solving or character work. It is unlikely that you will see this yourself, as it is more easily perceived through objective eyes. In the writing team you may find:

* The ideas man (brainstormer).
* The character poet.
* The story liner.
* The fixer/problem solver.

- The gagman.
- The polisher/script doctor.

The team must contain all these elements to be effective. Notice that nowhere do I include 'comedy genius' as this is what you get when these elements all come together (plus a sterling cast). If you are lucky enough to have met someone with whom you can work, then it will soon become apparent that each of you will fulfil certain roles. The partnership will not work if this is not a good fit. Two gag writers is not a team, it's a pissing contest. Here are some problems that can occur when writers collide.

The skills you need

The ideas man can have so many ideas that there is no quality control. Scenes fly off at a tangent and scripts may follow one bizarre idea after another. A good script editor will see where the ideas are all shouting to be heard and spot when one line of thought is taking the script astray. Another aspect to this could be that the characters are thinly veiled mouthpieces for the writer (soap-boxing or stand up). It is usually pretty clear when a line has been 'written' as opposed to one that has come from the perception of a character. The ideas man needs to follow the characters and plot with more rigour.

The character poet sees only character. All is subsumed in the wonderful complexities of those who people his script. Their sitcom is character all the way, however they do need to be involved in a story each week. What the writer is afraid of is dropping that catalyst into the story and having them react and then act. They need to think 'out of the box' and work on gags or plotting to divorce them from the character for a bit or at least until they can have some degree of objectivity. They are like the actor who proclaims 'my character would never say/do that' which is admirable in terms of depth of commitment and research, but 'method' is better suited to film.

For the story liner, thinking in terms of story is great if all the underpinning has been done – but again the story may hit all the right beats but lack character. The writer obsessed with the linear plot might benefit from doing some character exercises.

The fixer/problem solver is a master at sorting out the plot, but they might wrap things up too neatly. The solution arrived at is a good one but somehow it feels mathematical – like a man trying to give emotional advice to a woman ('What you need to do is leave him, and cut up all his clothes and steal his money and then sleep with me'.) The solution is pat and predictable. It works, but it is not inspired. It leaves us with nothing. The writer has not stretched themself. Life is messier than this and the answer is to push the fixer to keep coming up with solutions through character. The writer must go back and work from the page, looking for what was seeded earlier.

The doer creates a workaday efficient script but it lacks sparkle. They need to pick up the peaks and troughs – the high drama/comedy beats – and to be encouraged to work deeper and to think more to make it shine.

Finally, the gagman is used to firing out jokes, but they do not relate to the character or the plot. They are like the stand-up comedian who is never off. The one who is 'just as funny off stage as they are on'. But, they howl, sitcom is supposed to be *funny*. Yes it is, but the comedy is not why we watch. The funny people are funny because of how the character phrases things and not just gags, otherwise you end up with those sitcoms that play endlessly in the afternoons (you know who you are). The gag writer must be kept in a cupboard and released when needed. Alternatively, they might work harder on character.

When and when not to write

This is a section for the lone alcoholic as well as the pair of writers. Firstly, if you are working as a pair, establish a writing schedule that suits both of you – if one is an early bird and the other a night owl then emailing each draft back and forth or writing separate scenes is a good idea, using an agreed weekend time to meet up for editing and brain storming sessions. You will still be working in gainful employment up until the first series is aired, so you will have to forgo some of those 'socialising events' that you put on your CV. Three hours is enough for any writing session, as ideas tend to dry up – plus someone who shall be nameless starts surfing porn, suggesting bowling, talking about movies and a million other procrastinations.

Get all the rubbish out of the way before you start. Get the chit-chat done on your cell phone on the way over. This is what it was invented for. Have an agreement that you will only reward yourselves with pizza, beer or pizza and beer once the work is done. These things are not conducive to writing; they are conducive to a coronary episode.

Be realistic about how much both of you can achieve in a week or a month. Work and life gets in the way but both Dickens and Shakespeare seemed to manage – although they weren't trying to make a jokes out of the word 'peachy'.

Waste some time making a timetable and honour it.

Don't stem the creative flow of your partner by offering criticisms such as 'this is crap'. Accept that we all come up with crap from time to time and run with it. Embrace the crap. There is a time for creativity and a time for critique. A wise writer will perhaps express doubt but agree to keep going until they can prove conclusively to their partner that they were wrong. And of course, being in the right is so much more important than anything, isn't it? Ensure that there are tasty beverages around and permit yourself biscuits or cookies. Do not neglect your spouses any more than usual.

As for when not to write – being tired and fractious is anti-thetical to being creative. Personal issues and work stresses do not help and putting them on hold is a good thing. Dealing with them is better. Some writer's write in chaos and many journalists will only write when a deadline has just whizzed past. Some writers write in a chaotic environment, the heaps of 'research' (pizza boxes, soiled tissues, beer bottles, clipped out magazine articles and bookmarked books) helping them to 'get into the space' for it. Personally, I like to clear the decks before I start, ensuring that at least some of the domestic tasks are done and so I can begin 'fresh'. My partner likes to think by moving furniture. I am always surprised to find the bedrooms reversed but by then she is working. Let nothing help you procrastinate, even going off to find a quote about procrastination. There is no substitute, as Hemingway said, for the seat of the pants to the seat of the chair, though he wrote standing, up, naked, with a shotgun near to hand.

Do not write yourself into the ground. There are days when you write for five or six hours straight until your back hurts and your vision blurs. Throwing an all-nighter (along with its concomitant chemicals) is often the way to end up with endless pages of serial killer style scrawled diaries.

For a first draft you should write as fast as you can. I recommend the NaNoWriMo method developed by Chris Baty, which is based on the idea of writing a novel (fifty thousand words) in a month. The sheer energy and ruthless attack of this will surprise you. A first draft sitcom script done in this manner can be completed in fewer than ten days.

We all have a certain amount of creative energy each day for doing productive work. I have found, over the years, that two to three hours is enough and that you produce no better and no worse by grinding on for a full day. A cracking scene is enough. Some writers do all their best work in the morning, others in the evening. Find your best time and use it. Also, take time to think. The great benefit of having a writing partner is that you can kick the ideas back and forth into submission. If you do not have this luxury you will have to do it yourself, and this means taking your mind out for a walk. Take your notebook along. Find some greenery and walk or run amongst it. Get out and away from the screen. The brain, as does the body, atrophies when spending too long in one place. Run, or at least jog, you lazy beer-swilling hog.

Have a small cheap notebook on your person always. Why cheap? Because that lovely black moleskin cover doesn't want to be tarnished does it? Why small? Because it is portable; A4 is too big to carry everywhere. A policeman's notebook is best (and may get you out of embarrassing situations). The gadget conscious among you will already be using your Blackberry, iPad, iPhone, secret tape recorder and some doo-hickey with voice recording software, which instantly sends it to your Mac at home. Show-offs.

Do write by hand. The act of writing itself communicates ideas from your brain to your hand to the page and we learn better that way. We get a muscle memory. Some like to 'keep it all up there' (they say, tapping their head rather sanctimoniously) and for some this is the way they do it before they download it all – but us mere mortals, we forget. We lose inspiration because inspiration is will-o'-the-wisp and a tricky bugger at that. I would rather say to myself, 'Now why did I come in here?' rather than 'Now, what was that brilliant Golden Globe winning sitcom idea again?' Trap it. Your notebook is a snare. Build up a pile of usable ideas for the days when there is nothing in your head. There is no such thing as writers' block, only blockheads who don't write.

How to divide up the work and the spoils

Having a writing buddy has its advantages and disadvantages. You face the blank page together. If one is feeling like the script is going nowhere, the other can talk them out of it. You have more room to think things out together and because you have a real bullshit detector on hand, chances are you will have thought through your ideas before starting work.

You can divide the work; sharing out scenes and drafts, emailing them to one another for correction before coming together and thrashing out the final draft. You can agree on which literary agents to approach.

The disadvantages are that maybe one of you works more slowly, or maybe you don't see eye to eye on a project. If you have a falling out, then the writing stops, whereas the lone writer has no one to hold them back except their incipient drink problem or their PC game addiction.

Once you agree to writing with another, you ought to agree on a simple contract between you, stating the terms of your partnership and have it witnessed by a lawyer or solicitor. Yes, it is a pre-nup and in this sense it makes sensible provision should you split up. You must agree that for everything you work on together, you are 50/50 shareholders: the work is neither the property of one nor the other but a joint enterprise. As for the spoils, an equal spilt seems fair. It is true to say that in the case of Laurel and Hardy (not Laurel vs. Hardy), Stan did the lion's share of the work, writing most of their two- and three-reelers whilst 'babe' Hardy was out on the golf course, but when Hardy died Laurel never appeared again. They needed one another equally. The double act is symbiotic.

Once you start to get commissions and a literary agent hoves into view on his pirate ship, then more formal contracts will be issued. Like most rock bands you will, certainly, strike out with your own 'personal' projects but ensure that the ones you do together are equitable.

Finally, if you remain the lone author you will have to spend all that money on your own.

❖ Assign the tasks equally when it comes to pacing and writing.
❖ Divide the spoils equally, and have a contract between you from the start.
❖ Know what skills you have and what you lack.
❖ Write at the best times.
❖ Avoid procrastination.
❖ Be honest about the relationship.
❖ Keep a notebook and trap your ideas.

Selling the script

12.

The business of sitcom

> Make it original. Don't just copy what's gone before. Keep it simple. Never over-complicate the premise. Never send out the first draft.
>
> **M.M.**

> The function of the BBC writersroom is to find new writers. It is a talent search without the *X Factor* histrionics. It is still advantageous to try to get your work produced in one of the BBC's regional centres, with Manchester, Glasgow and Northern Ireland being the most likely entry points.
>
> **M.J.**

Contact information. Headers and footers

This is a bugbear. Put your name/address/email or some form of contact detail on every single page of your work. Get into this habit. Why? Because cover pages get lost. Scripts are often printed out nowadays and if they do not come with some form of identification then we have loose pages and no more. I recently received three scripts which had no contact details on anything other than the covering letter. I later performed a ritual incantation over the goat blood covered pages to the effect that the writers would be cursed until their fingers fell off one by one.

You have spent weeks, months, even years preparing your work and then you go and send it out anonymously. What does that say about what you think of your work? Perhaps that you think so little of what you have achieved that you cannot even put your name to it. Therefore, why should I be concerned about reading it? Please use a simple header and footer. This is a standard macro which can be applied at one keystroke. All you need is your name and/or email address. Put it unobtrusively in a top or bottom corner. Once you are up and running, and represented by an agent or have sold something to a production company, then you only need put your name/details on the cover page.

Until then, let us know who the heck you are.

The covering letter

Your covering letter/email is a simple request to a reader to read your work. That is all. There is no need to go into detail about how you conceived it or where your inspiration comes from or any kind of plea to save you from your daily drudgery. It should be as simple as a ransom note (do not send a ransom note). Make sure that you are writing to the right person. If it is a producer whose work you admire you may say so, but don't gush, merely tell them that because they produce X and you have written Y then you would opine that as it is of a similar comic bent, they might like it.

If you want to include plot or character breakdowns then you may add them, but not in the body of the letter. If you want to pitch your idea then write a simple sentence such as:

Feeding the croc.
Old college roomies, Bob and Simon live happily in student squalor, but when Simon's girlfriend moves into their flat, Bob realises that he doesn't like her.

This pitch will do. A teaser. Enough to intrigue the reader but not so much that they're swamped with information before they get to the four hundred page opus. Add your contact details and any relevant writing experience. By this I mean creative work sold or interest from other producers, not how you once attended a writing class and that the tutor thought your work 'showed promise' (we say that to get rid of you). If you sold a short story to *Woman's Realm* or *Carp Weekly*, this is not relevant. If you went to school with someone he might know, this is borderline. You may benefit from nepotism or the reader might think you're a grovelling little toady and crumple your work like the receipt from his expense account lunch. The work must sell itself. That is your calling card. The purpose of the script is to get a meeting and *that* is when he will ask you about yourself not before.

Let your work be your stall, lay it out well.

Email or snail

> Ask first. Drop a polite email to the producer to ask them if they will read your work – don't just batter them with proposals and ideas.
>
> **M.J.**

These days almost everything is done by email. Most scripts are sent on attachment and producers have the latest version of the final draft or other screenwriting software installed as standard on their fancy iMac. It is unlikely that you will have a producer's email address (unless it has unwisely been included on their website) and so your initial contact is likely to be by letter or phone.

If you meet a producer/script reader say, at a writers' seminar, forum, or industry event, you will of course ask them for their card. You can give them yours (the one you got for free off the Net or printed up cheaply in a service station) but trust me they won't get in touch no matter how much you schmoozed them. Why? Because no one gets back to you. No one returns calls. No one other than you is going to be proactive when it comes to your career. Put yourself in their position. They have been working a long day and have been sent to this or that event as a favour to someone else or because the BBC is publicly owned and someone has to be seen to be doing the right thing. They would much rather be grabbing some much needed free time at home or catching up with the pile of scripts or the endless list of things they have to do, not standing with a glass of warm white wine talking to bug-eyed crispy-breath fawning writer you. If you are one of those writers/stand-ups then its even worse as they try to keep the rictus grin pasted on their face whilst trying to get away to talk to someone else. This may be why they give you their card – to send you away. Harsh? Yes. An element of truth? That too. A script editor or producer is impressed by the work itself, not the person. They are buying your talent, not you. But you have at least made contact.

You need to meet and make as many contacts as possible and to be nice as pie, so make it your mission to get the business card and send the short, polite email follow up. Persist but do not pester. Let them know you are there and that you are a dedicated writer (not a stalker). Let them know that you will wait as long as it takes for a response. However, if you constantly call or email or make demands on their time or start getting snarky and demanding then they will block you for good.

Yes, it is like getting a date with a cheerleader.

Once they are interested, you can ask if you can send the script on attachment to be downloaded at their end. When you have a literary agent, they will print up copies (and charge you for it). At the same time, you will also be sending out bound hard copies to the production companies. Emailing companies is fine when they give an address but remember, be polite and succinct and above all, don't be too funny: be winning, friendly and approachable. Leave the good jokes to the script.

Don't write in your own mix tape as soundtrack

Music rights are expensive and clearing them involves a lot of work. You are not always going to be able to get that Bowie hit, Porcupine Tree rarity or Lady Gaga warbling so why impede your chances by writing it into the script? If your script is absolutely dependent on foppish 1980s New Romantic dross then God help you, but yes, put it in by all means. It is, however, cheaper for a production company to hire a composer to write sound-a-like tunes, which are compatible with the era. In your script it is better to give a flavour rather than name names. Write:

GRAMS. SEXIST GANSTA RAP. HELD UNDER

Maybe you have your own band or you write your own music, much of which you intend to include in your show, because you will be in it and writing the theme tune, and singing the theme tune (this is not likely to happen). Remember that to use any part

219

of a song needs permission from the copyright holder. The only exceptions to this are for research and private study, criticism and review, news reporting and public interest. Sitcom does not fall under this, which is why they generally originate their own song material. This leads us to ...

Copyright issues and plagiarism

Plagiarism is a nasty situation from which no one comes out smelling of roses. The merest hint of it can tarnish a reputation and destroy a budding career. Many writers ask how to protect their scripts, assuming that unscrupulous production companies will lift their work wholesale. On the other side of the coin before reading your work production companies will ask for a waiver or disclaimer. This indemnifies them against any court action should you have plagiarised anyone or made defamatory (libellous) comments.

Sometimes you see something on telly and it's just like an idea you had. Do you really? Did they actually break into your home and your mind and lift the idea while you were otherwise engaged? Plagiarism is far more rare than you might expect. The thing is, ideas find their time. In 2004, hospital sitcom *Scrubs* appeared in the US and in the UK, *Green Wing*. There are no similarities other than the location (and maybe the speeding up and slowing down of the action). Just prior to that time, two other UK sitcoms about hospitals were doing the rounds. One was commissioned and shown, but *Green Wing* was the one that succeeded. There is no copyright on a location, a profession or a situation – it's first past the post. *The Lad* sitcom has been re-invented numerous times, as has the fish-out-of-water, the funny foreigner and the one man against the world scenario. None of these are stolen, merely upgraded for a new audience.

It is highly unlikely that anyone is going to come up with the same concept, characters, trap, situation, plot and jokes as you. The odds are way too high. In other areas of TV (game shows perhaps) there is more of an overlap as all are chasing one elusive idea, which can mutate into millions of pounds.

As soon as you complete a piece of creative work it is yours. You own the intellectual property rights. You cannot just *say* that something is yours, you must patent it, and the simplest way to do this is to email it to yourself and not open the email. You can also email it to a friend, lawyer or other semi-responsible person thus ensuring the same protection. If you place a script with the WGA (Writer's Guild of America) for a small fee it is numbered and noted and thus protected. In the UK, the Writer's Guild offers the same service. You can also send a hard copy to yourself with a letter of providence co-signed in the blood of your first born, but we have in the main stopped that practice.

So what happens when you *do* see something close to your own vision hitting the screen? I suggest you treat it as a great compliment. It means you are well on the way towards getting commissioned yourself because you are clearly on 'the right page'. Sadly, this also means that your project is now scuppered and you will have to let it go. Sorry, but there is nothing more depressing than enthusing about a project to frowned expressions and comments like 'Isn't that a bit like …?' You will also have to let it go if, as a result of feedback or meetings, producers have told you that they have 'something similar in development'.

Whilst this is often a bit of a cop out and a catch-all excuse, it is also true. How many sitcoms are going to be about a couple of mates or a family? Essentially most of them. Yours needs to have that extra sparkle. It must be slightly off kilter, new, fresh. You do not need to re-invent the wheel (which was my idea actually) you just need to give it your own spin. But why give up on an idea close to my heart just because someone says it is a 'bit like something we have in development?' you wail. Because you are on the back foot. You are defensive. A lot of the game is being the first one to stake the claim.

Once you are in the position of having to justify your work you are working from a negative. Producers don't need this. They need to believe that this project is fresh and unsullied so that they can sell it to the network. They are salesmen too, ones who have to believe in the product. So take a deep breath and re-work what you have. There will always be material worth saving. Characters, plotlines, situations, the core of it. You will be amazed at how often you will have recurring ideas.

Reversion your own work – you cannot self-plagiarise.

Carpet-bombing versus individual send-out

> One hundred per cent of the scripts we take to broadcasters have come from people with whom we've developed a relationship over a period of time. Rarely will the first script we see by a writer be the one we take forward. Broadcasters want to know you, as a producer, are passionate about what you are sending them. Less is more in that regard. How many scripts you develop depends on how many you feel passionate about. Developing sitcoms can't be a sausage factory where you are churning out as much product as possible.
>
> **M.M.**

Should you send out your finished piece to one or a few agents and companies? How long should you wait? Do you carpet-bomb by sending a script out to all and sundry, hoping that one will hit? There are no hard and fast rules on this.

The production company or agent receives many submissions a week and it takes months to sift through them all. No one piece is more important than another unless it is higher up in their hierarchy, which means that a produced writer will always be read before an unproduced one. A writer who has sold will have an agent who will ensure their work gets to the right people and stays at the top of the pile. At the lower end, the unsolicited script is given little priority.

I subscribe to the seven projects rule. This means that at any one time you have seven projects on the go: this does not necessarily mean all of them are complete – indeed some may be in the thinking stages whereas others are ready to go out. To become a professional you must think and act like a professional writer. I was never more impressed than when as a newbie writer I visited the studio of sitcom writer Michael Aitkens (*Waiting for God*). On asking him for a sample script he opened a cupboard and inside were literally *hundreds* of scripts.

In order to beat away some of that disappointment you must have something else on the boil. Also, it means you'll always have something to talk about when you are called in for a meeting and asked 'What are you working on now?' It's embarrassing to say, 'Uh, you have it in your hand.' You need something up your sleeve and not just your armies.

Your work *will* get rejected. This is part and parcel of the writing game and a year from now you will have enough rejection emails to paper your trailer. You still won't have as many as me but you do have to undergo an immense amount of rejection before you get a 'yes'.

My suggestion is that once you have completed your sitcom (third draft), spell/grammar checked it and had it read professionally, only then do you send it out to four or five places. Then get on with something else until you start getting feedback. Once you have a quorum of opinion, you can decide what to do next. If they reject it with similar comments, then it's time to reboot the script. If some want minor tweaks or changes (running repairs) then do these before you send it out wider still. If you get a few positive responses then this too is a good reason to rewrite. Each comment is a building block to take you nearer to that sale. If you get pointers, comments and feedback, then use it. This is gold dust. The script editor is reading many scripts a month and they know what the company wants. As to major changes, this is something I will cover in 'options'. The act of sending the work out is a triumph of hope in the face of adversity. It is a brave act to offer up your babies to the fates but this is a commercial enterprise. If you never wanted to share your writing you'd be a poet or the late J.D. Salinger. It is horrible to get a curt uninformative email, but remember, they are not rejecting *you*; it is merely this project, which does not fit the bill. At the end of a long road of no, you only need one yes. Just one.

You could see all those nos as necessary. What if you sold your first script out of the gate? The first person who read it, called you back and said. 'Your script, The Student Who Inherited a Butler? I goddam love it. I won't have you change one word. We are going to cast Simon Pegg, Kelsey Grammar and Megan Fox and we go into production Monday. *Monday ... Monday ...*'

Hey. HEY. Not going to happen. What would you learn? Nothing. Each script has only one chance with a production company so make it your best.

Options away

The option is a written contract exercising the right to buy an original or adapted piece of work. This contract is between the production company and the writer or writers and sets out the terms of engagement and fees for a piece of television or film writing. This may be a comedy, drama, comedy drama or screenplay. It covers the work due to be delivered and the dates it will become due and the schedule of payments to the writer or their agent. An option agreement is around ten pages long and goes into every legal detail concerning the sale to a broadcaster, that is to say, if it gets made into a series, and/or second and subsequent series and format fees when and if the product is sold to other franchises or broadcasters (when sold on to cable, satellite and other terrestrial and non-terrestrial repeats). It will lay out the fees due to you in these eventualities. It may also refer to DVD and other sales, theatrical rights and in the case of any literary work, any foreign rights and translations. Much of your revenue, when you do sell something and it gets made, will come from secondary and tertiary sources.

It will also cover the grant of rights, the credits (you will want sole credit unless you are a pair of writers) and warranties to ensure that you are the sole creator of the work, thus protecting them from any legal action. It will also mention termination which happens if you do not deliver or do not deliver on time or deliver unsatisfactory work.

Scary?

Yes. This is why you need a literary agent before you sign an option agreement. In truth, most option contracts are what are known as boilerplate, meaning they are standard contracts that go out to all writers. They have been vetted by the Writers' Guild, PACT (the Producers Alliance for Cinema and Television) and in the US, the WGA – Writers' Guild of America. It is not vital to have an agent – you can join the Writer's Guild (details at the back of the book) and they have lawyers who will scrutinise the contract for you. Once you have signed and counter signed this contract (it is witnessed on both sides) the initial fees due to you will be paid according to the schedule set up.

Having said this, options are disappearing.

Formerly, a hot project would be touted around several production companies and the first to bite would offer a deal. The option is worth roughly ten percent of the final fee, so it means in practice only a few hundred pounds/dollars. This is where your agent earns their fiteen percent fee. The option stakes a claim, says that we like this idea and wish to develop it. Sadly, industry practice has changed and independent production companies aren't betting anymore. What is more current is that they will agree to take on a project but the agreement will be verbal, saying in effect that once they sell it, we'll all benefit. Their reasoning is that they are investing time and money in paying their production staff to work with you, just as you are (except you are doing it for free or 'on spec' as the industry calls it), so no one gets paid until it is sold. Whatever you think about this, it is now standard across the British TV industry. What is asked for is in effect a free option. I used to advise writers never to accept a free option because I felt that if a production company wasn't prepared to offer at least a token payment they weren't worth working for, but the industry has changed. It is all or nothing. It's a gamble for all of us. If you can get an option go for it, and don't worry, if offered, it won't go away. You have ample time to look for an agent and the production company may even advise you on some sharks they know. Writers often panic when a company shows interest. Don't. A sitcom has a long gestation period. You don't have to start getting greedy and difficult but you mustn't be taken for an idiot either.

Meeting and pitching

Before you are offered the option you have to interest a producer through your script, that or you have had it produced on stage or on the Net and a producer has seen it. They will then invite you in for a glamorous showbiz meeting in the shiny glass and steel headquarters in the business part of town. You must dress like a writer. Not how a writer normally looks (robe, stubble, bits of food caked on chest), but in your all-purpose Converse, black jeans, scruffy jacket and shirt without a tie. Be comfortable and casual. Arrive early so you can size up the place and negotiate your way past the grouchy security guards and uber-attractive

PAs. You'll have to sign in and will be asked which company you are from. 'Self' will do, rather than 'Megacorp', or 'Omni Consumer Products'. You will be offered a beverage. You may even be able to see your new producer through the glass door of their office as they chat away with the important people. Five or ten minutes later, they will emerge, shaking you by the hand and apologising effusively for a call they simply 'had to take'.

They will sit you down and engage you in small talk as they put you at your ease. You will praise their work, but not sycophantically. There may have been a new sitcom on TV the previous night, which you might chew over. Remember to make intelligent comments but avoid tearing it to shreds in case they say: 'I produced it. Here's the door.'

They will lightly praise your script. You will be thinking, *buy it, buy it, buy it*. They will have a few questions. We might call them reservations. You will need to keep your head and answer succinctly, clearly and truthfully. If you have not worked out what will happen in series two, then bland generalisations will not do – they'll see through them in a flash. Better to admit you don't know something than to bullshit. He's used to bull-shitters and doesn't need another one.

The meeting may go in one of two ways. They may announce that they would 'like to proceed' with the script and to 'develop it further' – which means that you can start the skipping and kissing strangers in the street and planning a suitable period of refreshment that evening. Or as they slyly question the motivations of your central characters, their dynamic or the viability of the situation, you get a sinking feeling they're not going to bite. You must in this case hide your rancour, rage and resentment and swallow it. They will outline why it isn't working for them and you will have your notebook out and will be making notes.

No one minds if you make notes. It shows you are serious and that you wish to deal professionally with your potential clients. Don't record the meeting – it's not an interview – but ask if you can jot things down as they speak. As it is, your pretty head is being turned by the impressive posters, the piles of scripts on the shelves and on his desk and by the uber-gorgeous PAs (did I mention them?). What they are doing is turning down your work. I know. Why the hell did they invite you in there if they weren't going to f*&^%g buy it!? They like your work. They want to get to know you as a writer. They want to check that you aren't the kind of person who takes rejection badly and starts screaming madly and covers the limited edition movie posters with bloodstains. They aren't convinced by this particular piece of work but they may be in the market to buy another, which is why you need to be ready to pitch the next project. Remember the seven projects you had lined up? This is where you have two or three of them at a stage where you can talk about them.

A pitch is a brief description in a couple of lines (as you would read in a TV listing) of the project, including its title and the protagonist's primary struggle. You should have rehearsed this enough to be able to tell anyone without hesitation or explanation.

Frasier is a sitcom about a shrink who can cure everyone but himself. When his ageing dad (a cop) turns up at his door following an injury, there is nowhere else for him to go.

Peep Show is a comedy about two guys who both want what the other has got. The USP of this show is that their inner monologue is always on display via mini cameras strapped to the actor's heads. We see what they see and hear all their thoughts. The comedy comes in the disparity.

All scripts need something in the way of a USP (unique selling point). This does not mean necessarily that it has to be high concept (*Space Butler*. It's a butler ... in space!) but a description of the project in such terms as to intrigue the producer. If you use the tired trope of cross-referencing (it's *The Office* meets *Scrubs*: the inner working of a hospital administration authority) then you aren't saying much. Your pitch must focus on a 'What if' or an interesting take on an emotional situation. You can suggest an area, which has not been well explored. What about a show about nerds? A bunch of competing brain boxes that live together? (*Big Bang Theory*.) Or a show about a loser drug dealer who is bullied by his girlfriend and taken advantage of by his clients? (*Ideal*.) You need to make your idea seem fresh so the producer will want to know more. If you get a negative response do not desperately try to justify yourself; move on to the next one. Remember, ideas cost nothing. They have no currency. They are all equal until recognised by someone else as having value. An idea only gains currency when agreement is reached on its value. If a producer shows interest, explain in more detail. Briefly outline the characters and situation in broad-brush strokes. They will not want plot outlines or details at this point, rather just a sense of the show.

- Who and what is it about?
- Is there an unresolved love/lust affair?
- What are the contentious issues to keep us watching?
- What will happen in series two?

If the producer continues to ask questions then you are onto a good thing and they may ask for something written down. A page will be enough. They will shop it around to gauge interest. It is a good idea to practice writing everything a newcomer would need to know about your pitch on a page. Take it in with you so you can leave it if you're asked to. Rehearse your pitch but sound natural. You should be able to talk confidently about something you have created. In the UK, it will be one-on-one; in the US, a panel or pitch meeting is more common and is a chance for the frustrated performer to shine. You may be a retiring wallflower, but if you cannot demonstrate the passion for an idea then who will? Enjoy it, because it is talking about the work that you love to do.

And enjoy the refreshment period afterwards.

Agents and other sharks

FX. Phone connecting.

CLIENT:
Hi. It's your number one client.

AGENT:
Eddie? I thought you were in LA?

CLIENT: (*beat*)
No, John. ... John Shrapnel?

AGENT:
Heeeyyy. How are things?

CLIENT:
As I haven't heard from you in months I thought
I'd call you. I've sent you three things now and you
never got back to me.

AGENT:
Soz. It's been chaotic here. I've had to sideline
my reading until I can get a clear week. Then, I
promise you –

CLIENT:
What about the sitcom? I thought the producer
loved it?

AGENT:
He did.

CLIENT:
So?

AGENT:
I'll chase.

CLIENT:
I thought it was all set to go?

AGENT:
Actually, I think he may have passed on that one.

CLIENT:
He WH -? You said it was in the bag.

AGENT:
These things are never done until the ink is dry. I'm sorry.

CLIENT:
I need that commission. I've got no money at all now. I gave up a decent day job for this, now nothing's happening and you don't return my calls.

AGENT:
I always return your calls, John.

CLIENT:
After three days.

AGENT:
I do have other clients as well.

CLIENT:
You're *my* agent. I expect you to be out there getting the work.

AGENT:
Listen, John, I've got a meeting. Can we talk properly later on when you've cooled off a bit? Catch up before the end of the day, OK?

FX. CLICK

The above is an agent/client relationship going bad. Please try to avoid the blame game. It is true that a client/agent relationship sometimes doesn't work out, but many of them do, producing fruitful and lucrative partnerships. Here is a more positive spin.

You have had interest from a production company or network. A producer has made an offer to option or to buy your script. Now you need a literary agent. These are to be found in your local aquarium swimming around waiting to smell blood or listed in *The Writers' and Artists' Yearbook*. Whilst some writers operate without an agent, most – not being finance people – prefer to let others deal with the financial side of things. The advantage of having an agent is they will stir up interest in your projects and present them professionally to producers who match your style and area of interest. They will negotiate the best deal on your behalf, shore up disappointments, filter criticism and pay fees promptly and fully.

In brief, an agent is responsible for clout, negotiations and contracts. They have industry contacts and a client list, which means that at the start you will ride on the back of these coattails and your work will get serious attention. Having someone else to be the bad guy when it comes to doing the deal is also a good thing. You get to be the nice guy and can always blame them for the horrible conditions and impositions they are making whilst secretly looking forward to the increased revenue and prestige they offer. Being objective, they can fight your corner, painting you as the tortured artist instead of the insecure loser who would accept any deal no matter how pathetic. You have an ally, a person who, if your project does get canned, you can commiserate with. It is in their interest to get you a deal that will pay you and them dividends for years to come, which is why they get ten to fifteen percent of your fees in commission. For this, any product you take to them and any you already have in development will earn commission for them. Sometimes a situation occurs when a writer finds a producer themself and does all the work up to and including the deal. They then wonder why they should involve the agent who has done nothing to secure the deal. The thing is, once you are in the water with a shark there's no getting away from them. The agreement is *all* your work goes through them. You cannot pick and choose where they make their fees.

Literary agents either work for an independent 'boutique' agency or a named firm, where they will have many agents covering many fields such as literary estates, screenwriting and 'packaged' talent – actors, directors and producers. An agent has a client list of around thirty writers and does not often take on new clients. They have to be very convinced of their potential saleability to do so. Remember, they are looking to represent you for life so it is not a decision made lightly.

This means rejection, and there are myriad reasons as to why you may be turned down, none of which are a reflection of you or your work. First, the client list is full. Second, their personal taste does not coincide with your writing style; they just don't 'get' your work. Thirdly, they may be about to leave the agency and do not need any new business. What you need is someone new to the agency who is trying to establish themselves. As people in television are constantly shifting, so are agents. They have to more forwards or they die.

If they like your work, you'll get a call or an email suggesting you meet. You may even be lunched (they will pay). What they are looking for is someone approachable, friendly and easy to deal with. They want a writer who writes consistently both in quality and in volume but they will understand that good things take time. If they take you on, there may be a contract but this is by no means always the case. It may be verbal or rest on a handshake (count your fingers afterwards). They will deduct fees at source, so when you receive them you'll get a breakdown of the agency's cut – sometimes this will include sundries such as the photocopying of your scripts. In the UK, it is wise to voluntarily register as self-employed and get VAT registered, which means you will be able to start claiming back all your work-related expenses (and those which your agent passes on to you).

There is a honeymoon period in which, as a new client, the agent will send your work out to lots of new people and you get to meet several producers and big wigs. Hopefully it leads to great contacts and a lot more work down the line. You can expect to keep in regular touch with your agent – a call once a month is about right and more often when you have 'live' negotiations. Otherwise, they will leave you alone to get on with it because in essence you are still that miserable writer at home in their sweatpants.

Once the contracts and money are taken care of you can concentrate on what you do best, which is writing and pro-crastinating. It is a healthy relationship and a fairly necessary one, but sometimes it does go bad. Some marriages of client and agent don't work out. I had one with whom I had absolutely no contact in two years. A year later, on phoning his assistant, I was informed that I had been dropped. The letter went to my old address, so I guess that's why I never received his Christmas card.

After the initial flurry of excitement is over, you may experience a dry spell and find that the producers aren't biting. Maybe your show did not secure a commission and you haven't heard from your agent in months. You start getting resentful, blaming them for your lack of success. They're off with their next fancy signing, squiring them around town. What about you? You gave up your job/partner/life for this and they just don't care anymore. Rarely will you find an agent with the guts to tell you honestly that this is what is happening. This is because it is their failure too.

Ideally, they should be in it for the long game, but they will of necessity promote their more successful clients. What can you do to stop the rot? I suggest calling the situation. Make sure you have a couple of cracking project ideas ready to go and arrange to meet them for coffee. Don't do this by phone or try to stretch it to a lunch. Be as positive as you were at the start. Don't apportion blame for anything but make it your joint problem. Explain that you are concerned about this fallow period and ask how *we* can get around it and move on? Offer up new ideas and ask what you can do to help them. No guilt tripping and no recriminations – just try to re-enthuse them in your work. Chances are, they've just been busy. They still love you, but they need to be reminded from time to time.

Hopefully you will get back on track and the next project will have you both skipping to the bank with wheelbarrows full of money. Why not? You're both human.

Script editors

Matthew Mulot is currently producing and developing scripted comedy for talkbackTHAMES and Delightful Industries. I asked how he got into script editing.

I got a job in the comedy department of a television company and asked if I could read some scripts. Eventually someone asked what I thought about them. The script editing part comes much later because a writer/producer has to trust you and your opinion for you to be able to do your job and that won't come easy. Gaining that trust can take any amount of time. It is a case of building up your own connections and relationships with writers, producers and directors.

233

How does a reader's week pan out? What duties are expected of you?

Comedy departments are so small you have to be a jack-of-all-trades. The thought you'd just get to sit in a quiet room and read all day is a fantasy and I've never met anyone solely employed to sit and read scripts. As a rule of thumb though, just try to read as many scripts as you can!

What about current developments and broadcast series?

In terms of meetings it is essential you keep up to speed with what is being broadcast, what has been broadcast, what your colleagues are developing and what other people are doing. The more you know about who is doing what the better. The BBC won't want to read ten separate scripts all set in a taxi.

How many scripts do you receive per month?

It is hard to say how many scripts we receive in a month because the main focus of our work is developing specific projects, not reading as much as possible. The unsolicited script pile can never be a priority for an independent production company, as at the end of the day they are a business. There is always a pile of scripts and when you have free time you'll take the one at the top of the pile and proceed accordingly. Saying that, I am surprised the department doesn't receive more scripts than it does. I think a lot of potential writers think they can write a funny script, some even want to write a funny script but surprisingly few are prepared to sit down and put the hours in, it seems.

What is the development process for a script?

The first step would be to meet the writer, if you haven't already. One of the most important things to consider is that if you are going to work on a script together this is the start of a year or two-year relationship with that writer. Then it would most likely be a case of re-writing the script that got your interest and developing a series outline based on new notes and conversations. There are no hard and fast rules though, that's what is so fun about the process. More often than not the first script you read from a writer is just the start of a dialogue.

The BBC College of Comedy

Michael Jacob is current Head of the BBC College of Comedy. This interview was conducted in 2010. The BBC is known for starting and stopping new initiatives, so before contacting this producer or the BBC College of Comedy please check the BBC writersroom website.

The BBC College of Comedy was founded in 2007 in order to train up writers who already have some kind of writing CV. The Head of BBC Comedy, Mark Freeland, noted that the Corporation was already running drama and journalism academies and so created the College of Comedy. There were three and a half thousand applicants in the first year resulting in six writers being chosen. Over the following year they each developed a script under the tutelage of professional sitcom writers and producers. There were two residential workshops wherein they learned about industry production, budgeting and the psychology of character and story structure. Speakers attending were Sam Bain and Jesse Armstrong (*Peep Show*), Susan Nickson (*Two Pints of Lager*), Kevin Cecil and Andy Riley. At the end of the year a showcase was held for the industry to show off their talents. In a live studio production, fifteen-minute extracts were read out of each script. Many media professionals and independent production companies, plus several literary agents attended the event.

Out of the six, five writers went on to write for BBC shows.

In year two, the bar was raised slightly and one and a half thousand applied. One residential workshop was held. One writer went on to write for the *News Quiz* and a four part radio series was commissioned by BBC Northern Ireland. In its third year (2010–11) more events are planned and more collaboration is projected. A sitcom, *The Inn Mates*, has been produced and broadcast by the College of Comedy.

So this is a foot in the door?

Whilst no guarantee to success, this route will get your name known to producers, commissioners and amongst the independents and agents.

What is the remuneration like?

In terms of payment for a script, the Writers' Guild and PACT agreement puts the fee at £5,125 for a beginner, rising to its highest tariff of £20,000 a script. You are still likely to be commissioned for two scripts if your first is liked. Sadly, budget cuts have swept across the board. Most programmes have had their budgets cut by twenty five percent, meaning that at the high end, a half an hour sitcom will now cost £290,000 and £200,000 at the minimum end. New writers are, of course, cheaper than existing writers.

What is the BBC looking for?

BBC1 is always looking for shows with mass appeal. It is doing well at producing stand-up shows (which means that narrative comedy shows like sitcom are currently suffering). *My Family* series ten will be twenty-two episodes taking us through to 2011. *Outnumbered* has been commissioned for a third series, and *Life of Riley* (starring Caroline Quentin) series two obtained excellent viewing figures of 5.9 million on a pre-watershed slot: narrative comedy (sitcom) is going to be after two slots – pre-watershed at 7.30 and 10.35pm. This means family shows.

BBC1 is piloting *Mrs Brown*, with Irish drag act Brendan O'Carroll. Also *2012*, concerning civil servants and dealing with the 2012 London Olympics. BBC2 has done well with *Miranda*, which has been re-commissioned. *Whites* is on BBC2 and stars Alan Davies. BBC3 is still a proving ground for new talent. A puppet show *Mongrels* began in June 2010. BBC4 is focussing on biopics.

Webisodes and the net

A webisode is a short (often ten minute) episode of a sitcom, either real or animated, which is broadcast on the web (currently YouTube is the most popular site). It is impossible to predict what will happen as regards the Net. Will it provide revenue streams for the individual, thus becoming the true punk industry of our era? Following the Napster legal case brought by the group Metallica, it seems that there will continue to be battles over the usage of music and content on the Net; one thing is for certain, the fastest rising area of law is intellectual copyright. As broadcasters put more and more content online for free (iPlayer, On Demand, listen again, etc) and TVs and home computers combine into one unit, it seems as though our future viewing is unsettled at best.

One surprising reaction to these increased viewing options has been the incredible growth in live theatre and performance. In the UK, comedy has reached arena levels and theatre is healthier than ever. It seems as though communality is something we strive for, the gathering, the warmth of the (metaphorical) campfire, the gifts of the storyteller and the story well told – face-to-face or performer to audience. However this continues to manifest itself, I believe that sitcom will continue, will find its form – the question is how. As terrified broadcasters batten down the hatches, thus reducing our options, we the writers may have to take matters into out own hands. Andrew Barclay, producer of Channel 4's *Pets*, believes that producing your sitcom online is the way of the future.

> You can work at your own pace, you can control every aspect of your project, and you can 'audience-test' it every step of the way. You can seek all sorts of help and advice from other writers, performers, and animators, and all before you do your 'official' big launch! I can't emphasise enough the need to 'test' your material before you start emailing broadcasters with links to your site. Unless you are already established, you need to find out if what you are doing is funny. Don't waste months or years of work presenting something that is not properly thought-out. If you have a good idea, but get lost on the way, be prepared to re-write! Think of your on-line site as being both your 'rehearsal room' and your 'TV channel'. Invite helpful people to the rehearsals, but don't launch your channel until it is the best it can be in your given circumstances. And remember – a web audience is potentially a lot bigger than just BBC1 or ITV! You could be reaching companies around the globe, and you never know – you may just have something they want!

A.B.

Audiences

" Where is sitcom going? More polarisation between mainstream BBC1 sitcoms, which aim to gather an inclusive
audience of all ages, and the more out-there comedy series
like *The Thick Of It*. Perhaps a bit more fusion of character
comedy and stand-up comedy following the success of
Miranda.

S.N.

Who are you writing for? Yourself? Your mates? A perceived
audience of like-minded souls who share your cultural references,
in-jokes and post-modern sense of humour? The chances are it
will be some or all of the above. It is a truism to say, to thine
own self be true, and good writers and performers will take great
pains and perseverance to create a world with which we want
to engage; however, sitcom is a commercial business and the
broadcaster wants good ratings above all.

This is not to say that you should ever pander to an audience
because then you are lost, because you are writing down, rather
than up. The art of sitcom is in finding communality, of emotion,
of desire, of needs, be it the inclusiveness of *The Royle Family*
or the urge of the four *Inbetweeners* to get laid. It is deceptively
simple and the writer who misses this will fail. Some get it
instinctively, as with the great Galton and Simpson or John
Sullivan, but for the rest of us, not everything is going to chime
with an audience every time.

Whilst you write about characters and in true emotional
scenes that you believe in, you must acknowledge that you are
writing for a market and that the market will, to a degree, let you
know what it wants. The BBC wants broad family comedy for
BBC1, slightly more quirky fare for BBC2 and more experimental
shows for BBC3. Each of these is different in conception and
reaches a very different audience. Most of the BBC's successes
were hated at first and placed on BBC2 (with a repeat) in order
to garner an audience. *Only Fools and Horses*, *Fawlty Towers*
and *Dad's Army* all suffered from poor ratings and unsupportive
commissioners. However, BBC comedy is a brand, and it does
have a certain sensibility and intelligence. Channel 4 spearheads

more radical fare, trying to reach a youth audience, a diverse one. It happily breaks taboos and is content with confrontation. It would not be the home for a cosy comedy about an old colonel with a ghostly butler. ITV has struggled to make any sitcoms of note since its heyday in the 1970s. They used to demand ratings of six million per episode, a commercial pressure that tended to result in crude, broadly comedic end-of-the-pier comedy.

Bear in mind that audiences are sophisticated and that the age of the family gathered around the goggle box to watch *Bilko*, *Fawlty Towers* or *Dad's Army* (or on BBC radio, *Hancock's Half Hour*) is long gone. Talent shows and reality TV are currently audience winners, but all things change: a wise Chinese saying once noted that if you sit by the river long enough, the bodies of your enemies will wash past. The danger is to try to create something radical and high concept (for example, the animated sitcom *Popetown*), but this can be self-defeating if the idea is considered too offensive for mainstream TV, or simply does not 'have legs'.

In my classes, as an exercise, I suggest that the students come up with the most offensive sitcom idea they can think of. This usually involves the disabled and various incestuous scatological elements that I won't go into here, but it does have the advantage of clearing the air (except for the flatulent ideas). It demonstrates that the puerile and amoral doesn't develop; it is a posture like the concept of black magic, which can only exist in opposition to the notion that there is a God. In trying to create the anti-sitcom, it merely shows us the holes in the arguments. Try it yourself and see. The Viking sitcom 'Only Fools and Norses' or the graphically obscene 'Felching Towers' are one-note jokes and my ghost butler pirate student sitcom isn't going to play either. Probably.

Audiences like to own a sitcom. There is an arc here. At first, resistance. If a new sitcom is 'hyped' or contains stars of whom we already have much knowledge, it is going to struggle. Sitcom does not have a good history of doing well with established star actors, as witness *Joey* or *Hank* in the US or *Babes in the Wood* or *Big Top* in the UK. If we 'know' the actor from another role – a soap or long running other show – it is hard for us to accept them in a new one, meaning that the first series is crippled by confusion. David Jason and Ronnie Barker are wonderful exceptions to this, but even the brilliant Steve Coogan struggled with *Saxondale* after *Alan Partridge*. A star will give the series a leg up, even guarantee great ratings in the first couple of weeks, but we are watching a star and not a character. *Whites* starring Alan Davies has recently suffered from this.

It is far better to make stars through the medium, as with Harry H. Corbett (*Steptoe and Son*), who was dubbed the English Marlon Brando by the press. In the UK we resent hype (whilst still taking a sneaky peek). We flatter ourselves that we are being terribly clever in finding a new show, such as *Spaced*. We claim ownership and discuss it over the kettle. Sitcom of course cannot exist in a vacuum, and so as we convert others we are delighted if the press then begins to respond, allying itself with our opinions. Broadcasters pray for this, as it is hard to sell sitcom by viral marketing. Word-of-mouth is crucial.

The cult grows and the media and broadcast magazines will be sensitive to this, using focus groups, studying website forums and gathering opinions from many sources. In the BBC, this will lead to the decision to promote a second (or third) series of the show from BBC3 to BBC2 and into a more accessible time slot. It may be hammocked between other shows or placed after a soap or panel game or other solid ratings winner. Channel 4, back in the 90s, used to premier all its new home-grown comedy smartly between *Friends* and *Frasier* on Friday nights. Good times.

Now the show has a solid audience, good ratings and the cast and crew are working in perfect synch. This is why a second and third series is often the best. It becomes appointment-to-view TV, and the media coverage is broader and robust. This is the golden time before the inevitable wane as familiarity sets in and this may go to explain why many UK writers are currently dropping the axe on their own shows after two series. Can we really imagine series six of *The Office* UK?

You are the audience. You pick up on a show and treasure it in the same way as anyone does. You buy the box set, or go off it, or then rediscover a much-loved show years later. Think of whom you are appealing to. Who is your target demographic? Is it actually people who watch TV? Some scripts I receive are so oddball that you know they were designed to be read out in a seedy pub to friends, and not for public consumption.

Think of the audience, and approach the most suitable broadcaster.

* Always consider the audience.
* Be clear which broadcaster you are writing for.
* Make sure that there is contact information on every page.
* Politely ask a producer to read your work. Do not pester.
* But do not let them forget you.
* Do not plagiarise.
* Consider the market when you send out.
* Approach agents when you are ready – not before.
* Use every opportunity to get your work seen and read.
* Persevere. This is a five-year plan at best.
* Have many projects in various stages of development.
* Don't wait for them to come to you. They won't. You must do everything you can to market you work.
* The fruit doesn't fall far from the tree. Get nearer the tree.

Conclusion

Working from a negative

> Never, never, never, never, never give up. See rejection as a comma, not a full stop. Watch lots of sitcoms, even ones you don't like, and see what works and what doesn't, write lots and be prepared to get it wrong more than you get it right. Never forget the importance of story.
>
> **D.H./S.W.**

The theme of *How NOT to Write* seems like an awfully negative approach to take when it comes to a creative exercise. Why tell us how not to do something when what we want is a book telling us how? OK. There are two ways of going about learning a skill set. One is trying and failing and then learning from it, working incrementally towards a piece that fulfils the remit of the creative brief. The second is to learn beforehand all the necessary skills and then, armed with knowledge, going in with eyes open. Both have their disadvantages. With the former it is that when learning as you go, you can often feel lost and that you are wasting time which could have been saved by reading up on the subject. With the latter – as may be the case once you have digested this book – you may feel so stymied by all the rules and regulations that you give up before you have started.

To that I say, good.

Good for you. Give up. You will have saved yourself a lot of heartache, unrewarded toil and rejection. On the other hand you will miss the excitement of the eureka moment, of building a character from the ground up and coming to know and live with

242

them in your mind: also the joys of playing God in your world, of piecing people together and seeing the dialogue and jokes flow out and finally the feeling of creative satisfaction when the piece is finished and ready to send out.

The writer is responsible for three parts of the process, firstly conceiving the piece. No one can do that for you; not a script editor, a producer, actor or a director; it is solely you, in your seedy apartment with the broken air conditioning unit and the faulty toaster. It is your idea and yours alone. Secondly, there is production. Again, you are the one who produces draft after draft (or you and your co-writer). This is the job of the writer, to make it happen. Without your words the actor, director and production company has nothing.

Then there is completion. If true happiness is absorption in a task then finishing it is true satisfaction. These three are in your remit – as well as pushing it out to as many people as possible, accepting criticism graciously and networking with as many people as you can.

Beyond this it's a crapshoot. You will have no decision in casting (though you may be 'consulted' but then I 'consult' my girlfriend about recipes) or commissioning or scheduling or set design or direction. All this is in the hands of the gods until you are a successful writer and the networks come begging to your door.

Your job is to find a way to create something of yourself, something unique of your world (not the media one or other stuff you hate on TV). Your job is to bring into the world a fresh vision about a dysfunctional brother, mother or father, co-worker, lover or boss. It is your job to make it the best it can be because you only get one shot. Once a production company or network has considered a script and unless they specifically ask you for changes then you cannot go back again with that same piece.

This book has been full of negatives and mistakes and ways of not doing it but the truth is that when you receive fifty scripts a month you have to operate a filter system. Networks also have other agendas to consider. The controller may have inherited other shows that they personally dislike but they are paid for and must be broadcast. The comedy controller may be forced to accede airtime to sports or news programmes. Comedy is easy to shift:

it's shorter than big drama productions and it isn't sequential. Beware the sitcom that goes out in the summer months or late at night – this is the comedy graveyard where they bury your work. Overall, the decision a comedy commissioner must make is – to quote from a former BBC Head of Comedy – 'a commissioner must ask herself not which sitcom shall I commission, but which sitcom shall I *de-commission* to put yours on?'

In this way, they are always working from the negative. What's wrong with this script? Why won't it work? You have to prove that it will.

Contrary to the belief of frustrated writers and critics, they don't schedule crap. No one goes into television wanting to produce rubbish. So much time and money is involved in making any TV programme that it simply cannot be done without passion – and it is that passion which you must express on every page. The passion for your project, your characters, your situation, stories and jokes. You must start the fire and once lit, people will come to build it higher. Then with application and talent and a lot of luck you will pen a saleable, successful sitcom.

They are always looking for new talent.

I hope it's you.

Now stop reading and get on with it.

Author details

Marc Blake is a contributor to the *Independent on Sunday*, *The Sunday Times*, *Evening Standard*, *The Mail*, *The Daily Express* and *Scriptwriter* magazine, as well as being the sitcom consultant for the British Comedy Guide website (www.comedy.co.uk). In this capacity, he reads hundreds of scripts a year and it is from this, plus his experience in writing and selling his own sitcoms that the content for this book is drawn. He was a comedy writing consultant for the SABC (South African Broadcasting Company) as well as leading courses in Europe and all over the UK. At City University he taught Sitcom and Comedy Writing for fifteen years with graduates including Catherine Tate, the co-creators of *Genius* (BBC2) and *The Thick of It* (BBC1). He currently teaches Sitcom, Comedy and Screenwriting at Kensington and Chelsea College, and Screenwriting at Solent University, Southampton.

He is the author of three novels, *Sunstroke* (1998), *Bigtime* (1999) and *24 Karat Schmooze* (2000; Hodder & Stoughton). He also wrote *The Little Book of Drinking*, *My Computer Hates Me* and *The Bastard's Bedside Companion* for Boxtree Macmillan, as well as the *Little Book of Failure* for Summersdale. His TV writing includes *The Swap* – a two-part drama broadcast on ITV in 2002.

He is a stand-up comedian with many thousands of performances under his belt over a twenty-year career. He wrote and starred in *Marc Blake's Whining for England* for BBC Radio 2 (1994) as well as his own show *Eurocomedy* for ITV (1993). He wrote for BBC radio's *Weekending* and the *News Huddlines*, as well as on *Spitting Image* (ITV) and for Frankie Howerd (ITV) plus for many other comedy stars who shall remain nameless.

Websites

www.bbc.co.uk/writersroom/ (BBC info + script/ template downloads)

www.chortle.co.uk/ (UK live comedy)

www.comedy.co.uk/ (comprehensive sitcom site)

www.comedy.co.uk/sitcom_mission/ (the sitcom mission)

sitcomtrialsco.uk/ (the sitcom trials)

www.imsdb.com/ (movie scripts)

www.nanowrimo.org/ (how to write a novel in 30 days)

www.writersguild.org.uk/public/index.html (Writers' Guild)

www.wga.org/ (Writers' Guild of America)

www.kcc.ac.uk/humanities/literature-and-creative-writing/ (My courses at KCC)

www.frieze.com/issue/article/tears_before_bedtime/ (Michael Bracewell article on Social Realism)

Suggested reading

Aherne, Caroline; Cash, Craig; Normal, Henry. *The Royle Family Scripts*, Granada Media (1999).

Allport, Gordon. *Inventing Personality: Gordon Allport and the Science of Selfhood*. American Psychological Association (2002).

Angell, David; Casey, Peter. *The Frasier Scripts*. Newmarket Press (1999).

Baty, Chris. *No Plot? No Problem!* Chronicle Books (Revised ed. 2006).

Blake, Marc. *How to be a Sitcom Writer*. (Ebook) Andrews UK (2010).

Bryson Bill. *Mother Tongue*, BCA, Penguin Books (1990).

Chekhov, Anton. *The Plays of Anton Chekhov: Nine Plays* Kessinger Publishing (1994)

Cleese, John; Booth, Connie. *The Complete Fawlty Towers*. Methuen (1998).

Field, Syd. *Screenplay: The Foundations of Screenwriting*. Dell Publishing, Bantam Doubleday. NY (1984).

Galton, Ray; Simpson, Alan. *The Lost Hancock Scripts: Ten Scripts from the Classic Radio and TV Series*. JR Books, London (2010).

Long, Rob. *Set Up, Joke, Set Up Joke*. Bloomsbury, London (2005).

Mills, Brett. *Television Sitcoms*. BFI Publishing (2005).

McKee, Robert. *Story*. Methuen (1999).

Nobbs, David. *Reginald Perrin Omnibus*. Arrow Books (2009).

Nye, Simon. *Best of Men Behaving Badly*. Headline Books (2000).

Sedita, Scott. *The Eight Characters of Comedy*. Atides Publishing (2005).

Simon, Neil. *Collected Plays Volumes 1–4*. New English Library (1986).

Silverstone Roger, Ed. *Visions of Suburbia*. Routledge (1996).

Turner, Chris. *Planet Simpson*. Random House (2004).

Taylor, Rod. *Guinness Book of Sitcoms*. Guinness (1994).

Vogler, Christopher. *The Writer's Journey*. Michael Weise Productions (2007).

Sitcoms and comedy dramas cited

The following is a list of the principal sitcoms and comedy dramas referenced in the text.

All in the Family (CBS, 1971–79)
Are You Being Served? (BBC, 1972–85)
At Home with the Braithwaites (ITV, 2000–3)

Beverley Hillbillies, The (CBS, 1962–71)
Big Bang Theory, The (CBS, 2007–present)
Bilko (aka the *Phil Silvers Show*) (CBS, 1955–59)
Blackadder (BBC, 1983–2000)
Brass (ITV/Channel Four, 1983–90)
Butterflies (BBC, 1978–83)

Cheers (NBC/CBS, 1982–93)
Cosby Show, The (NBC, 1984–92)
Curb Your Enthusiasm (HBO, 2000–present)

Dad's Army (BBC, 1968–77)
dinnerladies (BBC, 1998–2000)

Early Doors (BBC, 2003–4)
Fall and Rise of Reginald Perrin, The (BBC, 1976–79)
Father Ted (Channel 4, 1995–98)
Fawlty Towers (BBC, 1974–79)
Frasier (NBC, 1993–2004)
Friends (NBC, 1994–2004)

Good Life, The (BBC, 1975–78)
Goon Show, The (BBC Radio Home Service, 1951–60)
Green Wing (Channel 4, 2004–7)

249

Hancock's Half Hour (BBC Radio, then TV, 1956–61)
I Love Lucy (CBS, 1951–60)
Inbetweeners, The (Channel 4, 2008–10)
IT Crowd, The (Channel 4, 2006–present)

Keeping Up Appearances (BBC, 1990–95)

Larry Sanders Show, The (HBO, 1992–98)
Last of the Summer Wine, The (BBC, 1973–2010)
League of Gentlemen, The (BBC, 1999–2002)
Likely Lads, The (BBC, 1964–66)

Mary Tyler Moore Show, The (CBS, 1970–77)
M*A*S*H (CBS, 1972–83)
Men Behaving Badly (ITV/BBC, 1992–98)
Miranda (BBC, 2009–present)
Monty Python's Flying Circus (BBC, 1969–74)
Mork and Mindy (ABC, 1978–82)
My Family (BBC, 2000–present)
My Name is Earl (NBC, 2005–9)

Nightingales (Channel 4, 1990–93)

Office, The (BBC, 2001–03; NBC, 2005–present)
One Foot in the Grave (BBC, 1990–2000)
Only Fools and Horses (BBC, 1981–2003)
On the Buses (ITV, 1969–73)
Open All Hours (BBC, 1973–85)
Outnumbered (BBC, 2007–present)

Peep Show (Channel 4, 2003–present)
Phoenix Nights (Channel 4, 2001–02)
Porridge (BBC, 1973–77)

Rab C. Nesbitt (BBC, 1998–present)
Red Dwarf (BBC, 1988–2009)
Rising Damp (ITV, 1974–78)
Roseanne (ABC, 1988–97)
Royle Family, The (BBC, 1998–2000)

Saxondale (BBC, 2006–7)
Scrubs (NBC/ABC, 2001–2010)
Seinfeld (NBC, 1989–98)
Shameless (Channel 4, 2004–present)
Shelley (ITV, 1979–92)
Simpsons, The (Fox Broadcasting Company, 1989–present)
South Park (Comedy Central, 1997–present)
Spaced (Channel 4, 1999–2001)
Steptoe and Son (BBC, 1962–74)

Taxi (ABC/NBC, 1978–83)
Till Death Us Do Part (BBC, 1965–75)
To the Manor Born (BBC, 1979–2007)
Two Pints of Lager and a Packet of Crisps (BBC, 2001–9)

Vicar of Dibley, The (BBC, 1994–2007)

Waiting for God (BBC, 1990–94)
Will and Grace (NBC,1998–2006)

Yes, Minister (BBC, 1980–84, 1986–87)
Young Ones, The (BBC, 1982–84)

Index

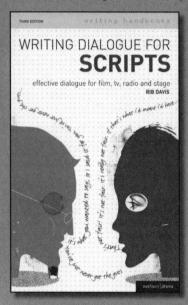